Conversations With My Father

GARY DUNCAN

FLYWRITE
- Publishing -

First published in Great Britain in 2010
by Flywrite Publishing
www.flywritepublishing.com

A CIP Catalogue of this book is available from
the British Library

ISBN: 978-0-9564954-0-2

Cover designed and typeset in Centaur MT 11½pt
by Chandler Book Design
www.chandlerbookdesign.co.uk

Printed in Great Britain by the
MPG Books Group, Bodmin and King's Lynn

CONTENTS

1

A Few Too Many

The *Few* are celebrated; that small band of brave and defiant to whom so much is owed by so many.

The Battle of Britain defines one of the great international battles of all time. It presented to a then still young Royal Air Force, mature in attitude but under-resourced, the justification for an armed aerial service that was effective not only in bombing, but in intercepting and eliminating an attacking enemy. Britain no longer saw battles as civil, between her peoples, or in a foreign field, but brought to her very shores and deep inland, terrorising town and city, inflicting on child, woman and man the indiscriminate affront of war. With fortune, the might of the Luftwaffe could have succeeded over this plucky band; history and culture, so much of it, would have been eradicated. For years subsequently, the populist relationship with the Royal Air Force would never be the same again. The individual pilot is a warrior of heroic stature.

Lying beyond the frontispiece of wartime history, of action and destruction, is a set of circumstances: of planning, logistics, actuarial analysis, mobilisation and implementation involving, ultimately, a Royal Air Force whose numbers would exceed one million. Far beyond the white cliffs of Kent in 1940, and for the next five years, *The Few* would become a vast force employing the resources of many countries united in the defence of liberties. By 1945, *The Few* had become the *Too Many*. Post-war economic policy, new domestic priorities, technological advances and the adaptation to the Cold War saw the RAF being reconfigured. The Force was too big, too costly and, as for the aircrew, there were simply more than were needed.

The romantic adventure of aviation, conflict, and the mere glimpse of being a hero was lost, as those trained were repatriated with their day jobs, if they could remember what that was.

This is one such story.

2

Blue Sky Thinking

Dark eyes and a slender face, narrow – not chiselled – and drop-dead handsome; looks that were probably his passport. Uniformed he was, blue serge and hair combed back precisely, the collar and tie so missing from other uniforms which he eschewed in favour of fulfilling his dreams of flying. With Wings proud on his chest he looked beyond the camera, not at it, a Brylcreem Boy, frozen for posterity and forever twenty-one. Now, round-shouldered, weakened in old age, shuffling, cardigan, drooping pockets and memories – an aged body, wrinkles, veins and thinning hair, but a sharp mind. Rage, if he sought it, summoning the energy, could turn his face, and sometimes, just sometimes, you would see a twinkle of delight in his eye. The same man.

Virtually house-bound, his knees and lungs racked respectively by over-use and indulgence, the telephone was never far from his side and apart from the daily, and sometimes disappointing, rise-and-fall routine of waking up and settling down, he would read and write: lists, poems, thoughts, philosophy and quotes committed to memory since childhood. Having, myself, left home years before, we would exchange photographs, newspaper articles, notes and letters. His would be carefully handwritten

3

in a fine, steady copperplate style. Such penmanship is all but lost now, but in these letters was something of a man who left school with nothing more than the ability to apply his mind, use his hands and find his feet. Flying was a recurrent theme in our correspondence, with the annual September birthday card enabling the assembly of an impressive collection of aviation artwork. These images formed palm-sized memories which, together with model airplanes, were placed in the back room, affectionately and reverentially referred to as 'the hanger'.

In childhood he was encouraged to write an essay every day and whether this was in some way to advance his learning and make up for limited education – and certainly no college education – I can only speculate. It was June 1937 when he left school at the age of thirteen years and nine months with no more than a talent nurtured through application, and doubtless some parental and a little bit of school discipline. This enabled expression not just through a carefully crafted sentence, but through opinion. Whether or not these opinions were scientifically or empirically informed is another matter. Later, letters and notes, short essays and treatises shared over a twenty year period outlined his views, and often far-sighted views they were, on political and economic theory, on war and famine and on personal triumphs and troubles. Here was a father-son relationship expressed in writing; words unspoken and a rare insight into not just worldly events or current affairs, but some of the actual events that had shaped him. To describe the discovery of these hidden parts of his life as a revelation would be to indulge in aggrandisement, but the story is no less revealing. This story is as much about uncovering something of the man, as it is of his ordinary and, at times, extraordinary life.

The first inclination towards his story stemmed from these often brilliant letters. I deliberately but respectfully put the more reflective and personal notes to one side, though. There was a taboo which was as much about things unsaid as it was things best not known about but always, intriguingly, there. The reality was that he actually wanted these more personal reflections to be read. He wanted me to know about him. Only once did he ask in his soft Scottish brogue, *"Did you get them, son?"* My reply was shy, with a laconic and incomplete excuse. Reluctantly I offered, *"Aye, I did, but…"* Embarrassed or saving his dignity, I was foreclosing on his offer. We carried on.

My own reticence in examining his writings, tucked away as they were in a box file, may suggest that I felt I knew my father better than he knew himself. I felt I didn't have to look. Somehow I knew, though I felt that if I did look I might intrude on his discretion, perhaps realising a different man. Fleeting glances provided snapshots of events and emotions, misjudgements and regrets. But without the detail of his story, I would not know him. I barely knew the more troubled side of my father: helplessness and worthlessness that were borne of circumstances I had yet to find out about and understand. The reality is that he wanted someone to know about his life and about him. Somehow shamed by his own conduct at certain points in his life, in his final years he wanted a form of absolution, pardon for selfish disregard and wrongdoing.

However handsome he was in the photograph, the total picture was incomplete and hidden. Stories, events, and circumstances were merely alluded to and not fully told. The truth was somehow veiled and this created a desire to realise his life. Answers lay dormant and waking hours asked many questions. Only the papers before me could provide some answers.

Growing up, there were areas where you did not go, topics of conversation which, for whatever reason, were never fully explored. There were half-stories and legends which were stored in recesses. Shame or embarrassment in their explanation, too complicated for a child, may have been the reasoning. The reality was that his life was a long time ago and its circumstances and events belonged to a different generation in a different Britain. Attitudes and experiences were clearly different then, but they had a profound effect on my father's upbringing and his career during and immediately after wartime. The 1940s and 50s had no apparent bearing on my childhood and teenage years. And yet they did. As a youngster in the colourful 60s and 70s, free of rationing and seemingly years away from the war, my life was being influenced, if not formed, by events never experienced; a sepia, then harsh black and white world of a previous generation. When I write this I realise that much of what I am about to convey reflects only the twenty or so years prior to my birth – eons ago, but seemingly just yesterday.

He had a gift for writing and an ear for good music. There is a love of 'Swing': of Artie Shaw, Tommy Dorsey, Glenn Miller; of Porter, Gershwin, Berlin. How many of us today know how to spell Andre Kostelanetz, let alone say it! And I don't think I have even heard a Jane Froman recording, but still I know her name. There was also an inclination to classical music. Why was I listening to Tchaikovsky and Rachmaninov? He would quote Shakespeare, Burns and Omar Khayyam, and not for the entertainment of memorising lines, but for the deeper meaning and philosophy. The fondness for words and poetry would find expression throughout his life, but would culminate in some words he wrote following a solo flight in South Africa in 1944. Here, he described the wonder and splendour of flight; a spiritual connection above the clouds. What he wrote would become, for him, irritatingly world-famous and his recollections of high flight above the bundu will challenge accepted wisdom and certain facts. I have no basis to challenge his assertion, but read on.

In adulthood I would be mature enough to comprehend what had been a lingering fascination for the fortune of war and the misfortune of my father's experience of it. In this terrifying, yet unifying, period of history for so many, in the midst of massive upheaval and disturbance, was opportunity. Yet his career heights of swoops and barrel rolls and the freedom of flight would combine with the depths of desperate depression. And in this was the undercurrent fear in examining these notes. Something had happened along the way.

There is no regret in unfolding the story, only sorrow that my father could not find an opportunity to fully share his experiences other than in seemingly confessional notes and letters. In what he shared was his personality and his story, both of which few knew. He had been through The Depression, had signed up for military service, had flown airplanes and seen foreign travel; his old suitcases were covered with labels confirming visits to far-off destinations by sea and by air. All of this is so commonplace now, but he was part of a rich, remarkably romantic period of what is now history. Such romance may be an ironic contrast to the poverty of 1930s Britain, the grind of war and the sheer effort of getting-by afterwards. In the midst of this long-forgotten daily life, there were events that would have a catastrophic effect on him and alter his whole approach to Civvy Street. Adjustment to a new Britain, *post-war*, of demobilisation and resettlement, and of the effect this had on him would be profound.

Growing up, what is uppermost is the military career and the image of the dashing RAF pilot in the photograph. These are my earliest recollections of my father. There was a glamorous side. Many military personnel had photographs taken, but here was a *portrait*. This was studio-style and in the manner of a Paramount or Warner Brothers-issued photo of a movie star. Still I barely knew him. I only know of the legend – perhaps even a myth – that I had created in a child's head. There are many facets to this story, and many questions.

Many sons and daughters look back and admire the struggles, courage and achievement of the period. We recognise hardship and adventure at a time of *Total War*, but we have no concept of the individual risks faced at the time or the consequences that would be faced. War is too often written about in terms of conflict and suffering, of active engagement with an enemy, of sorrow and destruction. It is not really written about in terms of aftermath, of adjustments, sometimes painstaking, so often frustrating.

Faced with many hundreds of years of history, Britain looks back to defining moments of conflict which have helped establish a national character defined by our centuries-old, battle-scarred history; more recently the hallmark cigar smoking bulldog and the Dunkirk Spirit. Active conflict in its many theatres on land, sea and air would be experienced by many thousands. For many thousands more, the period 1939–1945 led to huge and discomforting change that would linger into the 50s. Wartime, with its make do and mend optimism, straddled a period of poverty on one side and austerity on the other. Soft tone reminiscence of wartime belies the personal battles of many.

Yet life, and the opportunities it provides, is hugely complex. The Second World War provided massive changes in the ordinary circumstances of everyday lives, and so my father would have a role in the largest aircrew training programme ever, being one of the 170,000 from the Dominions who were trained to provide air superiority. With the RAF there was the experience of flying, matched only by the frustration of being trained for, but never actually being involved in, operational duty. There are no heroic acts in this account. There are no marvellous stories involving active service or of knowingly saving lives. All I can say is that he, like hundreds of thousands at home or overseas at the time, bore witness to the effects of the wartime years, and the aftermath, without actually being involved in armed conflict.

To a large extent this book is concerned with realising a life: my father's life as victim of domestic abuse, an ambitious young man, trained airframe fitter, and despite the waywardness and interference of his own father, by the age of twenty-one, RAF pilot. It interweaves family circumstances with the events of the time: the perilous financial problems of the 1930s, the build-up to war, and the aftermath. It is a story of questions. Why was he in Scarborough one minute and Manchester the next? Why was he in South Africa in wartime? Just how was it that he became one of the *Too Many*, his skills no longer required? Why was he working on cross-Channel ferries? And just how did he experience the summary justice of the French courts? What was his career with the infant British European Airways? What was his role in the Berlin Airlift? And what else happened along the way?

There is sadness in the honesty of my father's concealed emotions, of the feelings that I now realise. There are depths in his own admission of self-disappointment, fragility and a vulnerability. Crippled – or perhaps even *tortured* – by his upbringing, all he wanted to do was get on in life and to provide. Yet he seemed guilty for his own failures and wrongdoings, or at least was made to feel guilty.

I barely knew my father other than as that: he was my dad. But he was also a seeming hero with a rich romantic past of out-of-the-ordinary stories and events from another time. Circumstances have been explained to me and I have tried to understand his observations and feelings to the point where there is compulsion in putting this work together. The story is also told for those who did not meet him or even grow up with him. For all his feelings of limited self-worth there is huge desire to respect him as an individual and to tell his story.

There is irony, though, in the title of this book, for the conversations exist largely in the context of his memories and the things we wrote about. They did not take place at all. Sadly, the opportunity of having further conversation is delayed, though maybe I could get a 'long distance' to Heaven.

3

The Brace Position

You can expect a call like that one day. These are the words he said to me following an unexpected phone call at some obscure hour. If I called him too early, he had barely woken up and would not be fully *compos mentis*. A little later and the afternoon nap would be disturbed. Tea time? No, that would mean he was in the kitchen. From about eight o'clock things were more settled, but with the ever-present distraction of television. Telephone conversations could be punctuated irritatingly with *"yeh, yeh...oh, he's snookered behind the brown"* A pause as he repositioned himself in his favourite TV-side chair, then *"sorry, you were saying?"* But such phone calls carried a pattern. After ten o'clock was way out of sync, so when the phone actually did ring at quarter past I feared the worst. "I thought that was *The Call*," I said, emphasising some seemingly expected finality, an ironic scepticism of life:

"No, no, son, I was just..."

It did not matter what the pretext was, his voice was strong. *"Oh, I see, that call. No, no, it'll be a wee while before you get that one."* Such confident dismissiveness, I thought, as he said this knowingly. My father was a mixture of the prophetic and pragmatic. He knew of the certainty of death and with cynical black humour would sometimes be disappointed that each morning he had woken up.

He was a worldly, competent individual with time on his hands to write, to think and to prepare. He was a man of organisation and lists. But physically he was wearing thin. Just how serious his frailty was at eighty-three years of age was cleverly concealed. He had carried on working into his seventies, although he had effectively retired years earlier. Around him there wasn't much, but he had what he needed; a man of order and priority, stripping bare his life, easing his passage into the hereafter. He was now comfortably resigned.

I knew that amidst the simple accoutrement of crossword puzzles, pens and notepaper, of ultimately small things, the result of decades' life distilled into that which mattered most, he was being flippant. There was an undercurrent preparedness after eighty-plus years, often mixed with a weariness and an increasingly limited day-to-day life. Always mobile, always driving somewhere, but by now he was walking so little. He wanted others to be prepared too.

With all the foretelling and certainty of demise, it happens suddenly. I am now in the brace position: the part of your life you have awaited, the one you have been told to expect. I have dropped everything and booked the air ticket and a place to stay. The delay at the terminal is longer than the actual flight and I find myself filling time, doing what travelling people do: drink, eat something, look at duty-free goods, buy something utterly pointless and, in the process, confirm that there is a waiting-for-a-plane captive market of desperate, bored souls anxious to pass time. Thoughts turn to retail conspiracy and then my conscience pricks me: time, this time, is not real. An out-of-body moment tells me I am somewhere between a look of self-conscious pre-occupation and avoiding the look of shiftiness. When I least expect it the bing-bong of the tannoy announcement greets and the monitor confirms a late departure. The plane has been late in arriving and is late for take off, but I am now on my way, relieved from the tension of waiting. Distant and anxious, I walk towards the aircraft steps, across the runway apron and through a heady mix of aviation fuel and warm London air. Dundee next.

Pre-occupation marks the swift journey, but one that is never fully reliable; the last twenty minutes being the worst – it somehow doesn't feature on the timetable. Here I am for one hour and the seemingly extra twenty long minutes. Solitary. Seat F. Click. Magazine. Coffee. Thank you. Newspaper. View. Click.

The airplane passes from the limitless, bright blue of 27,000 feet and emerges under a low canopy of cloud; the ethereal becomes familiar again. The approach from the west leads passengers to crane for a view of what is a far from small town. It is now a buoyant city with a southward prospect to a beautiful estuary and Fife beyond. Bridges have been built straight to its heart. Some passengers are going home from visits and shopping trips, some have the look of 'research chemists' en route to the university, now famous for bio-technology. The stylish 'architect' – with the pretentiously 'arty' black polo-neck and portfolio – and his 'assistant' may be visiting or returning from a new development. To some passengers it will be a new city and a new experience. Click. Bump. Screech. As the plane touches down on the long grey runway next to the river, I compose myself and contemplate the new and life-changing experience that is facing me. However surreal the journey – and distance from home does insulate one's feelings – the reality of place and time grabs the heart and stomach. A life is slowing to an inevitable stop, yet the river keeps moving. The day is ending. The sky is sombre and fittingly grey.

In my head there is something of a phoney war going on. It is no longer someone else's life you are watching, you are in the middle of an event. You somehow know that death is imminent and you prepare to expect it and respect it. A life is fading, despite the best endeavours to make it comfortable. But life is also going on all around you. A personal drama is unfolding and you try to conceal the most honest of emotions, put on the brave face and manage just about to 'get by' in the single most emotional rite of passage in your life: the realisation that with your father pre-deceased by your mother, both parents will be gone. Another funeral is required.

I had seen the paperwork some ten years previously, but must now muster all energy and see through a thing called "wishes". There is the preparedness in action as the man of lists would have wanted it. Here is the long-standing, pre-planned, default position based on a series of practical steps to care for the man at a critical time. Emotion would follow.

It is fitting that as a practical man he would take steps to guide the manner in which his funeral affairs should be conducted; certainly without fuss or adornment. And yet in making very simple arrangements to be followed, there would be a twist. It was by chance, or maybe some higher intervention, that his life would turn full circle with a connection back to the place of his birth: the City of Glasgow.

The preparedness to meet his maker was established long before his last few days. Truth to tell, illness had laid him low on at least two occasions before his death. Oddly, the thirteen years of *Warfarin* – otherwise a form of rat poison – had done him no obvious harm, despite it being supposed to last for only three months! There was also the piece of cow artery that had been transplanted to his leg to overcome phlebitis, but even that had not stopped him playing golf, albeit briefly, and by golly he could still hit the ball!

He did, however, succumb to particularly bad health a year later and was hospitalised, but still he recovered. So all-in-all he was an indefatigable sort. But it was when he was most recently hospitalised during hip replacement surgery that he found himself bedridden alongside the Reverend Jack Mitchell.

Both men had bits of their respective bodies which needed fixing. Jack was having a knee replaced. At the time they were both in their seventies and seemed to greatly enjoy each others' company. Their's was not just the "hail fellow well met" easy-going banter of hospital food, dull aches and pains, or of sleepless nights, but of politics and religion, of life's hardships, of personal struggles, of philosophy and doubtless the matter of destiny. In my father's case, there were searching questions, deep explanations sought and personal apologies to be offered and explained.

Jack had humour and was an ordinary working class guy at heart. Importantly, perhaps, he had been a military man; a paratrooper with a sense of humour not lost if you consider the irony of him so used to falling gracefully towards earth and later in life being so readily disposed to despatching people upwards!

Never mind the finding of God or the theology coming out of his ears, here was a man who had witnessed personal struggle and someone you could commune with. He was good counsel. The, dare I say, Godly aspect to Jack is important; not in any way that he was like a god, rather my father wanted some reconciliation with something that had gone before. He wanted a man of God and some form of atonement.

I suspect my father actually knew he was ill long before anyone else did. Although not a hypochondriac, he did display a rather macabre, if over-simplistic, interest in things he might have, a favourite pastime being to match the undiagnosed condition with the textbook description, a sort of epidemiological trivial pursuit. He exercised self-diagnosis all too frequently, consulting various medical dictionaries and cross-matching how he felt with the symptoms he might have. The prospect of his departure was known in the matter of fact way that everyone can predict their own demise. Yet, with gallows humour, I see now a man searching for something he might have, something that would cause demise rather than perpetuate the routine rise and fall and the disappointment of waking up. My father fully understood the sublime temporary nature of life, but equally, to me, he was always *there*. In childhood and in adolescence life is interminable, yet with experience there is the realisation that the product that is 'us' has a limited shelf life: best before the euphemistic 'three score and ten'. Where there was knowledge of illness – and frankly he was wrong – and long-standing preparedness for death, the papers before me might confirm.

For a raft of reasons, which I believe I can now understand, my father was fundamentally a solitary man, but he placed a huge value on Jack's company. Similar ages, the same place of birth, and someone who had seen what Jack would later refer to as a *darkness*. The problem for my father was that he did not want to presume beyond the casual nature of the brief friendship.

I am saddened, and ironically my father was too, that the joy of that serendipity did not extend over the last four years of his life. My father would send Jack a Christmas card, but never ever put his address on the card or the envelope! Jack would have liked to have reciprocated and both men lived only a mile or so apart. To say this frustrated Jack would be an understatement. The Reverend Jack Mitchell touched my father's life in a way that few had. Jack was a fitting man to call upon to counsel and guide my father's last journey. As we prepared for my father's funeral we both laughed at the man with no apparent address, who signed his Christmas cards: *"Fae the man in the next bed"*.

Now, years later, I am anonymous, at the same hospital. No one knows the story. The hospital appears as a discordant assembly of 1970's white slab design sitting uncomfortably overlooking what to me is quite the loveliest estuary: the Firth of Tay. In his last few moments I am grateful for this architectural mistake as those within it do great work.

Somehow the significance of the nursing care and oncological expertise does not appear to be fully understood by the three desperate and nicotine-craving visitors, standing by the main door and drawing furtive, desperate lungfuls from their last cigarettes before entering the sterile world on the other side. I grimace and harrumph at the irony here as my father's self-diagnosis and cross-matching is fruitless now. The smokescreen of pernicious anaemia is replaced by the reality of virulent cancer. As I walk through the doors I have the look of the thousands upon thousands who have walked the walk to the ward and the staff, the blessed souls whose calling, not career, is to care. Staff who talk in hushed, reverential tones and provide quiet dignity in the face of the beeps and tubes and the faint aroma of cleansing alcohol and disinfectant. On the walls are fading photographs and paintings bleached by sunlight, long past their interesting phase; they are old and somehow only relevant to those who have donated them so many years before. They belong to other people and their emotions, but they are now pale, greying semblances of lives lived before: a metaphor for all that is now.

Beyond this calm and in a private room I see the desperate industry of an old man trying his damnedest to breath, fighting for staccato breaths through an oxygen mask. The hero is now a weakened, quivering, wheezing, foetal figure, holding on and letting go with every fading heartbeat. Two and a quarter hours later he took his final flight. No more the rise and fall. No more disappointment. With waxen skin and his teeth in, proud and restful, the nursing staff had prepared him. I hold his hand and make conversation, searching for words to say; things he might want to hear. And all the time I am listening to each word, expecting, impossibly, one last murmur. I saw my father's last moments.

The hospital window looks over the river towards Fife and I think of the plane arriving and flying past the window just hours before, gently tipping its wings, saluting the hero. Not so, but a nice thought all the same. My father would have liked that, but then dismissed the gesture as unnecessary: *"You shouldnae o' done that, son."*

The day before the funeral I am outside his flat. Twenty years before, as a student in the middle of my Finals, I had moved in there with my mother and father. In all that time the other flats had been occupied by older people. It was an area where good tenants with much in common could co-exist.

This was an older generation where the open door was still accepted, and where shared experiences could be remembered. So much had gone on in their lives. They too had stories to tell and wisdom to pass on, yet we are dismissive of old age. By now, experience and its values were a dwindling characteristic of these flats. Some had been bought from the Council. New windows and doors, replacement kitchens and bathrooms were installed, signifying personal choice and desire to remove the previous occupants' taste and smell. The improvements were not just physical, but social and economic – what had been occupants were now owners.

It was a fine day. The sun was shining and daisies punctuated the green grass. There was a cloudless sky and the view to the mouth of the river, over Broughty Ferry to Carnoustie, and the North Sea beyond, was all-too-familiar with bridges, spires and lighthouses animating the beige, green and blue. The places of my father's childhood were spread out before me, but to one side, only feet away, was a scene I had not witnessed before: a young mother sitting at the end of the close with her two toddlers playing in an innocent world of toy pushchairs and dollies.

She did not know me, but knew of what to her was merely the old man in the low door. The richness of his life and experiences were not known to her and perhaps not relevant to her younger age. Here was a new generation. Life was moving on.

4
Bastard

And so his life came full circle through a Glaswegian, Jack Mitchell. When talking to a seventy-plus year old former shipyard worker it is impossible not to reflect on the atmosphere of the Clyde in the 1960s when the great cranes, like the now monumental, iconic one at Finnieston, a huge squarely-built edifice that – platers and riveters having done their work – would fling these handcrafted ships across the globe. Here were the still-troubled twilight years of life on the Clyde – vestigial firebrand politics and the implored dignity of Jimmy Reid as *Red Clydeside* saw its last days. Yet in these twilight years it was still possible for huge tonnages to be produced each year, in the process supporting trades, trades unions and politics, as well as families.

Humour and the great stories of life in the shipyards are now legendary. One tall, bearded man in particular, of whom a little later, would forge a career out of these stories during the 60s and 70s. A rich vein of humour is also to be found in funerals.

Funerals are peculiarly emotional, almost *bipolar*, as we laugh and cry in equal measure; we make light and joke as we cope with bereavement. There is celebration without colour or festivity; there is ceremony based on a process of sad despatch, not happy arrival. Within their grief and sorrow, they are confusing and abstract. We are so used to a family life being around us that in the ritual of ceremonial send-off there is the shock of uncontrollable feelings of sorrow, regret, grief and the exposure and vulnerability of losing a parent. There can be just anger too. Yet amidst the tears can be found so much laughter as we reach for composure and conceal our sadness through humour as an emotional crutch. I know I do. And I certainly did that day.

My father's life had gone and outside the calm, nervous, but good-humoured expectation of the funeral director's office he was encased in mahogany inside the long patent-black Daimler at the side of the road. The hearse would lead and other cars followed. Jack was sitting beside me as I drove forward self-consciously.

I had discussed with him arrangements for the funeral in the previous few days. These were matters of ceremony, choices of hymn and biography. I barely knew Jack, but my father had effected a bridge with him that made their respective stays in hospital far from weary and almost enjoyable. This unassuming, short, greying man genuinely liked my father and his kind words enable some reflection on the qualities of my father whom he admired for wit, intelligence, his observations on life and thoughtfulness. Jack had wisdom and insight, summing-up my father laconically and with acute observation: charismatic and cantankerous.

With this limited amount of familiarity I wanted there to be an easy quality to the journey to the crematorium. This had got off to a bad start as he corrected my cross-town navigation. He wouldn't have gone that way and so I found myself a stranger in my hometown. Jack had a likeable, avuncular, yet gruff quality, and I was somehow wary. On one occasion I had greeted him with a cheery "Good Morning." *"Good Morning, yourself,"* was rasped in an unexpected, dismissive and swift retort, sweeping off the need for small talk. I questioned the descriptive 'good':

was life not for living, was not each day to be enjoyed? Must be a Presbyterian thing, I thought.

But what do you say en route to the crematorium? I wanted to make some routine getting-to-know-you sort of conversation. So I tried to get to know him a wee bit better. Nervously I ventured: *"So, Jack, when you were in the shipyards, did you know Billy Connolly?"* The reply was curt and indignant. How could I not know this? *"Work wi' 'im? He was ma apprentice!"* Small world.

Rivers are symbolic of life and continuity and yet curiously they are eternally still and constant. They are always moving, have start and end, and one is drawn to them. They are always there. You go back to them. Optimistically I had hoped the plane would tip its wings over the River Tay. It never did, but somehow at death there was a connection to another river: The Clyde.

I feel robbed now of the ability to talk to my grandparents about *their* grandparents, discussions that would enable me to touch the early nineteenth century and feel a little more comfortable in understanding a sense of familial place: a starting point. Quite where we came from was neither fully explained, nor, at a young age, fully understood. These relationships were of little concern to me growing up and this adds to an enduring mystique.

There is confusion in fully comprehending the geography of disparate family, though at the same time this creates a desire to explain certain of the complications surrounding my father's upbringing As a child, I knew of family connections with Glasgow and Aberdeen, but there were no groups of grandfathers or grandmothers around; great aunts and great uncles were equally absent. There was no wider family set-up and if there was, it was not apparent on a day-to-day basis. The precise relations between previous generations are far from clear and whilst the roots of family connections focus on Glasgow and its pivotal role in sucking-in the opportunistic of a century before, it is the remote, rural Scottish East Coast that presents the backdrop for my father's youth, which, in essence, was fearful, lonely and distant.

Without an understanding of events and characters two generations before, my father's dreams of the freedom of flight would not have been created, nor would they have been fulfilled. His childhood and upbringing owe much to events and relationships that seem to centre on expectations thwarted by bad timing and the two major conflicts of the twentieth century. Father, grandfather and great-grandfather play roles in a succession of circumstances that were borne of the effects of war, indiscretion and corruption.

The connection with Glasgow, and previous generations, existed in my childhood through a widow grandmother who seemed to be permanently old. If youth was older in years gone by, then so were the aged. Housebound and into her seventies, housed in a modern but impossibly – *hopelessly* – remote apartment right on the edge of Dundee, she would be isolated and reliant on my father for practical and financial support. Hers was a ground floor apartment with a main road to one side and a car park to the other. Distant views of fields to the north and the steady hum of traffic. What hope could there possibly be for a frail and elderly widow years and miles from any sense of belonging?

A saving grace was that the apartment was new – brand new, all mod cons provided: radiators, hot water, windows that opened and closed with no draughts. Yet within the architects' grand vision for homes, rapidly built and adopting the latest Swedish construction systems, there was rather less concern for social welfare. Built in 1969, these flats and houses were being demolished twenty years later. For my grandmother there was neither the familiarity nor faculty to enjoy what should have been a better-planned community. Ten thousand homes and no doctor's surgery, no shop, no high street, no community.

A far cry from the solid streets of Glasgow decades before and still pretty much intact.

My visits on a Saturday or, if at all, on a Wednesday morning during school holidays or perhaps even when skiving, would enable me to hear her voice and sit patiently as my father brought in some provisions, often a fish supper, sometimes a half bottle of Bell's or Famous Grouse. I would sit patiently, drinking the hot sweet tea made with Fussel's condensed milk, listening. The objects around her had stories too.

All about were odd trinkets and souvenirs, sometimes art deco and often 1940's. Postcards of the 1938 Empire Exhibition and cocktail sticks from romantic nightclubs and lounges in far-off cities would fascinate me. Memoirs from the First World War confirmed that I had a great uncle, John Brown, who had been killed at a young age.

There was a photograph of my great-grandfather being presented to King George V and so there is a memory of my great grandfather having some eminence within the community. Quite why she had a commemorative plaque from 1916 celebrating the Battle of Jutland, I don't know, but in her distinctive voice, an accent different to those around her – a sweet drawl of long vowels – she represented a connection to a previous generation and another place. A favourite catchphrase was *"No' fancy at aw, jist plain black"*. Feminine modesty or thrift are the order of the day, and maybe there is a good Calvinistic or Gothic reason for her customers in the Lewis's department store, where she worked, not to unnecessarily adorn themselves.

By the 1970s, as she became less and less able, it was easy to see her return to an almost Edwardian look of long skirts and shawl. Caring for her assumed a great responsibility and despite a few independent years in sheltered accommodation, she soon became dependent on professional care. My frail Glaswegian grandmother, with her poor eyesight, arthritis and, finally, dementia would be supported by my father for close to thirty years.

Although his brother and sister were long gone, having emigrated some years before, not once did he regret this. His concern was to avoid State intervention and an institutionalised life for his mother. Unfortunately, this proved unavoidable and to his regret she would succumb to the Council's social services practices which could not provide the familiarity of surroundings so important to the stimuline in the infirm and vulnerable. So she was exposed to a system so cruel that in a lucid moment she described the individual being treated like a sack of potatoes.

My grandmother was a bridge not just across generations, but between centuries. Solitary in her old age, she had neither husband nor brother or sister. She was remote from a past which was rich in memory if only I had tapped the recesses. Answers, now, could have been realised. The one thing that was not explained or discussed was 'the past' in the form of the parents and grandparents, cousins or brothers or uncles, schools, places, and events. I was disengaged from a past which, whilst of no real relevance to me as a child, is now curiously relevant to me through memories of her later life and of old pictures which are now recalled as puzzles.

My father is a product of The Clyde. The connection with Glasgow is something, though, that has to be explained, for the only reason the connection exists at all is in the economic migration of the middle part of the nineteenth century. Glasgow has a pivotal role in drawing together two sets of families otherwise in Ayrshire and Kincardineshire.

Like many other Scottish families, or those of Scottish descent, there is revealed a pattern of parochial, pastoral life in small communities in the early nineteenth century giving way to the industrial revolution and familial fusion in a rapidly-growing urban area. Glasgow would give birth to iron, chemicals, trains and ships and families in a cauldron of genetic soup centred on the magnetism of the city and the industry of the age. The transition and pace of that change would be massive, in a pattern of gravitation from village to city, of rural poverty or limited means giving way to economic growth and the opportunities of urban living where hard work was plentiful and income could be steady. No longer the seasons and working with Nature's ways.

This was a time of villages becoming towns and towns cities; massive urban expansion borne of huge accumulation of people, relatively good wages and further population growth. Hopes were being realised, dreams fulfilled, fortunes made and empires built. *The* Empire was built. This was urbanisation on, quite literally, an entrepreneurial, industrial scale, where in hard stone streets, families would settle and hands would walk to work. The tenement, city life, muck, grime and graft were the currency and conversation.

In the transition from primary to secondary industry, from the rigid stratification of farm-workers and propertied society, would be the emergence of different types of working and middle classes. This was a massive agglomeration of background, religion and language, culture and diversity in town centres formed of close-knit communities. The City would draw in huge numbers of Catholics and Protestants, homeland and European, young and desperate, lowland, highland, forming what we may now describe as a cosmopolitan blend of town with country, that would lay the foundation for society for generations to come. The glamour of city life provided dreams for many, each one no more than trusting to fate and avoiding charity. Destiny had varying forms. There would be hard work and reward for some, no work and nothing for others. There was hope and failure.

Domestically, new districts were rapidly being built and incorporated into the city's expanding girth, and new, longer roads were linking the country with the town. Twenty-fold growth in town size and population in the 150 years to the 1930s would see the Second City emerge as the dominant powerhouse of Empire. Glasgow by now was sucking people in from far and wide, fuelling its economy and growth. They would be drawn in and distributed upwards and outwards in a vast wave of seemingly limitless expansion in the second half of the century.

These communities were examples of indifferent-to-good quality working class housing constructed or made available through sub-division and the efforts of the industrialists who controlled vast estates. My grandfather's generation would settle in Govanhill. Basic housing was a prerequisite to meet the growing demands of an ever-expanding workforce. As for Govanhill, this comfortable part of Glasgow was substantially the work of the Dixons. They would develop foundries and ironworks and in due course would become not businessmen, but magnates whose decisions could make or break a community. South of the river, they were responsible not just for the provision of jobs, but schools and, after 1859, Govanhill. Williams Senior and Junior were the major industrialists of the time who would combine raw materials and labour, processing each, creating corporations and communities.

Their efforts would change fortunes and landscapes. As mine owners and colliers, as well as foundry owners, they were responsible for supplying an Empire and creating their own: trains, railways, ships, engineering works, plant and equipment, they all needed iron, steel and quality coal. The Dixons would buy up vast coalfields and in purchasing estates would be major landowners. Dixon Senior founded the Govan Ironworks on Crown Street, Govan, Glasgow, which would look immense and demonic. A fearful energy and presence, otherwise known as *Dixon's Blazes*, a firey hell on earth which was the basis for community policing, by reputation being the mythic foreboding destination for all naughty children of the day!

The difficulty in fully understanding the family history is demonstrated by the mistaken belief that my grandfather, George Duncan, was from Aberdeen: an *Aberdonian*. That was certainly my own father's understanding, but as a young boy there was never any other family member to discuss or verify this. Relatives were alluded to in Aberdeen, but never in Glasgow.

And yet there must have been previous generations: this is a simple matter of biology. The frustrations of my father's life begin with the birth in Aberdeen of Robert Duncan in 1867. Resourceful and ambitious, limited by his life as a farmhand, he saw his future in the 150 mile rail journey from Aberdeen to Glasgow. By 1889 he was a twenty-two year old locomotive stoker and settled enough to marry Agnes Tennant.

Robert was the first of his generation to jump from agriculture to industry. This was no mean feat at the time, but why not choose a town closer to home? One can only assume the scale of opportunity was too big to ignore. Robert sought a degree of fortune and a comfortable life in urban Glasgow. He was smart too: in the subsequent forty years, he would become a railway engine driver, subsequently an inspector. By 1913 he was a property agent and, later, a Ministry of Labour Manager.

A career in the Civil Service was seen as the height of respectability, affording station set apart from the otherwise working class. Expectations that his own self-endeavour would shape the next generation would be cruelly undermined by the Great War.

By 1897, Robert Duncan was a thirty year old railway engine driver. He and Agnes had been married for eight years when their eldest son, George Duncan, eventually my grandfather, was born. The misfortune of being born in 1897 would be revealed as war broke out in 1914. George Duncan, by then, would be seventeen and ripe for battle.

The relationship between Robert Duncan and his son, George Duncan, can only be speculated, though it appears obvious that Robert's career path from humble farmhand to being presented to HM King George V gave him standing, pride and a degree of will for his own family to do well. The concern for his offspring to do well was, however, severely interrupted by the events of 1914 and a certain incident involving an Arch-duke on a bridge in Sarajevo. George Duncan, like many, volunteered for army service. The understanding is that he survived Passchendaele. Doubtless good-looking, perceptibly charming, and in the Civil Service after the conflict, he was a catch. But the torment of war led to mental scars that would manifest later in his life.

George Duncan and Jeanie Brown provide the immediate family link with Glasgow. Jeanie Brown, my grandmother, was born in 1901. Both were essentially Victorian people, products of their own previous generations. The clothing, if not black, was certainly dark and practical. Victorian values of temperance and the fear of God may have prevailed, but this was also a time when there was an expected courtship etiquette. And so it came to pass that in 1922, George Duncan, bachelor, aged twenty-five years, and a Ministry of Labour Officer, married the twenty year old spinster, Jeanie Brown, a drapery saleswoman and part-time model.

The wedding ceremony took place at the United Free Church. It seems to have been a comfortable affair and photographs were taken – expensive at the time – showing Edwardian formality. The long exposure time forced no apparent pleasure from either the bride or the groom. The mood is shared by their attendants. George is sternly handsome, with dark eyes and hair, appearing fit and tall in a three piece suit, collar and tie. Jeanie is slender, waif-like, and be-laced but without undue adornment.

Married life began in a comfortable tenement flat on Westmoreland Street. My grandmother talked about Queens Park, which sounded quite respectable. The actual street is cobbled with smooth pavements either side. In the shopping areas the cobbles and storefront canopies mix at the heart of activity and commerce. These long sinews of activity are in fact linear villages for the industrial age.

The streets in the Edwardian era were in fact quite young, at least in architectural terms, and the actual colour of the tenement and activity in the neighbourhood is masked in sepia memories giving the often false impression of dour, continuous tenement blocks with older, blackened facades and plain-fronted sash windows where ground floor shops are interspersed with closes giving way to darkened, stinking stairwells of filth, shit and high-octane bleach lingering pungently and furtively alongside carbolic soap before back greens of washhouses, women and *we'ans*. In the streets a policeman on a corner deals in justice and directions, discipline and occasional cheek.

In contrast, shops have attractive window displays and painted stall risers. Ground floor shops of tobacconist, shoe-mender, wines and spirits merchant, grocer and general store form a plinth atop which can be found newer soft buff sandstone and others with bay windows. The soundtrack is footsteps, chat, horses' hooves, the clatter of carts and trolley buses, and distant factory whistles. To delight the eye and taste-bud, and to tempt the thirsty and wanting, are familiar names like Rowntree's jam and confections and Farola wheat products, Fry's chocolate, Whyte and Mackay's whisky, Tennant's beer. Staples of tea and sugar, bread and jam, are found alongside ham, bacon, semolina and cocoa.

George Duncan and Jeanie Brown are growing up in a new world; Modern Scotland with its knee length stockings for boys and girls, boots and bonnets, prams and coachbuilt tansads. Older men sport the bowler hat and the fedora or a trilby can sometimes be seen, together with the waistcoat and jacket, trousers and fob watch – shirt, stiff collar, well-combed hair and waxed moustache. Long black-skirted women, with tunic shirts and wide-brimmed dark hats, and bairns playing with girds, hoops, spinning tops and dollies.

More often than not a makeshift ball is being kicked around. A life long before the National Grid came along in the 1930s, of gaslight and paraffin lamps, if you were lucky; hard work during the day and, later, weary tiredness, a life of seeming and nostalgic darkness in the evening, but in reality with long summer evenings.

Before the Great War, George Duncan was a Telegram Boy. After it, my great grandfather's career paved the way for George Duncan to enter the Civil Service. He successfully passed the Civil Service Examinations and became a Ministry of Labour Officer. This was a good, safe, well-paid position in the emerging middle classdom of 1920's Scotland, with a public, if still junior, role in the community.

The future looked promising for someone still young – in his mid-twenties – and with the good wages he was receiving, marriage to Jeanie Brown anticipated a settling down to domestic life, children, and career progression. Their first Christmas was to be celebrated in some style and with seasonal recreation: my father was born nine months later. A sister, Jean, followed in 1926 and in the midst of the General Strike there were at least some things to look forward to, with a move from a downtown location to the suburbs: a semi-detached and brand new three bedroom house with bathroom. The reward for surviving the Great War: a home for a hero.

But the apparent domestic bliss hid a darker, aggressive side to George's character. He was not shy in coming forward. This was evident on his first day with the Labour Exchange as he was being shown around the new office by his boss.

"When you address me, you will call me Major Smythe."

Legend has it my grandfather replied with Great War pride and equal disdain for pompous authority. He 'trumped', Major Smythe, cutting right through any haughtiness:

"That's fuck all, I was a Colonel!"

George was known to me only through two photographs, one of which – like so much of the photographic family records – was lost or destroyed.

There was a particularly handsome soldier dressed in tunic, polished belts, boots and webbing gaiters sitting by a desk and looking back at the camera. This was a stage-managed photograph, perhaps in a studio or, alternatively, it revealed vanity or good amateur photographic skills. It was a kind image, giving the impression of someone who had a caring disposition.

The other photograph, which survives, shows him later in life, fuller figured, perhaps even burly and smiling. Here is a well-dressed, even successful looking man – he did have some standing, or maybe wished he had, in the community – well-dressed in overcoat, hat, suit and vest. Jeanie was by his side in Crichton Street, Dundee. Despite these kind-looking images, he was by all accounts cruel, selfish and unpredictable, with a predilection for beatings. If I didn't know him in the photograph I would swear it was one of Al Capone's contemporaries.

There is a domineering, proud, if perhaps, too confident look and this is not just revealed as a result of what I now know or some misinterpretation of the old photographs; he does carry himself with more than a degree of arrogant authority. This arrogance, bolstered by a military career, Civil Service responsibility and apparent respect within the community, would set him apart. That, and an ability to throw his weight around. He was a bully.

It is now realised that the mental state of military personnel can suffer as a result of battlefield experience. Post-traumatic stress is now a recognised condition, but clearly George Duncan survived and carried a violent legacy into married life and fatherhood. In the 1920s, and at the hands of his own father, my father was not just the errand boy, he was the whipping boy – the object of sadistic pleasure and pathetic reliance.

Often in a drunken state, George Duncan would retire to bed and awake at all hours desperate for more drink. Dutiful as ever, my father at such a young age would search the various cupboards for whisky, often in the middle of the night when stupor and mental torment would lead to orders and threats.

Whether the cruel violence of childhood was an innate characteristic or a function of war or the economic conditions of the time were speculated. The parental imprint was irremovable, embossed on my father for years afterwards. He would question this dark side and speculate:

> *"I have long tried to come to terms with the spectre of my father – how it formed from his early years into the change that brought about such a tyrannical transformation…volunteer service for the first World War – four years of that experience may have given birth to his outlook on life, I don't know."*

Events and experiences had sharpened an anger. George Duncan was a violent and particularly, predictably, vindictive man. You knew it was going to happen. You didn't know when. And so my father, clearly always on his toes, would always do as he was told. There were no means of escaping the entrapment of a dastardly web of deceit, suffering and abuse.

By the late 1920s, Britain has seemingly got back on its feet after the Great War but there are social tensions and political unease. High unemployment emerges as the country returns to the Gold Standard. The economy is weakened and deflation sets in. Interesting that, at the time, the Chancellor of the

Exchequer is one Winston Churchill. The Trades Union Congress has demonstrated the power of the Unions and workers, bringing the country to a virtual standstill as proposed wage cuts in mining lead to massive support and the General Strike of 1926. These are unsettling times with food shortages, high prices and military and police presence on the streets. During the General Strike, Churchill was reported to have suggested that machine guns should be used on the striking miners.

These events had huge effect on the domestic economy and the authorities feared revolution. Speculating on the effect of this on my grandfather's state of mind would require some more of an insight than merely through the eyes of his frightened young son. On the face of it, home life for my father could have been comfortable. What better life than to have the main breadwinner in the family working for the Ministry of Labour?

Alas, the possibility of physical home comfort borne out of emotional and financial stability was not to be. My father only speculated, later in life, on the effect – the *emotional* effect – of the Great War, or the General Strike or, later, the Wall Street Crash of '29. There were, however, other domestic strains borne of George's business dealings and philandering ways.

Here was the possibility of rational explanation, but there appears little point in such analysis, for the daily treatment, at the time, of one so young seems to deny such a dignity. The actual way of life was irrational, with no outward demonstration of a loving father-son relationship. There is a recurring disgust with my grandfather, and his controlling and fearful ways seem to have indoctrinated and corrupted the memories of my father's childhood.

The spectre of parental abuse stayed with my father for many years, a painful imprint on body and soul. Life at home for him as a child appeared normal to outsiders, but there was shameful suffering and humiliations at home. There were 'goings on' behind closed doors. For one so young, there was no actual, rational reason at the time, let alone an excuse for my grandfather's behaviour at home.

Only afterwards, with the Great War receding as a memory, was there the understanding that suffering, sights and emotions on the Western Front may have been to blame. Given the career stability and now suburban lifestyle for the Duncans, there were other factors at bay.

Years later, and into his eighties, my father still bore scars and carried the pain of his childhood through sharp memory. It was not just the bruising, but its crazed administration:

> *"My existence centred on servility and obedience to the dictates of my parents. Dad was a cruel monster. If perchance I failed him in any way whatsoever, the outcome was inevitably a taste of his fists or a good hiding across the buttocks with a leather belt. The black and blue weals on my body were evident for many a week after I had endured his maniacal wrath. The rule always was to submit to his power, obey without question and never, but never, transgress. This atmosphere was the breeding ground for fear and submission to authority."*

The 'lesser' form of punishment was to stand face to the wall until he nearly dropped. These sessions would feel like hours and incessant pleadings from his mother —sometimes even from guests who witnessed the behaviour — would not get his father to relent.

This was obedience to the point of control, based on a mental and physical cruelty, like that of a dog answering to the master's call: his voice, his apparent sadistic pleasure in humiliation and his control. A phrase my father used from time-to-time in relation to dogs was *you don't bite the hand that feeds you*. Perhaps this phrase had been picked up from his own father. George Duncan was a man who could not and would not be forgiven for the damage he administered so freely, unjustifiably and so forcefully. In later writings my father refers to events which affected him and his reactions to parental behaviour. It is 1927 when the indelible imprint of hatred is stamped.

My father is only four years old at the time, yet there are graphic images and sounds – recalled seventy-five years later – of the effect of George Duncan's affair with a woman who happened to live just a few houses away. According to accounts, this love affair was physical and passionate, desperate and selfish, and in the brief description offered by my father, must have caused an awful lot of upset to say the least. This was the 1920s and such brevity presents a curiously understated description.

Imagine the effect on a young wife aged just twenty-six and already with two children, far from her immediate family, isolated and fearful. The instance was not a one-off. There were affairs with female office staff and very often he would not come home. Whatever wayward lifestyle he was enjoying would have cost some money. His pig-headed, vile arrogance would lead to tension and violence at home; his explosive attacks on his wife were horrific. In an era of female emancipation and an emerging middle class with opportunities for women, these Victorian values lingered.

Whatever Jeanie Duncan had done or stumbled across, it was clear that she had found out about George's infidelity, but this was not just mere dalliance or infidelity. Worse than that, a woman in the street was pregnant with George Duncan's child. Shame and ignominy rained. George Duncan was a married civil servant and a neighbour was bearing his child. At the time, she would have been ostracised and cast adrift from her family, facing the prospect of an illegal abortion. She was not just a young woman, though. She was a young *married* woman. What happened to the child, whether he or she survived and how it grew up are not referred to. However, it appears that Jeanie Duncan had found out about it and confronted her husband.

At the age of four my father witnessed the ensuing violent quarrel and assault which, had the police been involved, would have had profound consequences. Perhaps George Duncan foresaw and was sobered by the thought of the Sheriff Court and certainly prison before he embarked on this tumult of abuse. Wife beating it certainly was and, there appears, grievous and actual bodily harm. He was very lucky that his actions did not result in manslaughter.

The actual event had force and the description years later presents a sustained attack of punching, beating and violent shaking, even perhaps being thrown across the room. The whole house, by now, would be shaking and Jeanie Duncan, slight, frail and unable to flight against the flail of raining arms and fists would be crying, shrieking, pleading for a merciful end to a suffering that would leave her beaten senseless and motionless. What may have started as a question or an accusation led to her being so badly injured about the head that she now lay crumpled on the floor, unconscious, her face unrecognisable, covered in blood, the walls spattered. Effectively left for dead, she may not have recovered, she may even have died. Years later, Jeanie's eyesight would fail.

She was left like this as George Duncan went out slamming the door behind him. He went off to the other woman's house having made up his mind there and then that whatever punishment he had meted out he, personally, could take no more of his wife's prying and accusations. He had had enough.

Divorce proceedings were initiated and the outlook for Jeanie and George did not look too good, but an agreement of sorts must have been reached and the petition was withdrawn. What life for a young mother at the hands of such generous, freely given and unloving brutality. Later it was revealed that a baby boy had been born, leading the *other couple* to divorce. The earliest emotion revealed by my father is of deep loathing in context, an anger tempered by practicality.

> *"Such were the complications at that time, but even then I could not forgive my father for the way he treated my mother."*

There are no family records of the police intervening and certainly George Duncan did not go to jail. If he had then my father and his sister Jean, born the year before, would have been effectively orphaned. The youngest, Ronald, was not born until 1930.

What is now absolutely clear is my own father's deep-rooted hatred for the man who not only had beaten him, but had pummelled his mother – my grandmother – into a blood soaked immobile heap on the floor. He had beaten her unconscious. Here was an event so permanently marked on my father's memory that it can only be a root cause for his desire to leave home and years later would curiously contribute to his return.

My father felt cursed by the memories of his childhood and particularly the physical and mental abuse which prevailed in dark secrecy in his family for years. This hidden violence and violation he would have to endure, manifesting as it did on a day-to-day basis. The father-son relationship of my father and his father went far beyond parental discipline.

This was a cruelty dispensed freely with an added and well-rounded measure of self-gratification. From the age of three or four my father realised the folly of not doing as he was told. There were persistent, degrading and humiliating assaults and insults. It is impossible for me to comment on his brother's and sister's experiences. It would be foolhardy or naïve to expect that they avoided the flair of temper, the back of the hand or throw of a fist, the inexcusable psychological and physical mistreatment of tormented childhood. The family home was not a happy place to be and fear, tension, hunger and shame are the adjectives my father uses in describing his childhood in the 20s and 30s.

Britain sits, in 1928, between the General Strike and the Depression. The Prime Minister at the time was Stanley Baldwin. He and Neville Chamberlain would see matters through until the next conflict. This is the Jazz Age: *The Jazz Singer*, the 'flapper'. Women now had the vote. Moving pictures were supplanting the music hall and broadcast radio was in its infancy. The confidence of the age centres on art, architecture and aviation. Only fourteen years prior, Bleriot had flown the Channel. Lindbergh and Amelia Earhart have now flown the Atlantic. Penicillin presents a medical breakthrough. My father is five years old. Jean, his younger sister, was two years old and Ronnie, their brother, not born until the following year. Ronnie would be born into the family just as panic selling of shares on the New York Stock Exchange sent a shock-wave around world economies, leading to the Great Depression from 1929 to 1934.

George and Jeanie relocated to Broughty Ferry on the Scottish east coast, and I can only assume this is to do with the Labour Exchange offering a new position, an opportunity for career advancement. Far from the commotion of Glasgow, the young family would be isolated from friends and relatives, in exchange for George's career progression.

The insecurity of the time and the senseless cruelty provides a less than sound basis for learning, but my father found that 1928 brought with it his fifth birthday and so it was he entered the big wide world of education. Growing up required learning, and learning required school. My father started his schooling in Broughty Ferry, a handsome and still desirable suburb now, but at the time a wealthy haven of fading millionaire status. Fine mansions and Jute Baron's castles were set back on the hill above the town, far from the fisher cottages and artisans' houses at the waterfront.

The small stone built Western Primary School building remains, but it is no longer a primary school and is now subsumed within a larger school complex. This public school – not in the *private* meaning of the word – provided the basis for my father's formal education.

In the inter-war years, when so much of what we accept today had not yet been conceived of, designed or invented, the austerity of that classroom would be a complete contrast. Bare floorboards, teacher's high desk, blackboards secured to the wall and one on wheels which, with gimbals, would pivot through 360 degrees. The first day at school, for so many, is filled with fear and anxiety. The limit of technology in that room was probably the blackboard, though perhaps the teacher had a fountain pen. The *Three Rs* or reading, 'riting and 'rithmetic would form the curriculum. The room was filled with dark wood and brooding authority, well-drilled, obedient, forward-looking children and a teacher. For all the hardships of a violent home life, school recollections centre on incursions with discipline of a different kind: firm, not cruel, and more acceptable.

Although schooling was an accepted part of growing up, for my father there remained a memory of a very uncomfortable first day for him. There was, he later supposed, trepidation and fear in his first few days. There were school rules which were strange and new, misunderstood or plain disliked. He had no school uniform other than short trousers, shirt and a jersey. During summer months he did not wear shoes or socks and attended barefoot, on his back a simple leather satchel within which was a ten inch by eight inch slate and slate pencil.

There is pride, perhaps not in his attire, but certainly in learning. Here we see the young boy wrestling to be free of family and school:

> *"These items were the only equipment as I ventured into the realms of universal knowledge: to be instructed in reading, writing and arithmetic, the foundation tools of all future education — and how I hated it!"*

As you read this you can probably hear the stomping of an indignant five year old's foot!

The subsequent move, five miles up the coast, to Carnoustie, in the County of Angus (until the mid-20s, *Forfarshire*) would require him to attend a new village primary school at Barry. With the Cairngorms to the north and Perthshire to the west, Angus falls to the Firth of Tay and the North Sea. This area of Scotland has a soft landscape compared to the wild ruggedness of the Highlands to the north and west, the mountains providing shelter and capturing the ever-present from the west. As a result, it is a place more given to blue skies which arc above fields of green and gold. Here the hedgerows, crops and trees have a clarity and sharpness beneath a lucid northern light. This part of the coast is a rolling barley and potato-filled landscape set back from the wide stretches of beach and dunes in the memories of my own childhood, where the marram grass, if cupped and blown, can provide a rasping whistle. Scotland, mistakenly dour, is given colour.

Located between the sublime, low-lying, triangular sand 'spit' that is Buddon Ness, and its military firing ranges, and the fine red sandstone cliffs which wrap around past Arbroath – features which 'bookend' this part of the coast – Carnoustie has said farewell to its dour, conservative gentility. With its sweep of bay, hotels and guest houses the town offers a strange, if limited, mix of beach curiosity for city children and fresh, bracing sea air for adults.

Stone cottages and fine houses or town mansions are the order, and a relatively new order it is too. Carnoustie is not an ancient place, but born of the development of a new village to settle in the eighteenth century. The sub-division of the Panmure estate would lead to a sort of new town developing. It is a comfortable town out of season and the railway station meant that Dundee or Arbroath were short commutable distances for those who had choice. There were shops and certainly pubs. The Kinloch Arms was a favourite haunt for George Duncan.

Since the mid-nineteenth century the town had the benefit of the railway that would be bringing holidaymakers and day-trippers to what was once capable of inexplicable description – or *aspiration* – as 'The Brighton of the North'. In the absence of a pier, royal patronage and with an inhospitable wind, I suspect it never did reach such a zenith, but at least it lay just above a nadir of equal distinction. Branding emerged and the marketing men were either disposed to irony or brutal frankness, with the town being described as 'the least-dull town in the north east'. Bracing conditions, ozone and community singing may have reflected in the description 'Home of Health and Happiness'. In reality, the seaside joys owed more to temperance than temperature. A short summer season and lack of real investment would seal its fate.

Circumstances were changing rapidly in the 1920s and 30s. Recovering slowly from The Depression, the Pierrot Clowns and modest bathing would be replaced with new and modern indoor facilities. The town began to see art deco beachfront pavilions, halls and sports facilities, replacing the genteel modesty of formal black promenading attire. Suddenly, the town was modernising for the modern age. Old photographs show a degree of bustle strangely absent in today's dormitory for Dundee or, further afield, Aberdeen. As the economy recovered in the 1930s, the horse-drawn bathing machines would all but disappear. Golf, and its associations, would be a more secure future.

Carnoustie would bring settled instability for the Duncans. School gave freedom from the discomfort of home, but this respite brought with it the obligation to study. However, at home there were different obligations. When the violence stopped, the servile nature of my father's existence would start. There were demands born of the emotional frailty of his parents and the need to supply a thirst for whisky, even in the middle of the night. As the eldest of three my father had the role of some sort of domestic prop for well-concealed dysfunctionality.

Both parents were troubled; George by the effect of war and Jeanie by the effect of the effect, like some form of matrimonial referral injury born of circumstance. This compounded an erratic, unstable, unpredictable and less-than-calm household. They contributed in unequal measure to the vicious circle of home life. George Duncan invested to a greater extent and had a cavalier disregard for a normal secure family life.

Instead he seemed to lead a high life down the railway line and sufficiently far from home to indulge in wayward pleasure. Without a car, or any form of personal mobility, the journey into Dundee for work concealed the ability to enjoy the landside night-time entertainment of a large port. The Ministry of Labour office on Dock Street was yards from the railway station and the main harbour entrance. This provided opportunities to satisfy his continuing infidelities. Young women of a given persuasion would abound, or could be procured. Such girls were not just interested in disembarking seamen. There was a carefree other life for George Duncan.

There would be more affairs at work and nights away from home, doing what can only be surmised. George Duncan would go to work under a mask of peppermints and Jeanie Duncan would lapse into a drunken stupor. Maybe this was how she coped. As a result, household chores would become neglected. The first two weeks of the month were the worst with money squandered on drink and the subsequent two weeks reserved for scratching and scraping for credit from the various sources which sustained them. Hand-to-mouth could have been avoided and why-oh-why was there not some careful planning and household management?

Money was all too often at the heart of things and my father, as the eldest of three, was the one who would be sent to various places with note in hand: a request for some cash on a loan basis. Alternatively, it was a trip to the pawnbroker. As for George Duncan, he was a Ministry of Labour employee – *a Civil Servant* – and would have had a good and steady income. Any fiscal problems he did experience were of his own making. Money was being spent, but not on the family. This resulted in fear, uncertainty and anxiety. My father was unsettled and frightened, growing up and noting this feckless behaviour.

Wartime experiences may explain George's *laissez faire* attitude to life. He could do what he wanted, apparently and without impunity or punishment; a lifestyle choice centred on bombast, discipline and a selfish arrogance in being one of one both at work and at home. His wife was very frightened, as well as alone, and would have no one to fall back on, a stranger in a small town with two young children and another on the way. No wider family and a husband who was working some miles up the line. But the remarkable thing is the ability to conceal or disguise the reality of the domestic plight.

A desperate cycle emerged with personal shame and probably a good deal of laziness meaning that George Duncan never went out himself looking for loans or handouts of cash. My father was known to be the son of the Civil Servant, so the attempts to conceal the shame of borrowing, although a major consideration, would not succeed. But right up until the age of sixteen my father was doing the menial and insulting work of securing funds otherwise squandered by his parents. Throughout his childhood and into his young adult years, my father, at the time an ambitious and intelligent lad, was being manipulated in a life under duress. He was growing up in the manner of the servile, ever-obedient, fearing errand boy:

> *"It was always me who had the unenviable task of going round the shops to get the usual shake of the head which meant our credit had ran out. Then the pawnshop loomed up on the horizon to provide ready cash. Each day after finishing school and returning home I was to take a case or wrapped-up parcel to the pawnbroker before it closed at 5pm.*
>
> *"A good deal of household equipment was lost. Hire purchase goods would be sold before completing any contract. The willy-nilly chain of events went on and on, day after day, night after night."*

The despair and loneliness of that upbringing would lead him to question why, on the face of it, his family life ought to be more comfortable and normal – and to the outside world it was – whilst on the inside he could see right through it. As a result, not once did my father regret the death of his father. The cruelties that were inflicted fuelled such sustained and pressurised hatred to the point where he actually wished him dead anyway.

To think of going to the authorities highlights his desperate plight, but how could a young child get the point across, let alone believed, in 1920s or 30s Britain?

My father soon realised that any approach to the equivalent of the NSPCC would be fruitless, with an investigation being mounted, truths concealed, normality portrayed and an outcome almost certainly with State-sponsored consequences. He would have been beaten mercilessly or, at worst, placed in care. Somehow philosophical, there was acceptance that a lot of what was happening at home was probably happening in other homes.

An insight into my grandfather's ways is also revealed in the relationship he had with one Freddie Hood, a five feet tall hermit/dealer who lived in disgusting disarray in a unkempt cottage just off Kinloch Street, Carnoustie.

Freddie was straight out of Dickens, someone who could have been one of Fagin's right hand men. Aside from his ability to accumulate what can only be described as 'stuff', and lots of it, his other distinguishing characteristic was his appearance in stature and attire: trademark greasy derby hat, black vest and tight-fitting trousers:

> *"What a character! Those three words could never adequately describe Freddie, for he was something special and really had to be seen to be believed. He was dirty, dishevelled and despicable."*

His home was described as a total mess from the moment you walked in the door. Collections of everything lay all over the house with piles of found objects being stored in every nook and cranny. His bed lay in the middle of the room. The fireplace was not used as this was valuable storage space for brown paper packages, the walls were a mass of shelves, boxes piled high: a veritable Aladdin's Cave or magpie's nest. Aside from the involuntary sponsorship of apiary, nothing in the house moved amidst the musty damp infested odour. It was only added to.

A single gas ring on a table was the only means of cooking. Culinary skills were not high on Freddie Hood's list of domestic activities and no awards would have been forthcoming from Good Housekeeping magazine. My father said of his culinary skills:

> *"I well remember the bacon in brown paper which when I opened it had maggots crawling all over it. He maintained that once fried the maggots added a sweetness to the flavour."*

The contrast between the Civil Servant and the dirty tramp-like Hood is there to see and my father could never quite make out the relationship. My father suspected it was his father who made the initial approach as both would frequent, somewhat regularly, the Kinloch Arms in the High Street, a short walk – or stagger – from the rented family home at Church Street.

George Duncan's lifestyle, paying men and women off, meant that steady income would be lost to his liabilities. Making up such losses meant he was a compulsive gambler and on one occasion lost his whole salary to the bookies. So presumably he latched onto Freddie Hood as a means of getting funds, either through borrowing or trading. I suspect that when all else failed, when the pawn shop was unwilling to broker, then Freddie could provide a discrete reliability.

Freddie had no relatives or friends as such and in my father's words was vulnerable for association especially with one so prominent as a Civil Servant with the Ministry of Labour:

> *"Poor Freddie, poorly attired, dirty, shunned by his neighbours, probably lonely and probably grateful that a new-found friendship was bringing a glimmer of excitement to his otherwise drab existence."*

The relationship continued for a number of years and was a convenient basis for mutual survival. Freddie became a trusted friend, evident in pivotal roles as my father was growing up. But it was not just Freddie who would be experiencing a drab existence. As George Duncan's lifestyle became more selfish, a house move was justified.

The hundreds of acres of fertile agricultural and shooting land surrounding Carnoustie formed the Panmure Estate, a centuries-old landholding comprising arguably the finest farming enterprise in Scotland. Set within the rich productive soils of the

Dalhousie Family were steadings and cottages set back from the sea behind the East Coast Mainline. It was here, to an isolated and more primitive life, that the family moved next. I can only assume this is as a result of infidelity, shame and the prospect of a fresh start. Maybe, though, debt got in the way and a moonlight flit resulted.

Panbride seems an odd choice for a house, where the comparative comfort of a relatively modern house on Church Street is all too noticeable. The brand new home for the hero in suburban Glasgow was by now a fading memory. The remote, isolated rural experience of an estate cottage at Panbride and of the beach at East Haven would be a complete contrast to life in Glasgow. Even Carnoustie's High Street in the least dull town in the north east would seem exciting, with the possibility of seeing a film at The Pavilion Picture House or having tea and a cake at de Marco's Café. And what of the holiday season? Well, visitors could enjoy the adventure or pleasure of the beach, model boats and a model railway, and the privileged cosmopolitan occupants of the Bruce Hotel could enjoy fine service. Unfortunately there is no mention of such delight, as deprivations were the norm in this and other communities during the hard, depressed years 1933-1934, and such hardships only emerged as *flashbacks from a long time ago'* later in life.

Back then there were no comparisons and so acceptance was a default setting in what was, after all, Britain coming out of The Depression. Panbride was a pleasant enough place in the summer, but dreadful in the winter. Having been there I have a recollection of the Craigmill Burn running eastwards to the beach and the North Sea. The beach was small, pretty, and comprising a narrow strip of fine sand beyond which there was a treachery of sharp, ribbed low lying rocks hidden by tide and revealed to seafarers only through local knowledge; an authentic strip of coastline, close but remote, not *seasidey* in a day-tripper sense, just an honest stretch of low dune, rock and grass sharp enough to scratch young legs. The Dundee to Aberdeen rail line and the coast road to Arbroath ran virtually straight across the low-lying landscape not much above sea level. A level-crossing permitted access to the beach, but beyond this to the north was fine agricultural land. At the side of the main road, a track leads inland through a wooded dell and passed a shallow, rocky cleft with a paddock running the length of the Craigmill Burn. At the head of the burn was a steading and beyond a row of cottages. Further to the east lay West Scryne and the small group of cottages, one of which being the new family home.

There are no romantic pleasures in the recollection of the hardships endured in the matter of simply living under the roof of that cottage. Conditions were considered normal at the time, but with hindsight these were basic nineteenth century farm workers homes plain and simple. The interior was similarly plain, although such a word cannot do justice and a more apt description would be 'in need of substantial refurbishment'.

A fireplace of the range type existed in each property. There was no central heating and the bedrooms were heated when necessary by a portable paraffin heater that would provide limited, if transient, comfort on a 'need to heat' basis. One heater was transported from room to room as required. Paraffin was also used as fuel for lamps.

Although there was a fireplace, coal was virtually non-existent. Charcoal was rationed and had to be collected from the gas works two miles away. An old pram was apparently used for this. My father recalls a four mile round trip at thruppence a bag. Shortages of available money meant that all-too-often there was need for 'supplementary fuel'. My father and his brother and sister would walk along the rail line looking for fallen – unspent – pieces of coal, but walking a mile in either direction would result in just enough pieces for one small fire. Fuel was so scarce on occasions that they would even resort to burning gramophone records. The beach provided another fuel source: sea coal. This could be found on the other side of the railway line. Every Sunday there would be a collection of odd wood and sea coal from the beach. My father, his father and brother and sister and their two Alsatian dogs scoured the shoreline. The sea coal burned well enough according to my father, but was basically tar and would spit small stones.

Looking back, my father was incredulous at the memory of his childhood: life without newspapers, without wireless and certainly no television. There was no bus service until the Alexander's Bus Company provided one later on and that was only one bus per day. When a second-hand policeman's bicycle was bought for 2/6, a whole new world opened up:

> *"I could get home in the school lunch hour for a hot meal instead of the unappetising jam sandwiches I had so long endured. It also meant I could ride into the village, two miles away, and bring home much needed groceries before getting off to school."*

Groceries at the time were probably sufficient to feed the family, and but for the wayward tendencies of George Duncan could have been so much better. Breakfast consisted of porridge oats. Milk was a luxury usually delivered by a local dairy farmer who called once or twice a week. He had a chariot, horse drawn, either side of which was a large urn containing fresh milk. One had to take out a jug, and give the horse a slice of bread from an open palm. My father somehow hated this due, apparently, to the size of the animal. He never did take to horses. One would then get the measured half-pint of precious liquid. This was diluted with an equal measure of water to make a whole pint and even then it was severely rationed over the porridge.

All other milk requirements were satisfied with tins of condensed milk made up with water. Here was a characteristic that stayed for a further fifty years, to be succeeded by a flirtation with powdered milk and ultimately the realisation that pasteurised milk was readily available. At other meal times, food was rationed. At teatime it was not unusual to get just two slices of bread. On this might be spread either jam or margarine – never both together. That and tea until porridge the next morning.

The water supply consisted of an outside pump connected to an underground source. This supplied a constant supply of fresh, but cold, water to the adjacent cottages, but although it was free and plentiful it had its drawbacks. Firstly, it had to be primed with a supply of water poured into the neck of the pump: a *Catch-22* situation, when you think about it.

Vigorous pumping of the handle was necessary to actuate the suction by expelling the air pressure inside the pump. Here was the coughing, wheezing spluttering approach, with huge effort resulting in the reward of a throaty belch of water. Once drawn, the water would continue to flow so long as the pumping action continued. In cold weather, the pump would freeze and had to be thawed using hot water. When the pump was frozen, the only free flowing water was from the nearby burn.

Cold water had to be carried from the burn in whatever vessels were to hand, then transferred to a larger pan that would be heated on the range. Sufficient quantity was required to maintain a thawing action, so another transfer from the range to buckets was necessary. A ferry system developed: people carrying tin bathtubs, basins, buckets – just about anything that could carry water. By the time the water got to the pump it had lost much of its heat.

Come the autumn, it was tattie picking time and this would mean hard work for families, and particularly children, if they were to supplement whatever meagre income they had by picking potatoes.

If George Duncan was a relatively comfortable Civil Servant whose pay was squandered, then it is all too apparent that his children would suffer. And so off to work they went in the sharp, eventually bright, cold mornings of October and November, awakened firstly by the five o'clock alarm and darkness. Stirred by this, the next experience was of just how cold the cottage could be. It was freezing. A meagre breakfast next and the parcelling up of sandwiches – *'pieces'* – which would provide the midday snack: the longed-for break – *piecy time.*

Having had breakfast and packed up the pieces, there was then a two mile walk to the field. The first drill (or *dreal,* in local dialect) would be turned at about seven o'clock. The tattie harvest was well-managed, efficient and frequently you would be told "yir up the wrang dreal!".

Back-breaking work for bairns until twelve o'clock was only broken by a ten minute break at about ten o'clock. Then from one o'clock until five o'clock a repeat of the monotonous and painful wide-legged, arched-back posture. All this for a child rate of two shillings – half the adult rate. But, hey, wasn't it nice to have continued pain as you carried some potatoes home with you afterwards?

By the end of the working day you were completely knackered, hungry and facing that same two mile walk but this time carrying 10 lbs of the stuff you were probably sick of the sight of. And to round it off, a cold wash when you got home. Such good fortune and so luxurious a lifestyle. Tatties and mince maybe for tea. No supper and porridge at five o'clock in the morning – again!

It would be impossible to write about Carnoustie without reference to golf: the Great Game. Within the darkness of the 1930s where my father experienced the rapid and painful growth from boy to man, from play to work, there were daydreams. Carnoustie provided two seminal moments in my father's life: the introduction to golf would be one of them.

The Open Championship first came to Carnoustie in 1931 when my father was just short of his eighth birthday, Tommy Armour winning with a four round total of 296. This was something of a sentimental win, for Tommy Armour was Scots by birth and American by naturalisation. Resplendent in kilt, he graciously accepted the Claret Jug. Where my grandfather had seen service in the Great War, so too had Tommy Armour, losing his sight temporarily and having metal plates fitted to his head and left arm. With such a reinforced body in the tank corps in World War I the name 'Tommy Armour' is somehow fitting. The tournament returned in 1937 when Henry Cotton shot a total of 290 to win. A championship golf course would put an otherwise small coastal resort on the map. Carnoustie was now world famous and the frequent golfing visitor to the town would want two things: accommodation and a caddie.

Jeanie Duncan would make available spare accommodation of questionable comfort. As for my father, his brother and sister, well, they would be put to bed in one room. They were not paying, the guests were. It would be a somewhat meagre bed and breakfast arrangement in the shelter of the Duncan home, by now denuded of many appliances and comforts following the frequent trips to the pawnbroker. But, still, it was money up front and this would pay for the guests' meals and maybe a little would be left over.

As for the caddying duties, my father, as a young enthusiastic entrepreneur, would compete with older golfing sages, well-versed in the game, its subtleties and etiquette, and if you believed all of them they had each helped Tommy Armour along the way.

The actual game of golf had not been experienced by my father. He had never actually hit a golf ball as his own father had not passed the game down to him in the usual way that fathers do.

Peering over the fence towards the fairways he would see technique of varying quality, players hitting the ball short and long. Caddying would bring him closer to the game and there was the possibility of some financial reward too. All my father wanted was a few pennies or a couple of shillings to carry the bag. Alas, the work was not very lucrative, as visitors would always incline towards the older, knowledgeable caddy. But still, he was gripped:

> *"Nonetheless I had a particular desire to play golf, although I knew little of the game and its rules. I watched, fascinated sometimes at how far that golf ball could travel with a seemingly effortless swipe."*

At the age of ten years my father became interested in this esoteric game, a game of rules and practices, a craft if you like, that would have to be studied. A strange language emerged of slices, hooks and shanks. As an inquisitive child he would leave the house and have privacy and freedom. Lonely trips to the links would pass the time and allow escape from the pain of home. At the time, golf captured the imagination of many. Golf also absorbed my father.

Professional golf as a spectator sport was in the ascendancy and the titans of the era were Walter Hagen and Bobby Jones in their fancy clothes and fancy cars, rich at the time and beyond the dreams of many in the 20s and 30s. Here was American romance on our dour shores. In the meantime, for my father, caddying duties failed to provide income to compete with Mr Hagen and Mr Jones. This did not hinder a lifelong interest in the game, the entrée for which was quite humble in origin. Very humble in fact, and possibly even opportunistic on the part of one Freddie Hood.

Freddie had passed by the house, perhaps to collect some money, maybe just to pass the time of day. During the conversation between my grandmother and Freddie the subject of golf came up. It transpired that Freddie was knowledgeable about the game and its idiosyncrasies and wouldn't the youngster like to try the game? Freddie sensed the enthusiasm and my father confirmed his desire to try the game. Freddie, conveniently for him, had a spare set of clubs and a small bag which he would give my father if he was serious about this new found passion. This caused quite a bit of excitement and my father could not wait to get his hands on some genuine golf clubs; no more the stick or driftwood and imagination.

My father had access to the equipment and Freddie rounded this off with the suggestion that there was also the links practice ground where in the evening it was quiet and he could get used to hitting the ball:

> *"So without hesitation I accompanied him to his cottage whereupon he extracted a brown pencil bag complete with golf clubs sticking out the top. Apparently they had been lying for a number of years under a pile of old trunks and although he hadn't forgotten about them they hadn't seen the light of day for a very long time…a very, very long time."*

These clubs were probably hand-forged and not the standard set we know today. Spoons, brassies, niblicks and strange 'combed' clubs for bunkers where the sand would filter through forged tines enabling contact with the ball. I suspect if you had looked in the pocket on the side of the bag there may have been some 'featheries' in there! Quite what they would be worth today is anyone's guess. They were his now and a dream was about to be fulfilled. The young lad, heart racing, his head rushing in a state of excitement, has the clubs and the bag. He is planning the execution of every shot. In his mind he is Gene Sarazen or Bobby Jones:

"So I rushed down to the golf course, and being unable to participate on the real golf course, I made my way to the practice ground which lay parallel to the sixth fairway and close to the rifle butts of the Barry range. What feelings overcame me as I swaggered round the fences with my bag of clubs, jangling around my waist.

"This was heaven, even though it was only a small canvas pencil bag and it did only have a few clubs and a couple of golf balls. When I finally reached the practice ground I stood facing the sunset which I thought wasn't a good idea, so I walked to the other end of the field and playing down sun would enable me to watch where the balls were going."

The apparent simplicity of playing golf is not matched by any ease in the execution of shots. Swinging a club, trying to keep your head still and make contact with a small white ball, whilst standing at ninety degrees to the line of fire is a highly unusual approach to pleasure. Nobody had taught my father, he had watched whilst sitting on a fence or loitering outside the clubhouse. He may have been lucky enough to see newsreel footage of the stars of the day. Fertile imagination and naivety were met with the realisation that whilst he knew what to do in front of the ball, after all he had watched and noted a hundred times what others had done, he had never actually hit a ball!

Having played the opening shot over and over again in his head, he knew only one club would provide the effortless drilling of the ball down the fairway. The driver, yes, it had to be the driver. Pride and ambition combined as he lustily prepared to propel that ball a full 300 yards.

In the days before plastic tees (or tee pegs as some call them) there were wooden ones. Before that it was a small pile of sand upon which the ball would be 'tee'd up'. You can imagine a small boy going through some reverential preparation. The ball was a 'Silver King', virtually new at the time, with, unusually, square indentations rather than the now conventional round dimples. The ball was placed neatly, and with this the reverence turned into ritual: a little wiggle here and there, an adjustment to the stance, look in the direction of the shot, pull the club head back a little.

If you believed the advertising of the time, the Silver King's patented core gave absolute cohesion. The promised extra twelve yards and scorecard sixes turning into fives turning into fours would require the use of this unique ball. Measure twice and cut once is the maxim of the craftsman, and so he adjusted his stance once more, thought about his grip and looked down the fairway, eyes narrowed, hopeful that his vision of that first shot would be expertly executed:

> "I stood over it doing what golfers do. Then I let go with an almighty slash — crash, the club hit the ball full in the middle. As fine a swing as you'll ever see. But suddenly, like a shock-wave that passes throughout the whole of the body, the club felt a bit light."

Something was clearly wrong, and although golf is an exercise in ballistics, it is also about enjoying the sport. In his first foray into the game my father learned more about materials science:

> "I had finished the swing and was left with a golf 'stick' and some wax threads hanging from the end. The club head had gone ahead about twenty yards, lying on the grass pathetically useless. I had to face the fact that the clubs were rotten, eaten away with age and lack of usage.

"The ball meanwhile had gone about 50 yards and I couldn't believe it when I found it – it had no skin on it. The skin was completely fragmented. All I had in my hand was a round mass of elastic. After the elastic is removed there is a wee bag in the middle which is filled with liquid rubber solution. And that, my friends, is how I learned how golf balls are made."

So much for Silver King's claims of 'absolute cohesion' and Freddie Hood's approach to quality control and after sales care. Serious and competitive golf would not re-appear in his life for another thirty years. With experience and the investment of his childhood years, my father would eventually play off a handicap of sixteen, but I recall this was reduced to eleven at one point. Even sixty years later, he had developed a grooved swing and could still drive fine and straight.

5

Sweet Dreams

F lying, flight and flying machines occupy a special place in my father's life. After 1945 he flew only one aircraft and then only through a combination of chance and charity. This was no mean feat after a gap of some forty-three years and what better memory than in the plane that had recreated Bert Hinkler's London to Sydney flight of 1928. In response to a newspaper article in the summer of 1988, and just before his sixty-fifth birthday, he piloted Squadron Leader David Cyster's Tiger Moth at Glenrothes Airfield. Looking, by then, a little arthritic he raised his leg onto the wing and struggled into the tiny cockpit. No longer the rationed frame of wartime, he settled-in more snugly before the familiar set up. After the short taxi, he fumbled, stumbled and bumped along the grass strip and at last he was airborne. He could still do it.

It would be an understatement to suggest that my father missed flying airplanes in the period after 1945, but ever the pragmatist, I suspect that as the years passed by he was happy with the consignment to memory and pleasure as an armchair pilot. He loved flying and the sight of a plane in flight gave him huge delight. He could be transfixed with equal longing and envy at the sight of a Pitts Special being flipped nimbly and severely around the skies, all the time working out the combination of stick and rudder to create such motility. He recalled the flying boats on the River Tay in the 1930s, the Short Mayo/Maia Composite and its record-breaking flight to South Africa and, in wartime, the military seaplanes at Woodhaven. In more recent times he would marvel at passengers getting on planes – through flexible bridges connecting them to the terminal – without realising the size of them, and merely accepting that they flew! And from time to time, he would assemble odd scraps of wood, knives, glue and paint and create model planes as if he was still ten years old.

In his youth he would become conversant with aeronautics and would understand components and instrumentation, strength, thrust, drag, lift, weight, wing load, cord and centre of gravity. His head understood the physics of flying, but his heart was in the cockpit. In the fast-moving world he grew up in, speed was everything – the future was flying.

This innate, almost primeval, desire to fly seems to have affected much of the nation as he grew up. After the Great War, and for the next twenty years or so, flying had fascinating popularity. No longer was it a defiance of gravity by the Wright Brothers and their sole preserve. Many pioneers emerged across Europe, in manufacturing, piloting, endurance and speed. Aviation history was developing and not just in terms of feats of endeavour, but the wider popularity of flying. Pilots were feted as stars of the day, with merchandising emerging as a money-spinner. The 5th August 1930 edition of 'School Days' ('The Chummy Paper for Schoolgirls') included a free stand-up photo of the *Queen of the* Air, Amy Johnson. Even specially commissioned songs were penned. 'Amy' was written by Messrs Gilbert and Nicholls to commemorate her homecoming following the England – Australia Flight.

My father was the first family member to fly, ever. Growing up the way he had, flying was also freedom. Whether he was inspired by Lindbergh or Johnson or Earhart or Hinkler is a possibility; certainly there was a lot of flying going on at the time. Lindbergh and Earhart provided Atlantic endurance records in 1927 and 1928, the Schneider Trophy gave speed records in the 20s and 30s. Records were being set and flying was a temptation to the well-heeled who could afford to actually buy an airplane. De Havilland had crafted an industry based, in part, on private ownership of small planes. There was a free-spiritedness in the *Jazz Age*. Thirty years after the motor car, and with rail providing the only popular experience of high speed, flying was the new fascination. In one London store it was possible to buy a Tiger Moth for £730. This was quite a sum and probably represented the cost of a substantial house at the time, but the retailer would not have taken the risk without recognising what was a 'must have' for the jazz generation.

As for the dreams and ambition of the nation's youth, this is summed up in a succinct, if rather clipped, quote from the famous and distinguished officer and author, Captain A O Pollard VC MC DCM. In his 1935 book *The Boys Romance of Aviation* he offers the following observation on contemporary ambition:

> *"There is no doubt that the youth of today are taking a very real interest in all matters pertaining to aviation."*

This was also the era of air circuses and displays, the adventure and excitement of magnificent men and women in their flying machines. Powered aviation was a new experience, a completely different and unprecedented thrill. For most, the experience of seeing, let alone being *in*, an airplane was limited at best. To sit in one was the stuff of dreams and at worst, illusory. If you were in the right place at the right time, with the right half-crown, there was the possibility of having that experience in the form of a *joy ride.*

Despite huge popularity, the sight and sound of an aircraft was a rarity. The sound of wind in the trees, a timely railway engine, or the infrequent motor car or bus provided familiar background sounds to semi-rural life. The skies of Angus in the 1920s and 30s were not yet full of white powderous lines of military airplanes commonplace during wartime or the more frequent commercial traffic of later years.

My father, a fascinated young boy, was by now dreaming of flying. Whatever emotional or sentimental associations there are of my father's relationship with flight, what better way than to leave the description of that real and wonderful part of his life to him:

> *"I cannot explain the passion I had for wanting to operate a flying machine. In my young mind I suppose there was a curious desire to understand how wonderful it was that a machine eventually transpired that conquered the invisible air mass which surrounds us all. I wanted to share this thrill, be a part of it, and actually perform the skills required."*

Being by the coast, Carnoustie sits solidly behind a long sandy beach and greensward, beyond it fertile fields. There is a defining moment on a summer's day when my father was not yet ten years old. As he lay on his back in the headland of one of these fields, the sun being warm under a clear blue sky, he was slowly drifting into that comfortable semi-slumber. The air was fragrant with the smell of mown barley. Wind and birdsong filled the trees and hedgerows. No parents. Here he lay, gently comforted by heat, calm and peace.

Suddenly, the peace was broken with the sound of aircraft engines. No, not one, but two! As he swung round and jumped to his feet, clouds of fine dry dirt kicked around his bare ankles. Squinting into the summer sun, hand peaked over his narrowed eyes, excitement and panic combined as he searched the vast open sky, with eyes and ears. Then suddenly the two biplanes were found circling round each other. He dusted himself down and ran like hell back to the cottage for the bike and rode down to the beach.

The planes had, in fact, been travelling up the coast and were offering pleasure flights – flight experiences that took off from the links at Carnoustie. These pleasure flights lasted maybe ten or twenty minutes and for those who could afford the half crown it cost at the time, it was their moment to enjoy the thrills of flying. A small crowd had gathered, mostly the usual assortment of flat caps, *bunnets* and bowlers. He elbowed forward, then marvelled at the sight, sound and smell of these magical, defiant machines.

As one of the pilot-showmen placed a small sandwich board on the grass, the other shouted through a conical megaphone imploring a reluctant public to take part in an experience of a lifetime: a circus barker and a pilot rolled into one. Listening intently to every word it quickly became apparent that a spare half-crown was never around for my father and so the twenty-minute thrill was always someone else's. He could only survey the scene with silent envy. That moment kindled the fire of ambition – it had to be flying.

If you were a young boy then you could enjoy scaled down enjoyment of airplanes, as aircraft model kits would emerge. These would be costly, though, but my father would improvise with paper and imagination. Where money was scarce, which was most of the time, my father just improvised and built his own with available materials, a little skill and some flair. My father's parents kept the models for a while, but later, when he had left home, the models gradually disappeared, perhaps given away, pawned or sold. Sixty years later he was still making model aircraft with available materials, a little skill and lots of imagination and, by then, lots of memories.

At school amidst the running, chasing, marbles and football, he would be competing with his classmates, making paper airplanes with all sorts of designs, a favourite one being fashioned from not one but two pieces of paper and, in the manner of origami, folded. This introduced weight to the nose, but there was also a tail and wings where the fold in the paper gave the impression of a wing profile. Even then, there was a rudimentary understanding of aeronautics:

> *"We competed against each other for height, gliding distance and general performance. In odd moments at home I would build squadrons made from clothes pegs. Always it was there, this flying bug."*

At the age of ten, he was building models of all kinds, sometimes, and if money permitted, from kits where the painted all-action image on the box would be far more exciting than the simple wooden components on the inside. These were sold on the basis of what you imagined and were bought from pocket money put to one side over a period of weeks. How advertising and marketing could seduce the ambitious dream-laden youngster. Little did he realise that events were taking shape in other parts of the world that would shape his future career.

As my father was becoming ever more fascinated with flight and building squadrons for his own private air force, tensions on the world stage would lead to major questions being asked of Britain's military condition. Far from the confines of Carnoustie, my father's career path was being mapped out.

Since 1923, coincidentally the year of his birth, the Royal Air Force had been looking to the future, with expansion plans unfolding and the need to patrol the Empire. By 1933, Hitler was planning to redress the apparent injustices of the Great War. The foundations for an RAF career were being laid. He did not know it at the time but Air Commodore Arthur Tedder had been installed as RAF Director of Training in 1934. Tedder would become one of the key air force leaders ten years later. Across the water, in St Andrews, another major figure was being installed as Rector of the famous university. His appointment in 1934 was almost prophetic, as we shall see later. The new rector at St Andrews University was none other than Jan Christian Smuts, Boer War veteran, politician, lawyer and Statesman. He also understood flight and its advantages. Unknown to my father, who at the time was just eleven years of age, Tedder and Smuts would be the architects of his future.

6
Clipped Feathers

A peripatetic and insecure life carried on and George Duncan's financial situation was going from bad to worse. Still in his late thirties, his twisted and selfish ways continued inexcusably. As a result, there was a subsequent move from Carnoustie to Dundee.

The trademark features of 1930s Dundee were the hill around which the town spreads out below a low cloud base formed of black, smoking chimneys and the second rail bridge, still young and sweeping reflectively northwards from the Fife shore. The town is considerably smaller than today's sprawling mass, but like the Glasgow of my forebears, it owes its fortune and livelihood to nineteenth century entrepreneurship, industry and manufacture. First flax, then whaling, merchant trades and routine buying and selling and then the water-driven jute processing on a massive scale and supplied through the dock area from India and Pakistan.

Ships would make the long passage from India round the Cape of Good Hope and despatch their loads of raw unprocessed jute. From this would be made rope, sacks and, during the Napoleonic wars as well as during the US Civil War, sandbags. To the north west and north east of the town centre, burns (a stream or brook) following the broad alignment of the appropriately named Brook

Street and Dens Road, fed the mills with fast flowing water that would drive the plant and machinery. Fine mansions were built alongside vast fortunes. Philanthropy emerged and the town owes much of its public parks and buildings to jute money.

Pullies and belts and steam and graft were the energy and drive in the laborious mill work that created profit for few. The painful corollary was low paid and hard work for locals: men, women and children, and often for migrant workers. Irish labour was a key resource in these essentially working class communities. Dundee had its own Irish quarter with, believe it or not, postcards showing daily life in what became known locally as *Tipperary*.

Labour was drawn-in on the prospect of riches and housed, again, in the ubiquitous tenement. Typically three and four storeys on radial routes emerging from the town centre, in Dundee they were as high as nine storeys. Urban villages were created and existing communities were subsumed within this expanding mass of world-leading exploitation. Although cleaner suburbs began to emerge after the Great War, in the 1930s the town centre remained a dirty, working class place, with men and women 'sooted' and booted or covered in the fine fibres of the textile industry.

Beyond the large dock area, with its three railway stations and gothic revival architecture, vast areas comprised huge textile processing mills and manufactories for carpet, bags, rope and all the sundry service industries, foundries, sawmills and engineers. The town's industrial heritage was emerging and the dominant economies were now widely – if euphemistically – regarded as jute, jam and journalism. Chief was jute and its support industries, certainly a massive employer in the nineteenth century, but as jute processing in the Indian sub-continent grew, Dundee would begin to lose its position as main supplier of textiles.

Jam exists on the back of world-famous marmalade manufacture spawned, through legend, on the tale of oranges washed-up from a Spanish galleon providing a new epicurean opportunity from an otherwise pithy waste. Journalism results from the endeavours of Mr Thomson and Mr Leng. Throughout the twentieth century D C Thomson & Co Ltd would become a major publishing house centred on a distinctive red sandstone office block adjacent to the Albert Square.

In the midst of this cacophony of filth and people, the family moved into a ground floor apartment on Constitution Road. Again, whether it was shame or lack of money or simply the prospect of secondary education is not clear. Maybe all three. Given George's lifestyle, perhaps it was the ready prospect of saving money or paying someone off.

Despite the shackles of parental ineptitude, the violence and the frustrations of not being able to escape the despair of domestic disharmony, there were personal dreams to be fulfilled. Had he been somewhere else, had he been more aware of opportunities, even for fifteen year olds, in the Royal Air Force, had he the money, the supportive parents ... so many questions.

There was hope in a dream of aviation and the freedom it could provide. These dreams would be suppressed as he was manoeuvred into his first job upon leaving school. In the summer of 1937, and not quite fourteen years old, he left school and was installed, through connections, as an office boy with J & J Ogilvie, Solicitors and Notaries Public. For all the effect of The Depression, there were opportunities for my father as a young man about to enter the world of work. As an introduction to the responsibilities of a working life it was a safe, if perhaps dull, way of passing the day. It was a far cry from the open spaces of the Angus countryside, but at least he could walk to work, he would be earning eight shillings a week, and he should be lucky.

Amidst the dark suits and waistcoats, large desks and portraits of late senior partners, would be heard the ticking clock and the sound of the typewriter busily transcribing notes or dictation.

As for the young school leaver, well, it was copperplate writing, ledger work, copying, mail and minor errands.

It was a start and, with hindsight and better judgement, he could have worked his way up. Night school, for example, could have led to a career as a solicitor. A good, well-respected and morally-upright career could be pursued if he was willing to forego decent earnings for a few years. But courtesy of the circumstances at home, the immediate and frequent requirement was money and the second job, working at W Smith & Son, a shoe wholesaler, in Bell Street, was better paid and much more interesting.

In contrast to the solicitor's office the second job gives an insight into the rather more, shall we say, *entrepreneurial* side to my father's character, a characteristic which would recur, beneficially, in later years.

Shoes were everywhere in the warehouse, thousands of them piled high on racked shelving, awaiting despatch to the high street stores of the day. Deliveries, loading, unloading, stacking, ladies', men's, boys', girls': thousands of them. Experience at the solicitor's office may have given him an eye for detail. Surrounded by all these shoes, though, temptation would creep in. Ever the quick learner, in this situation my father was able, literally and metaphorically, to take stock. Who would miss the odd pair? Or more accurately, who would miss the *odd* pair?

Recovering from The Depression, money is tight, so my father would supplement his income by taking two sample shoes, which were often different sizes and styles, and place them neatly in a brand new shoebox. Inside the box, tissue would wrap over and conceal one shoe, revealing the other gleaming, polished shoe to admire. Ladies', gents', brown, black it did not matter. This was currency and could be exchanged for money through a pawnbroker. So with the two odd shoes in the brand new box, he would proceed to the local pawn shop.

Initially nervous, a comfortable and easy routine emerged. The pawnbroker would open the brand new shoebox and being, to the eye, spanking new, the pawnbroker would only examine one shoe, assuming the other shoe was the same. But, of course, little did he know. My father would walk away from the shop, and having no intention whatsoever of retrieving the shoes, would discard the ticket. As a sole trader, he was now five shillings the richer!

The comfortable suburban house in 1920s Glasgow had given way to the neat homes in Broughty Ferry and Carnoustie. The shabby cottage at Panbride and now a tenement flat in mid-town Dundee continued a downward trend perhaps not appreciated in the economic malaise of the time. The dire living conditions and sustained dreams of flying created such frustration that in time – at the right time – he would be off.

Constitution Road ran northwards from the town centre and connected the courthouse and legal district, the High School area, and printing works with the well-to-do suburb of Dudhope, though pronounced *Duddup*. In this part of town, smart tenements would give way to town mansions and villas the farther north you went. Smart is relative, for essentially tenement life had little amenity.

Some had fancy tiles in the communal hallways, bay windows and even, if you were lucky, front gardens. There are a few still standing with the original ornamental doors to the pavement. The more middle class people had bay windows and were finished in a smooth outer facing stone. A good tenement was prized. As for 63 Constitution Road, well my father described his family home as "a time gone by". Here was perhaps one of the motive forces: the desire to move away.

All my life it was simply known as '63', a numeric shortening of the actual address, perhaps a euphemism for bad memories. Here was a house – a ground floor flat – that had been the family home as my father and his brother and sister were growing up in the latter half of the 1930s. My father's recollections seem so much more detailed. His memories are indelible, ingrained pictures of a hurting childhood borne into his adult years.

Number 63 was not the worst tenement in Dundee but certainly it was far from the best. It was built for what my father termed a more sophisticated occupant. Despite being just rooms – a hallway, no inside toilet, no bathing facilities, no kitchen – it would become the family 'home' for the next thirty-five years. The lifestyle was bleak, frugal and austere. No more the golden fields of an Angus summer's day.

The flat was entered by a massive and heavy dust-covered door. Stone flags were on the floor and the musty smell of rotting timber and poor sanitation greeted. A dim gas mantle on the upper wall provided some local illumination, whilst the round skylight window far into the roof, three storeys above, struggled, rainforest-like, to feed any light to the ground.

Once inside the actual door of the flat conditions became more apparent as dampness and the lack of home comforts typified the slowly decaying property. There were two rooms to the front: cold and uninviting. And two equally large rooms to the rear but only one of which was occupied.

It was the kitchen that was the main focal point. The fireplace was a large iron grate structure covering half a wall and surrounded by an equally heavy iron mantelpiece. The chimney would frequently fail to draw the smoke from the fire. Very often the room was full of smoke before the fire was sufficiently under way to draw it into the flue.

The house had no hot water, no electrical immersion heater, no radiators, no proper bath or shower. The long zinc bathtub filled with boiling water from kettles provided the only means of a reasonably thorough wash. One fill had to wash three children:

"Later on, as we grew older, it was possible to enjoy a proper bath at one of the public washhouses. For a small charge one was provided with a towel, soap, and a plentiful supply of hot water. This public service also had a swimming pool."

There was also an old, and I think it was in brown hardback, New Radiation Cookbook kicking around which contained a photograph of the 1930s gas cooker – an upright with a plate rack at eyelevel – that was used to augment the range.

The range cooker was useless. Heat from the fire was drawn into various ovens and compartments for the purpose of heating water and cooking. It never really worked. The water was red with rust and the baking "was a joke and a waste of good pastry".

Old *Westerns* and Laurel and Hardy were also what I recall. The Saturday visit where the sixty-eight year old grandmother, yet for all the world seeming so much older, would sit three feet from the television screen, with shawl around her shoulders. That and a smell of streaky bacon lingering, most probably smoked for reasons that will become all too apparent.

This was a large tenement, quite unlike the 'single end' that many would occupy. A single cold tap provided running water into a small pot sink situated next to the coal bunker. Coal dust would permeate the room every time this was filled. Invariably the bunker was full of coal dross which was never disposed of and could not be burned. So between the smoke and coal dust, who needed cigarettes? And it was quite probable that the flat could have rivalled Arbroath or Auchmithie in the smoking of food.

Walls had plaster coming loose, exposing lathe and more crumbling plaster. There were gaping holes that were routinely "fixed" with wallpaper covering a makeshift 'papier mâché' mix of paste formed from household flour and newspaper. In turn, this would go mouldy.

Outside, the 'back green' would be not just a play area or clothes drying area, it was also the communal point for waste disposal and a breeding ground for disease:

> *"No amount of description can fully reveal the agony of trying to survive under such dire conditions, for as it was so it had to be endured. One midden for nearly twenty-two tenants, never tidy, never cleaned out and an environmental threat with mice and rat infestation."*

In the meantime, the use of the communal toilet was a constant source of embarrassment. Bear in mind that toilet tissue was unheard of. Newspapers cut into hand-sized pieces were the order of the day and then only if a newspaper was available in the first place. These scraps of paper were neatly threaded on to a string and then hung on the bathroom door. Towels for drying were invariably full of holes and there was the difficulty of finding a towel that was dry enough.

The toilet was situated in the 'close' (the main stone-flagged and plastered hallway leading to the stairs) and immediately adjacent to one of the bedrooms. With no extractor fan it was a matter of leaving the door wide open to get rid of the odours:

> *"If you were unlucky to arrive when the toilet was in use it meant a sudden surge of odour, breath held fast, and a race through the foul smelling atmosphere."*

Although uncomfortable, this ground-floor flat was the family home. It is hard to suggest that my father was hard done by. With hindsight, and by comparison, it was one step up from a hovel, but at the time there was some degree of benign acceptance, for that is how many people lived in an economy bereft of largesse, where spare cash was scarce. Years later he would rationalise the memory in terms of the effect of The Depression and wider arguments of armaments leading to a redistribution of wealth. Although we did not trade many political views, this sort of Marxist line would suggest a leaning towards the left:

> *"It must be remembered that conditions were in part attributable to the economic circumstances of the period. The finger of 'J'accuse' points to a government of the day which held wages to an absolute minimum consistent with the inflationary paralysis. From 1932 to 1938 the hard times continued unabated. It was not until the outbreak of hostilities that money began to flow into the pockets of the poorer classes who found employment in the armaments build up."*

It must come as no surprise that one would want to get away from this very rudimentary form of living. My father left school weeks short of his fourteenth birthday.

Financial circumstances remained dire generally, but this was made worse by the feckless and irresponsible behaviour of parents. For the young boy who had left school without any path leading him to college or university, there were two choices: hope to get better paid jobs over time, or knuckle down to some studying. These stark choices were easily understood in peaceful peacetime, but in the uneasy peace of 1938/39 and knowing full well that war was not just a possibility, but an imminent prospect, there was another scenario.

Attitudes of previous generations – ever-present, haunting and confusing for my father – manifested as war drew nearer. His own father was a survivor of the Great War, suffering and given to despicable torment and rage. As for his grandfather, well, he was a self-made man. Robert Duncan was a boy farmhand in 1880s Kincardineshire, but had bettered himself through study, career progression and, finally, through entering the Civil Service, affording opportunities for his son, George Duncan, to follow him. Robert Duncan was not exposed to conflict as a current affair other than through the Great War. By then he would be in his late forties, a respectable and trusted figure, a driven, ambitious man who had come a long way from the rural, doric existence of his youth, the unmechanised, labour-intensive, long days of summer and the harsh, biting, very short days of winter.

Throughout his own youth, married life and professional career until then, there had been no major conflict. With the exception of border tensions, territorial skirmishes and Anglo-Boer fighting in Southern Africa, Britain was at peace with the world and domestic and business life in Glasgow was stable. Whatever ambitions he had for his own son, George, to study and enter the Civil Service would be shattered as Germany marched on Luxembourg, Belgium and France.

In 1914, George Duncan was seventeen years old, brimming with enthusiasm to get to The Front and ripe for harvesting. He would not enter the Civil Service until after he had witnessed the horrors of battlefield, returning to 'Blighty' in 1918.

The Great War had been hellish and seemingly bloody pointless. George Duncan had entered military service on the back of the politics and peer pressure of his generation, only to witness the scale of barbaric suffering in primitive conditions – the glorious mud of the Great War. He bore witness and survived to realise that twenty years later there was some unfinished business in Europe. Haunting scars would be permanent wounds and my own father's perturbed childhood would be a consequence. He had witnessed, noted and survived the Great War and, though in one piece, was scarred profoundly. The man was now fearful as he realised that the nature of future combat would be more intense, mechanical and technical.

The natural concern of a parent for their offspring emerged as an irony. Robert Duncan had been concerned for his son in the Great War. Whatever he had experienced in the run-up to that conflict, my father would experience similarly in 1939.

There was misfortune in George being born in 1897, as there was my father being born in 1923. Despite the cruelties George Duncan had inflicted on his son, there was now emerging concern for the career and welfare of his eldest.

War on the home front centred on the kitchen table. One generation was saying 'better yourself ', the next was saying 'my son will not go to war'. Frustrated, my father wanted to get away from the kitchen table. He saw a future in war!

Even if my father had left school short of his fourteenth birthday and had pursued a factory-to-factory career, his priority short term money over long term gain, it would still be possible to learn and improve one's lot. And so encouragement was given, at the age of sixteen, to attain a Civil Service career. This was a far cry from the ready and realisable money to be obtained on assembly lines. The motive force appears to be George Duncan, who was, by now, keen to see his son follow in his footsteps. After all, a Civil Service career had been forged by two previous generations, and could, in the prevailing circumstances, be a deviation for a young volunteer or conscript; not so much a career step, more a *side-step*.

With only the distinction of the bare minimum secondary school education and with only limited office experience, as well as factory and warehouse work on his two year career resume, the challenge was to prepare a candidate for the Civil Service Examination. Despite the lack of money in the family, strangely, conveniently, and with an expedience just short of contrived manipulation, a private tutor was found in an attic office atop a run-down tenement block. Some coaching from the School of Accountancy – a correspondence course through Glasgow – was also secured. You set your own timetable and you studied at home.

At the time the concern was to amass and retain, apply and be examined in knowledge: administration, law, accounts. The objective set by George Duncan was for my father to get a qualification and, by the age of eighteen, be in a position to take the Civil Service entrance exams. A fantastic opportunity lay here, but not in the circumstances of the Duncan household of 1939. Studying at home would be fine if the conditions were right. However, the contrived eagerness to project his son into a safe and secure position in administration was overwhelmed by his own lifestyle choice; the apparent selfless generosity in encouraging tertiary education was frustrated by selfish and unshakable personality traits. Opportunities for study proved difficult in the drink-fuelled, dysfunction of the household, where constant demands, interruptions and arguments were all too prevalent. And, of course, my father was still doing a day job.

The uncertainty of the times leading up to September 1939 manifested in desperation in George Duncan's mind. He had seen the heroic departure of young men – boys – in 1914 and who would return in lesser numbers four years later, if they were spared, carrying the pain, cost and waste of war. War clouds were gathering and intensifying from grey to black. The forecast was ominous, yet curiously, for my father, at age sixteen, the turmoil of war created opportunity.

Following a further spell as an office boy, this time in a jute factory, my father found himself trimming the cones of twenty-five pounder shell casings in a munitions works. This was heavy work, but by now the wages were £2 a week. Oddly at this time my father notes his health beginning to show signs of strain. It is not clear what is meant by this, but there may have been some weakness or ailment which would affect him later, significantly, in 1943. Further 'war effort' work followed including the making of jerry cans. But with so much work being available and factories paying the best rates, one was always on the look out for more money.

For a time, my father worked in a jute factory, but the suspicion here is that parental pressure wanted him out of factory work and into the safety of a what would become a white collar job in the office, usually making tea and keeping inventories of all transactions; more copperplate than copper bottom.

Study carried on as best it could, but fruitlessness, no, pointlessness, was an ever-present thought. Domestic difficulties and the wider tensions of European politics were busy creating an exciting future.

It is 3rd September 1939 and war has been declared, but there is little sign of actual engagement in conflict. Despite this phoniness, armed conflict was, by now, believed to be inevitable. The Phoney War was paradoxical: certain conflict and the uncertainty of when, how, by what means, and how bad? Gossip, hearsay and fertile imagination fed trepidation and then fear emerged. The war was becoming gradually more serious as the months went by and the Civil Service career was becoming less important. My father joined the Local Defence Volunteers as a runner, carrying information from one patrol to another. The dysfunction in family life was about to be terminated by the prospects of war.

Suddenly, two sons and one daughter could escape the gravity of patriarchal oppression. Ron and Jean, both younger, were evacuated and for my father the Civil Service studies receded in importance as the streets were filled with troops on call-up and sandbags seemed to be 'everywhere'.

War required men and women to do their bit. Whatever ambitions George Duncan had for his son were dashed as criteria were used to determine the future of young men across the country. The momentum, expectation and imminence of war had, in August 1938, created a state of national readiness with the Emergency Powers (Defence) Act being put into place. Defending the nation, ensuring law and order, and establishing powers of requisition would be vital. Assembling land, sea and air power was essential. Resourcing conflict was a major national, strategic priority. Readiness for war had resulted in planning both militarily and domestically.

In April 1939, further legislation was introduced, the Military Training Act put in place legislation where twenty and twenty-one year old men would be con- scripted for military service lasting six months. This had obvious but limited effect, with less than 900,000 being called up into the army. However, by the late summer, the effect of the National Service (Armed Forces) Act was to make all men aged between eighteen and forty-one liable for conscription. Between June 1939 and June 1940, the total might of armed forces had risen from 480,000 to a massive 2.2 million.

By now, the requirements of war had swollen the ranks by 1,700,000. Legislation was sucking-in the nation's youth, sending shock waves into the kitchen of 63 Constitution Road, with the inevitability that a young family, not just my father but his brother and sister, would be sent to war. In September 1939, at age sixteen, 'call up' for my father was within touching distance.

A Civil Service career would be put on hold; certainly there was no more studying for exams. The private tuition ceased. Meanwhile my father reflects on the innocence and hope in the Angus field five years previous. A ten year old with dreams of flight, now sixteen years old and a factory worker. He was growing up, making money, and contributing to a family life, but there was always the latent and inexorable desire to get away; to be free. In time, aviation could fulfil this.

"Normally family ties are pretty strong and as a rule, one would expect the bonds of love to be unbreakable, but as our family grew up and the war years were upon us it was an opportunity for us children to seek release from the demands of intolerable parents."

All was not lost. WWII was a springboard for a new life:

"...With the war in 1939 came the chance to see service in the RAF with only one aim in mind – pilot. Nothing else would do."

The deep seated desire, if not hunger, to fly verged on a craving. Some physiological need had to be met; an appetite which could only be sated by a safety harness and an open throttle. Timing was against him. In any other circumstance the opportunity to fly would perhaps have been acceptable at home. But not in 1939. A career in flying could lead only to one thing: armed conflict. The risk was that a son would be lost. This was a risk too far for George Duncan who has survived the Great War only to mete out physical and mental cruelty on the home front. War and aviation were not readily acceptable to Jeanie Duncan either; she could also foresee the loss of her eldest.

George Duncan was hell-bent on frustrating the favourable circumstances for a flying career fostered by Adolf Hitler and Benito Mussolini. Some stark choices would have to be made, unless, of course, there was an angle. A three year dogfight emerged, with George Duncan and my father trying to outwit each other. The enemy axis consisted of Adolf, Benito and George.

Unspoken memories and fears, dormant and prevalent since 1918, would now emerge and taint the judgement of the Great War veteran, now a Civil Servant. In the midst of fear, uncertainty and, bizarrely, opportunity, George Duncan would see his role change from being in charge of the local Labour Exchange offices, managing the supply of and demand for labour, to being involved in administering the selection for 'call up'. Logic dictated that sooner or later my father would be called-up, a circumstance George Duncan wanted to avoid. But the law was the law.

However, anyone knowing the law would be able to see a way of overcoming obstacles and, let's face it, the law can be perverted. George Duncan had an insight into how the labour market would be affected by conflict, and the certainty of war meant a diversion of labour into the armed forces.

Air war was still a new and effective weapon and throughout the latter half of the 1930s the Royal Air Force had grown in response to the re-armament in Germany. George knew this and for the next three years intervened protectively, if to my father's irritation and anger. George's mind was not just on career guidance for his son, but a strategic positioning of his son within the economy to avoid battle. Both saw vastly different futures, and so they would be pitched against each other, unknowingly at the time, in a cat and mouse routine of one trying to outsmart the other: the desire to fly versus the manipulation of administrative processes to prevent a son going to war. George had a conflict of interest: he had to administer Government regulations specifically aimed at managing domestic labour for the war effort and ensuring a steady supply of entrants to the army, navy and air force. On the one hand there was conscription and on the other there were reserved occupations.

The Schedule of Reserved Occupations had emerged in 1938. George Duncan could not avoid its presence; again, it was the law. However, it and its subsequent variations provided not just a chance to guide his son's career towards an exempted position, but would also enable George Duncan to act as agent in the local application of the rules.

The key to this was that from November 1939 onwards, an employer could defer the call-up for men in reserved occupations. As a result, and what a result it was, George Duncan evolved a scam to profit from his role as Civil Servant. Somehow he never missed a trick.

Having betrayed his sexual politics and his financial motives throughout my father's boyhood years, George Duncan appears now to be corrupt not just morally, but professionally:

> *"With the threat of war Dad found a new way of making money. This was by way of his position at the Ministry of Labour whereby he would use his knowledge of clerical procedures to advantage."*

If the employee's job was deemed to fall within the schedule of reserved occupations then both employer and employee would be satisfied. The employer would not have to suffer a disrupted labour force, the employee would be spared military life – or, at least, its certainty would be staved.

In a small community, George Duncan had a position of some standing. Although not a particularly senior Civil Servant, he was in his early forties and had some say in how procedures were followed, who followed them, and who could benefit. Routine administration in the preparations for war would include managing figures and processing individuals. Some would go into the military, some would not. Some may not be good enough, whilst others could be so good at their civilian job that their loss to an employer would affect how that business was run:

> *"When an employer wished to retain certain members of staff, approaches were made whereby bribery involved delaying certain compulsory call-ups for the services. Money was passed to Dad who in turn rubber stamped an order releasing the staff member for reserved occupational work which meant the employer could carry on without losing any male employee."*

George is on the take. This practice would continue through the war years and would have the effect of delaying entry to military service for those who did not want to go. It was not just the employer who was being looked after. It was justified in terms of freeing labour from the commitment of doing compulsory military service, but it certainly compromised George Duncan's position within the Ministry of Labour and, after the war, the newly-formed Manpower Services Commission.

In mitigation, it is probably worth stating that George Duncan had seen and disliked the effect of military service. Whatever scenes he had witnessed during the Great War may have resulted in a desire to spare certain of the young fodder around him from the humility and horror of a major conflagration. There is an irony here, for despite such pacifistic leanings, the life-threatening, domestic violence of 1927 told differently; his punch could stretch as far as his wife.

There is an interesting insight here into George Duncan's psyche, for if he was quite happy to take a backhander from employees and employers, what sort of protection from war could he afford his own family? At this stage we begin to see the acts of George Duncan as creatively opportunistic, at all times conniving, corrupt and capable of exploiting his own fear. Conscription, for him, exposed the horror of war, the frailty of leadership and vulnerability of youth. Mental wounds, still weeping for the so-called Great War, meant, ultimately, that he would be protective of his eldest son.

Any young boy or ambitious youth lucky enough to pick up a copy of Monk and Winter's 1938 introduction to careers in the RAF would be enthused by its buoyant, hopeful approach and its portrayal of a service which was expanding in the face of the worsening international situation. It was not concerned with the 'ten year rule' of financial restraint on military spending or of inter-service rivalry. Here was a book of increasing numbers, of access to the world of flight, education standards and most importantly for many, rates of pay. The book was firmly pitched at recruitment and exploring the appeal of the RAF to a younger audience.

It has to be said, though, that to become a pilot was not without difficulty, presenting massive logistical and academic problems. My father wanted to fly desperately, but this was a rarified and exclusive pursuit only for those deemed suitable for this privilege. Certainly at age sixteen, my father could have been apprenticed, learning an RAF 'trade', but lack of school-leaving qualifications presented a major barrier.

If flying was an ethereal world, the standards of entry for pilots were no less lofty. The central theme of quality in the service ran through the recruitment of pilots and skilled workers, but you could only become a pilot if you were bright enough, or wealthy enough. In reality, unless you had good results at primary school, had a grammar school education, had gone on to university, and, more importantly, could afford the Officers' Course at Cranwell, which, costing £300, was the equivalent of two, maybe three, year's wages, then you did not have a hope. Even the award of a Prize Cadetship required the sum of £40.

Academic entry standards were high and way beyond those attained by a fourteen year old school leaver. Those with a degree would have to make sure it satisfied the requirements of the Examination Boards of Oxford, Cambridge, Durham, Bristol, London or Scottish/ Northern Ireland standards equivalent to Oxford or Cambridge. Though candidates had to be academically strong, they would also have to be physically fit and mentally able.

But within those two thorough years of study there would be concentrated military and imperial history, aeronautics, engineering and most importantly flying. In addition to a bolstered ego, fine uniform and, of course, flying, the Pilot Officer would be rewarded with at least fourteen shillings a day. If you did not want to become a pilot or simply couldn't (strangely, on the back of the huge popularity of aviation at the time, who wouldn't want to become a pilot?) it was possible for boys to become an Aircraft Apprentice, Boy Entrant or an Apprentice Clerk. These posts were not open to all, but one could be nominated or take an examination. This opportunity presented itself to boys of fifteen years of age, with three-year apprenticeships at Halton or Cranwell. The output was young men with skills as fitter, armourer, wireless mechanic, or instrument maker.

Study and application was necessary, as the courses were not just concerned with the development of trade skills, but of academic, sporting and social skills. Examination took place in various subjects: maths, physics, chemistry, biology, mechanics, and English. Those with genuine talent – apparently *volunteers,* but in actual fact benefiting from a *recommendation* for this distinction (i.e. singled-out) had the possibility of a cadetship at Cranwell.

During the 1930s, entry to the RAF was limited and unless you had knowledge of the system, could afford the courses or merely the cost of travel to the establishments, let alone have the basic academic qualifications, it would remain a dream for many. Leaving school in 1937 at age fourteen, waiting for war in 1939 – *waiting to get away* – what hope for my father by 1940? Flying was privileged and seeming impenetrable career and class barriers were in the way.

Meanwhile my father is getting older and the pace of war preparations is quickening. For him, dreams of flying may yet be fulfilled, but also for him George Duncan is about to make the single most important tactical move of the early war: he wanted to dash those dreams. With the prospect of my father's eighteenth birthday not far away, he encourages an application for a place on a Government Training Programme located in Glasgow.

These were government-sponsored six-month courses aimed at improving the supply of skilled craftsmen as part of the wider war effort. Munitions, aircraft, automotive and manufacturing industries would have to sustain themselves with the ever-present threat that the supply of sea-borne materials and hardware would be uncertain at best and, at worst, interrupted. U-boat and aerial attack would see to that. George knew how the system worked. He knew the rules, the regulations and had the contacts. He had prior knowledge of legislation and knew the government's objectives; he knew the figures.

In 1940, the War Cabinet noted that, as a result of mechanisation, twice as many precision workers were required as in the last war. Ernest Bevin had authorised forty training centres, seventeen were in operation and premises for a further seven had been secured. 700 skilled men were being turned out every week.

What was apparent to the political leadership at the time was that conscription needed to be more effective, but there was a delicate balance between military and domestic priorities when the country was at total war. What George would have been aware of is that of the hundreds of thousands of young men in the labour market, most of the exemptions to military service were probably to be found in primary industry and in engineering. Accountancy exams and ambitions for the Civil Service for his son in peacetime were one thing in terms of career advancement, but even professional staff could be called-up for military service.

A career in engineering was clearly a manipulation designed to defer or prevent call-up. George Duncan had, by 1940, frustrated a passion to fly that was about to be satisfied by conflict. He had displayed sound engineering skills himself: in fabrication, shaping situations, bending rules and turning matters to suit himself. For George, this was a delaying manoeuvre aimed at preventing, or at least impeding, call-up. The gamble was that as a skilled engineer, my father would not be called-up.

For my father, the opportunity lay in this skills training adding value to someone who was otherwise doing unskilled factory work; labouring. The reality was that the twenty-eight bob a week he was making was only moderately more than previous factory work.

On the plus side, though, digs were fully paid and there was no longer the 'tap and borrow' mentality of his parents over and above the usual board and lodging allowance. But why on earth Glasgow? Why send his son to a major industrial city in wartime: the biggest industrial target in Scotland? But that was not the issue. It could have been anywhere, it simply did not matter to George Duncan if Clydeside engineering works were a target or not. Every city was a target.

My father was happy to be on his own in the big wide world. He was away from the misery of childhood and his own domineering father. Home now would be Springburn on the north side of Glasgow. So long as there was engineering training and a qualification, call-up was avoided and there was a fighting chance of avoiding direct engagement in conflict.

By now seventeen years old, my father was independent and establishing a trade at least, maybe a career, in a world of grease, oil, and the distinctive mustiness of metal filings. Banging and beating of panels and the steady whirr of the lathe provide the soundtrack. Friendliness and workshop camaraderie was borne of youthful excitement and talk of war; sparks flying only through the use of welding equipment. Amidst this activity he would become an airframe fitter.

Engineering capacity was a critical component of the war effort and, through the insight provided by Bevin, my father would have a grounding in how airplanes were put together and how they worked. By now, aircraft production across the country was adding vital new resources and reducing the reliance on aircraft being shipped across the Atlantic, whole or crated, ready for home assembly.

Here is a unique aspect to my father, for not only is he the dashingly handsome pilot in the photograph, he had trained in and would work on airframes. He knew how these things were made before he actually flew them.

But Glasgow in these early war years is itself coping with destructive menace and unprecedented aerial bombardment. Much is written of the London Blitz which somehow fixes images of war- torn urban Britain: abiding iconic images of a smoke-enveloped, seemingly haloed, St Paul's Cathedral, buses in bomb craters and the Underground used as deep shelter. Yet the Glasgow area had already seen the effect of air raids, particularly the Clydebank area where heavy engineering and shipbuilding dominated the local economy. At the outbreak of war in 1939, Glasgow was preparing itself not for the arrival of my father the following year, but for the departure of over 120,000 of it residents in a mass evacuation on some 322 special trains. But home, in whatever form, always seems to be more safe than anywhere else and by 1941 some seventy-five to eighty per cent would return only to be met with the onslaught of carefully targeted further mass bombing.

By comparison, Springburn was relatively safe. Springburn lay to the north of downtown Glasgow and maybe six or seven miles from Clydebank to the west; a place that would be attacked at various times between 1940 and 1943, but brutally ravaged in the Clydeside Blitz of 1941. This scale of suffering is not recorded by my father, and mercifully his training was not in Clydebank, but he did bear witness to these air raids, and it does not appear that he was a reluctant bystander. If conflict can demand attention in its awe, then my father found Springburn afforded an excellent vantage point over the city.

The might of the Luftwaffe rained heavily on 13th and 14th March 1941. These raids were not comprised of just bombs falling, but of initial incendiary devices to identify target areas then waves of substantially larger firebombs critical to larger scale destruction and intense heat. Emergency services simply could not cope with such extremes and any attempt to deal with the situation was thwarted by damage to the water supply. When the cold light of day finally appeared, tens of thousands were without homes, 4,000 of which had been destroyed, a further 8,000 homes were damaged to varying degrees. Over 500 people died, with many hundreds more seriously injured.

The tenements of my grandfather's time remained, substantial and stone-built, on three or four levels and with the communal close giving way to an internal stairway serving the individual flats. Sometimes a half-landing would present a doorway into a shared outside toilet, its characteristics being indifferent plumbing, smell, cigarette smoke, newspaper, string and, in the absence of a secure lock on the inside, perhaps whistling of varying quality from whoever the occupant may be.

These large runs of housing would back onto a large open area where children would play and mothers would talk. Washing lines would string between cast iron poles on the ground. Ingenuity manifested in the massive wooden poles rising fifty feet in the air and enabling clothes to be hung out to dry on a rope and pulley system connected to the stone surround of the kitchen window. The 'back green' was a hub of daytime domestic activity. Two, three or four streets, depending on configuration, would use this area. Literally dozens of families, hundreds of people, would form these tightly-knit communities. Aside from the children playing and the women gassing away as they did their laundry in the communal washhouse, these large open areas would be seemingly safe from building collapse or fire in the event of an air raid. Reinforced concrete air raid shelters would be built above ground.

In shared accommodation, my father would be bored, restless and curious. Hundreds of people living high up in wide streets concealed the scale of human concentration. Only when two or three generations from hundreds of flats emerged into the streets and back greens was there any idea of what an air raid meant. The risks and ravages of air strikes were fully understood, with a well-practiced rush to the air raid shelter replacing initial panic.

Whatever claustrophobia there was in digs would be exacerbated during these raids. When the siren sounded, the air raid shelter would become a very crowded and noisy place. Emotions running high, babies crying, mothers surrounded by people were beside themselves with worry and fear; men and boys equally scared and excited. Better the raid than such discomfort, thought my father. There were people around him, but in the shelter there was no family, no parental control.

He was a young adult of determined mind, on his own and Hitler was about to demonstrate his air power. Idle curiosity borne of intrigue and the shelter's all-too-close discomforts led him to the rooftop where he saw German bombers above the city. They had flown across the North Sea and up the Forth Estuary. They would then bear south-west to pick up the River Clyde. On a moonlit night this silver vein would lead to Glasgow's heart. The crews' objective was to destroy the engineering and shipbuilding capability of the river and its people. Weather conditions did not favour a discrete German attack:

> *"Being young and curious I could not suffer the claustrophobic atmosphere of the air raid shelters, so I made my way up to the roof of the building in order to see some of the action which was taking place. From where I was I was too far away to see the bombing effect. All I can say is that the sky was lit up with a full moon and hundreds of searchlights traversing the sky."*

Later, the tumult of war and an air raid on the city where he was staying provided indelible memories:

"The noise was unbelievable. Bomb explosions are one thing; but what was more frightening was the bursting of anti-aircraft shells. The guns surrounding Glasgow had all opened up and were firing seeming indiscriminately into the darkness of the night sky. I had jammed myself between a wall and a chimney stack and every now and then banged my face up against the chimney stack every time a gun close by fired another shell.

"The whole raid lasted probably half an hour but seemed like eternity until all the bombers had passed over and flown down the Irish Sea on their way back to the French coast.

"One plane which did not get back was on display in a car park near St Vincent Street. I well remember visiting and sitting in the cockpit of a German bomber — a JU88."

In a guest house in Frederick Street he experienced the effect of a bomb which had exploded in George Square, about two or three hundred yards from where he was staying. The explosion blew him and his bed across the room:

"The next day I discovered that, apart from the crater in the square itself, nearly every window for miles around was broken and although such extensive window damage was apparent, the strange thing I noticed was that it was every alternate street that actually saw the worst of it, as if the shock waves hammered every second street in a radius of about half a mile all around George Square.."

Despite the ravages of war and the effect it had on the home front, my father continued to want to fly. Although at the age of seventeen he is being trained in engineering — in the engineering centre of excellence that was Glasgow — a series of events is unfolding that will set back his flying career, denying a more full role in the war.

The simple fact is that George Duncan had blatantly, but unknown to my father, contrived entry to engineering training that was destined for a reserved occupation; his son would be protected by statute. Yet the prospect of a life of factory work loomed large unless steps could be taken to get into a cockpit.

With two men vying for one future, the career path at this time did not reflect single-minded determination; certainly not as long as George Duncan was influencing things. But the sole objective remained: to fly. It would be an unsettling observation that Mr Chamberlain and Herr Hitler provided expedient career opportunities which George Duncan could thwart! Luck was on his side.

7

Fortune of War

On completion of the engineering course, fresh from the engineering workshop in Springburn, my father was assigned to the Civilian Repair Organisation, a vast federation of forty-three firms including famous names such as motor car manufacturers Jaguar and Morris and furniture makers like Parker-Knoll. All were responsible for aircraft repair work, reporting to the Air Ministry and enabling the RAF to do what it did best. He was offered work with one of the lesser-known British aircraft companies, Cunliffe-Owen. Still a teenager and destined for a safe post away from the risk of call-up, my father looked forward to being amongst aircraft, but he harboured dreams of flight and knew that soon he would have to fulfil that dream.

Following his 'graduation' from the government training programme, his first posting with Cunliffe-Owen was to their outstation at remote, small, stone-built Edzell, in the north of Angus and not far from Montrose. George Duncan was placated by the belief that his son would be safe and 'just up the road'.

Edzell is in the foothills of the glens separating Angus from Aberdeenshire and Kincardineshire. Quite distant even now from larger towns, so one can only imagine the difficulties of getting there in 1941. The journey back from Glasgow to the east coast was a relatively swift affair with the train journey from Glasgow involving a stop in Dundee and the obligatory visit to parents. The war was visible in the sandbags, the taped windows, the signs, and for my father the impact of rationing at home. From Dundee East Station, the journey to Montrose by train was less than an hour in duration, but Edzell lay further inland to the north west. The windblown coast and tidal flatlands embracing Montrose gave way to distant mountains.

Formerly a Royal Flying Corps aerodrome, RAF Edzell was, in later years, commissioned by the USAF and until 1997, was one of many Cold War 'listening posts' located around the globe the role of which was to monitor submarine activity. Similar secrecy seems to have been reflected in the pair of meet and greet guys who welcomed my father to strange new surroundings. The impression given was one of fedora hats and overcoats, collars probably turned up for added effect.

Meeting my father on neutral territory in the local hotel did nothing to dispel any feelings of foreboding anticipation. The expectation was that one would report nervously to premises, form a view, meet colleagues, understand the work, find someplace to stay and settle in. Not so, in 1941. The meet and greet proceeded, a sort of interview ensued and the following day, armed with a note, he was directed to a guest house back in Montrose, then instructed to report to the base. The two men who had interviewed him the night before in the Edzell hotel had conveniently disappeared once they had put him in digs with a Mrs Murray in High Street, Montrose.

Somehow shady in retrospect, I wonder if the two who disappeared were concerned with security? Screening a potential spy, perhaps, or was Cunliffe-Owen activity a cover for some clandestine research? Certainly there was a different form of clandestine activity where my father was concerned. An older woman took his virginity.

Edzell was, in strict RAF nomenclature, No.44 Maintenance Unit (44 MU) formed in August 1940 and was basically an aircraft storage unit far from the front line and a safe enough depository for hardware. Unfortunately for my father it was not used for flying at that time and strangely there was only one old Lockheed Hudson and not even the complete aircraft! It seemed to be recognisable as Hudson, if only because he had been told it was one. There was no tail unit, no wings. It was, quite simply, a shell with the belly torn as if it had been in a belly-flop landing with its wheels up.

Having trained in metal fabrication, it became clear rather quickly that Edzell was a cast-iron disappointment. Matters got worse. There were no spares, no tools, no equipment, no office, no stores. Nobody seemed to know what was happening. Needless to say he learned how to repair aircraft. Spares did eventually arrive and a career emerged in milling, cutting, rolling, and fitting. A career was forged and the work was, well, riveting. He worked on the solitary Hudson and managed to get it looking like its old self again. Pay was very good and he was able to send money home each week. He was no longer a product of an engineering training centre, but a fully paid Airframe Fitter, part of the war effort. This was just what George Duncan had wanted, and there was a comfortable coincidence that the initial posting was not so far away from home.

After many weeks turned into six months of experience and expectation, the posting to Edzell remained a dispiriting experience. The longed-for dream of working in aviation had become a somewhat dull reality. The vision yet to be realised was to pilot an aircraft, not merely fix it! Was he ever going to fashion a flying career as far as possible from Scotland?

Courtesy of new priorities, my father found himself transferred to another Cunliffe-Owen outstation at Silloth, on the Solway Firth.

From a childhood in Carnoustie, an independent working life in Glasgow and then Edzell, my father wound up in the remote and rural far north west of England, in Westmoreland: what is now called Cumbria. Only a few miles across the Solway Firth, and as far away from Scotland as he could get.

Cumbria conjures up images of mountains and lakes, but by contrast what greeted him was a very low and vulnerable piece of coastline; an area of dangerous, shifting, Solway sands and unpredictable vulnerability. Tide and sandflats merge, with the Irish Sea and the rivers Wampool and Waver, giving way to what appeared to be poorly drained land relieved only by an uninterrupted panorama back to Scotland, seven miles away. Far off and landward to the south-east is the Lake District, with its verdant – quintessentially English – fells. But here on the Solway there are drainage ditches and dykes, sea defences and a landform that can in places reach barely above thirty feet. In this landscape so far from what mattered most – the sky – he was one step away from a flying career.

Silloth does not sound a very romantic place. But for the fact that my father was there in 1941, it would remain an unremarkable place; remarkable, if at all, only for its anonymity. The current anonymity of the place belies not just the scale or importance of the place for a military base, but the significant piece of training apparatus that was named for the town. Curiously, there is no mention by name of the 'Silloth Trainer' in my father's notes, though.

To some extent, the town is a bit like Carnoustie: small, tidy and new. The town is a surprising place with a *planned* geometric look that only town planners defiant against the medieval haphazard can ensure. It is also relatively modern and a function of maritime, railway and health resort attributes. Coastal, with good anchorage away from the sometime ravages of the Irish Sea, the Admiralty recognised safe haven in the Solway Firth's waters.

An inner and outer harbour was built, all square and cut out of the coastline, and the first wet dock on the Cumbrian coast in an area which was without such a facility. Years later the town would grow as a railway town, born out of the Carlisle and Silloth Bay Railway and the development of the port.

It was also a resort with air fresh enough to rival the Angus coast. An eminent contemporary physician declared "the air to be cleaner and more health giving than anywhere else". And so the local economy developed on the back of the port, the railway, and tourism. Large grand hotels were built to accommodate visitors and Silloth became a Victorian seaside resort. In wartime, Silloth's role would change fundamentally.

To the east of the main town lies the airfield, now home to various businesses and the Sunday Market. Otherwise, today, it is a cold, less-than-welcoming, place with massive hangers in an open flat landscape commanded by too much sky and too many memories of war effort and the many who died in all-too-frequent accidents. Amidst the wind and memories, nostalgia enables the sounds of plane motors and rivet guns to be heard. Initially it was an Aircraft Storage Unit (ASU) and maintenance station, its function to receive and store new aircraft like Lockheed Hudsons. Constructed on the wave of RAF expansion of the late 1930s, RAF Silloth was purpose-built, reflecting the latest Air Ministry specifications for an ASU, including vast new reinforced concrete hangers for the storage of more and larger aircraft, some one hundred yards long and fifty yards wide, equivalent to a football ground or seventy-five cricket pitches! Cunliffe-Owen occupied one of these vast D-type hangers.

For my father, this was a new air force base, the scale of which he could merely marvel at. The site was identified in 1938, the facility opened in 1939, but construction carried on until 1941, providing a thriving facility where hundreds of aircraft would be stored, prepared and repaired. By April 1940, Silloth's official title was Coastal Command Station No.1 Operational Training Unit. It was bigger and better than Edzell and was cosmopolitan in a way that only wartime can create. Canadians, Americans, Kiwis and Aussies could be heard. No longer would my father have just one relic of a Hudson to play with, as an important function of the base was that of converting pilots to fly the Hudson type. The airfield would also train aircrew for reconnaissance and rescue. The intensity of the operation was immense, or so my father thought: modern runways and dozens – ultimately hundreds – of the latest aircraft, hundreds of staff – civilian and military – a real role for him, with a genuine glimpse of what the RAF could, just could, provide. Grease and aviation fuel may not sound so seductive, but the curves of aeronautical beauty and seeing others in the cockpit created envy.

Silloth was a strategic location; far enough – literally as far as one could get in England from the south east coast – from immediate Nazi threat. It was also strategic as it aided the command of the North Atlantic and was handy for incoming planes being flown over the Atlantic should they be diverted from the Air Ferry terminal at Prestwick. He was busy. He was doing the same as at Edzell, only more of it! The sustained flying in inhospitable coastal and Atlantic conditions resulted in considerable wear and tear and damage to the Coastal Command airplanes. This required swift and ready repairs to compensate for what the 'top brass' might see as questionable and regrettable flying practice: all too frequently the aircraft would crash on approach or take off. As a result he was kept busy, and to a degree was enjoying what he was doing. It just wasn't enough. He had a transient association with these birds when all along he wanted a physical relationship. Airplanes would land, airplanes would take off. The Hudson was doing important work and was a key part of the Islands' defence, but airplanes required pilots and lots of them.

These guys would have to be trained and the demands of maintaining a steady supply of flyers meant that new technologies developed. The aforementioned 'Silloth Trainer' was the forerunner to the flight simulator we know today. My father merely described it as a Hudson fuselage with electrics and pneumatics fitted to simulate instrument readings, engine sound, and movement for 'realistic' training.

The desire to fly ate at him. At the age of eighteen, independent and with experience of bombing raids under his belt, my father was out there in a big world, applying what he knew of airframe engineering and instrumentation. He was also earning money, watching movies, dancing and meeting girls. Far from the farmhouse lodgings that was home at the time, the dizzying cosmopolitan aire of Wigton would provide opportunities to grow up free of the strictures of the family home. He wasn't free as a bird yet, but he was working on airplanes. He was enjoying a life he had not known before. He felt he was doing what he had been taught at Springburn and applying that which he had learned at Edzell. Unfortunately, this was as exciting as war could get. Overall, sheet metal, rivets, wiring looms and undercarriage repairs could not sustain him. Flying was so frustratingly, temptingly close.

As impatient as he was, he did not appreciate the significance of his associations with Cunliffe-Owen. As an airframe fitter, my father was a tiny part of a wider initiative that saw the US marshal its politics and resources in support of the war effort in Britain. At the time, there was a crying need for modern aircraft in vast numbers to meet the forces of the Third Reich and Lockheed and North American aircraft were part of the response, slow to begin with, but by 1941 vast numbers were being supplied. My father was not just repairing aircraft, but preparing them fit for duty following delivery. Cunliffe-Owen were part of the war effort and though their name may be less well known they were critically involved in bolstering defences using US hardware.

Cunliffe-Owen Aircraft Ltd had been set up in 1938 and chaired by Sir Hugo Cunliffe-Owen, engineer to trade, racehorse breeder and owner, industrialist and by then, Chairman of the vast British American Tobacco corporation. Unlikely as it was, the diversification from tobacco into aviation led to vast purpose-built facilities being constructed at Eastleigh in Hampshire. Sir Hugo was an entrepreneur and in the imminence of war he saw an exciting opportunity to build new aircraft, strikingly bold in design and with unparalleled performance.

Years later my father would talk of their involvement in a 'flying wing', a radical concept way ahead of its time, or so he thought, and one which fired his imagination. For years, the words 'flying wing' were synonymous with Cunliffe-Owen and its marketing of a remarkable-looking and dynamically superior American aircraft the manufacture of which had been secured under license. The airplane was otherwise the work of a Texan, one Vincent Justus Burnelli; an unsung genius of modern aviation.

In Britain at that time, the flying wing aircraft most readily identified with Cunliffe-Owen Aircraft was the OA-1, otherwise the quaintly alliterative *Clyde Clipper*, an ungainly looking plane, quite unorthodox in look, and in behaviour, too, a breed apart. Cunliffe-Owen came by the aircraft in a quite odd way and one with an interesting Scottish twist. In 1936 an existing design, the UB-14, was licensed to the Scottish Aircraft and Engineering Company. However, this was a short-lived venture and despite the dynamics of the design, production never took off. The company went bankrupt in 1937 and the following year, in 1938, the rights to the design were obtained by the newly-formed Cunliffe-Owen Aircraft Ltd.

The performance of the Burnelli designs, in terms of load, lifting capability and safety, was seductive and doubtless this appealed to Sir Hugo when he secured the license to build. With Burnelli as consultant and Sir Hugo providing the investment, the UB-14 design was adapted and became the OA-1. By 1940, and unique in being the only aircraft of its type, it was flying routinely and would become General de Gaulle's preferred choice during the war. It had a wing-profile fuselage, extending to port and starboard towards the wingtips. Twin-engined, these were set into the leading edge before giving way to twin booms and the tail structure.

Aside from the normal 'wing and fuselage' designs for aircraft, where the wing merely provides lift for an essentially tube-like fuselage, the early part of the twentieth century saw much fascination with alternative forms of lift. Different configurations of wing and aircraft body were being designed, tested, perfected and produced. In the case of Vincent Burnelli, the potential for the fuselage itself to provide additional lift was the basis for virtually a lifetime's work. Efficient aircraft design meant that more parts than merely the wing should provide lift.

Burnelli was designing and producing wide-bodied biplanes and, as photographs demonstrate, by the early 1920s these were flying above Long Island. The Burnelli models RB1 and the RB2 of the period were otherwise large biplanes with wide bodies, something like fifteen feet wide fuselages, rectangular in cross section and with a side profile not unlike a wing. The body had the appearance of two aerodynamic caravans, or trailers, bolted side-by-side. The nose of the aircraft was the *leading edge* with two piston engines providing propulsion. Behind this, the massive body tapered to a trailing edge with built in ailerons and rudders. Fixed upper and lower wings made this ungainly looking plane look like an airplane! Into the late 1920s and 1930s, the contemporary, more aerodynamic, look of the Burnelli was establishing itself, with the subsequent evolving designs – faithful to the basic concept – setting the tone for the more famous OA1, the Clyde Clipper, as used by de Gaulle.

For a number of reasons – political and financial – the Burnelli flying wing was not a success. Despite its capabilities being recognised by the military and Burnelli being a leading aeronautical designer of the time, in wartime there was no support from the US government. A degree of mystery surrounds the precise reasons why, but a range of factors are cited.

Despite winning US Government competitions to supply aircraft, with noted support for Burnelli from the senior US General, 'Hap' Arnold, a 1941 Washington report sealed its fate substantially, with the designs being deemed to breach established aeronautic practice. What were deemed subsequently to be inefficient had been described by Arnold in 1940 as "essential, in the interest of national defense". Dismissively, the design was no longer of interest to the Air Corps and, perhaps most conclusively, no consideration was to be given to the designs 'ever again'. Politically, it has been suggested that President Roosevelt did an about turn, cancelling the contract for the Burnelli planes when he realised that the project funding was being provided by a benefactor to a political opponent. Industry interference has been alleged, with knowledge of the aeronautical benefits being suppressed by other manufacturers. Undefeated, Burnelli carried on.

By 1945, a Burnelli plane, the CBY-3, though continuing to be unconventional, was outperforming the hugely popular Douglas DC-3 in terms of payload and short take-off capabilities. The CBY-3 was airborne after 650 feet, the steeply swept tail fin booms indicating a steeply angled take-off.

Burnelli was far-sighted and brilliant and many to this day argue that his designs outperform the orthodox wing and fuselage. Whatever lack of success he had commercially, his designs were critically acclaimed and despite alleged conspiracy, corruption and interference, somehow did influence – to the point of being close to copy – high-performance aircraft design from the 1940s onwards.

A lot depends on how you define the 'flying wing' concept. Certainly my father was familiar with the work of Cunliffe-Owen in a *sort of* flying wing otherwise known as the *lifting fuselage*. Junkers and Burnelli, and others too, proved that alternative aircraft forms could fly, offer a different flight experience and compete in performance against conventional forms. These innovative approaches, at the time, would pave the way for the genuine flying 'delta-wing' with absolutely no visible distinction between the fuselage and the lifting surface and de *minimus tail*.

In a 1930 publication entitled *Aviation of Today – its History and Development*, the authors J L Naylor and E Ower refer to a tail- less machine invented and built by Dunne in Scotland in 1911. This was the Dunne D5 constructed by John William Dunne, a pioneer of unorthodox aircraft design, and built by Shorts. A picture of 'The Pterodactyl' is contained in the frontispiece. In look, it had a short, stubby body with delta wings swept back 'resembling an arrow head'. Apparently it was flown successfully, with the controls locked in order to demonstrate its stability. The magazine, *Flight*, published 18th June 1910 extols the craft's natural stability and confirms the aircraft's flight of 2.25 miles at Eastchurch on the Isle of Sheppey, with Lieutenant Dunne, then thirty-five years old, at the controls. The 'pterodactyl' design appeared in the subsequent work of Westland Aircraft.

The more genuine flying wing concept would be further developed and perfected after 1945, the key, as ever, being to understand the fundamental matter of stability. We somehow take for granted, largely because we now know how to manage stability and control, the later work of Grumman Northrop and 'Stealth' bombers which really were flying wings. But at the time there was hugely influential work underway pushing the boundaries of aeronautics.

The ifs, buts and uncertainties of the Burnelli aeronautics – put bluntly, interference and the lack of orders – meant that by 1941, Cunliffe-Owen's business operations would have to alter. The remainder of the war years for Cunliffe-Owen were spent in aircraft manufacture, including Tornados and Spitfires, leading to the development of the pretty, but unsuccessful in sales terms, Concordia, a twelve-seater civil aircraft which first flew in 1947. Lack of orders for this model echoed the earlier experience with the OA-I. In the early years of post-war civil aviation the availability of surplus and better aircraft saw the demise of the company.

However, for my father in late 1941, Cunliffe-Owen's associations with the 'flying wing' were a thing of the past as they carried on performing more-routine sub-contract work via the Civilian Repair Organisation for the Air Ministry. This involved the supplying, modifying, maintaining and repairing of Lockheed Hudsons, a twin-engined variant, with modified tail fins, of the Lockheed Electra, but adapted for use as bomber, escort, and by Coastal Command for patrol and reconnaissance duties. The Lockheed Corporation of Burbank, California, were supplying these aircraft: gifts from across the Atlantic. And not just Lockheed, not just a company based somewhere, but the Lockheed Corporation, of Burbank, California.

My father recalled this in his notes; strange that a company name can conjure up a celluloid memory of the era. By comparison with the staid, stiff upper lip, Cunliffe-Owen name, Lockheed – a phonetic spelling of the old Scots, *Loughheed* – represented romance and Cunliffe-Owen were justifiably proud of their associations. Advertising of the time made play of the place of manufacture which was, after all, located at the heart of not just Californian aviation, but the movie industry. So far as the British were concerned, one could easily have advertised these aircraft under the banner: *'They're American, they're good, and they're all the way from Hollywood'.*

But what is clear is the emergence of American airframes supporting British defence well before their entry into the war in December 1941. Hardware was required in order to fight the enemy, and with British manufacturing capability being limited, transatlantic partnering programmes were established. Lockheed were involved very early on in the supply of planes to the British Government. The Hudsons my father was working on were part of the supply chain dating back to the initial order of 1938.

The resourcing of the European war required not just personnel but airplane production and aside from domestic manufacture there were agencies abroad, such as the British Direct Purchase Commission who would procure aircraft from US manufacturers at a time when the US Government's official position was one of neutrality. It has to be remembered that this was pre-Pearl Harbour and Britain relied upon its Dominion family as well as whatever resource could be made available from the United States. Creative procurement routes emerged from diplomatic to-ing and fro-ing to overcome the officially neutral position. But inevitably Britain was on the edge of the European land mass and had to look west if adequate resources were to be presented against the Third Reich. Philosophical difficulties were borne of the complex American interpretations of the war. States-side politics were frustrating the war effort. The vast Atlantic Ocean separated Washington from London, the Channel separated England from France. Yet it was a much smaller watercourse that focussed minds; smaller than an ocean, smaller than a sea or a lake, not even a river. Britain was up a creek.

On 15th May 1940, Prime Minister Churchill had made clear to President Roosevelt in a telegraph that if necessary the war would be continued alone and that the voice of the United States "may count for nothing if withheld too long". The withdrawal at Dunkirk two weeks later somehow sets the tone in subsequent strategic claims upon the US.

Despite Churchill's case to Roosevelt, Britain was far from alone but, in reality, its geographic position was far from anywhere. The nearest Dominion neighbour, Canada, was at least 2000 miles to the west. To the south of Canada lay the United States whose production capability and military and economic resources could assist the European conflict. Personal and official requests for transatlantic aid were made. Lord Lothian to the State Department on 3rd July 1940 made clear the request for immediate and long term aid: weapons and action required at once and "those tools to finish the job". Destroyers were requested, also motor torpedo boats for coastal patrol, rifles, machine guns, field guns and mortars. The Government asked for American aircraft.

The war, in July 1940, is ten months old, European states have fallen to the Third Reich and major death and destruction is unfolding. That Britain would be 'next' was a palpable reality and certain fear.

Despite the difficulties presented by American neutrality there were concerns about the illegalities and aggressions from Germany, neutral impartiality and certain elements who could be interpreted as pro-axis. Some even thought of the Royal Naval interventions as anti-democratic. Urgency and desperation led to continuing frustration, with the British Government, through Lord Lothian, launching an apparent scathing attack on US concerns such as contraband control and trade protection over the war effort. The US position would be clarified by 1940. Against the difficulties faced in time of conflict, President Roosevelt, in June 1940, committed the United States to extending to "the opponents of force the material resources of this nation". Subsequently, 'Lend-Lease' was born in December 1940.

This represented a turning point in the war effort. Despite a phoney start, the significance of the German threat and Whitehall's limited resources meant that by 1940 the political, economic and logistical factors of what could be a long term war were being converted into requests for military aid. British requests were acted upon by the US and 85,000 machine guns, 25,000 automatic rifles, 21,000 revolvers were released from US stocks, aircraft were flown through Canada, training facilities were established in Florida. British warships were repaired in American dockyards. The value of aid in the first nine months was estimated as $1 billion. *All aid short of war* was the strapline. Aid was not just major strategic gesturing measured in thousands or millions, quality was a factor too. With rye cynicism, distinguished historians Hancock and Gowing referred to the quality of the US ordnance: they were *American rifles* – not quite so familiar and handy as Lee-Enfields, but they shot straight.

From 10th November 1940, Hudsons were being supplied by air across the 'Atlantic Bridge'. Until then, the aircraft had been manufactured in the US, flown to the Canadian border, hauled by horses across the border (thereby overcoming strict neutrality codes) then mustered, prepared and flown across the 2000 miles of ocean from Canada's eastern seaboard. This meant more planes more quickly and without the huge risk of losses, not to mention taking up valuable space on ships. As a result, the three month lapse between Stateside test-flight and operational duty in Britain was significantly reduced. Hudson delivery was a key part of the British coastal defences. Other airplanes, such as the North American Harvard/AT-6, were manufactured in the US and manually shifted across the border into Canada prior to despatch across the Atlantic Bridge and onto British soil.

Supporting Churchill's stirring, political rally of defending our island, never surrendering and fighting on the beaches was the practical and very real position of the British military structure supported by Dominion and European men and women as well as US military aid. The 'special relationship' was emerging. In return for this aid, Britain leased to the United States naval and air facilities in British possession in the western hemisphere. After 2nd September 1940 the tensions surrounding the Great Britain/US negotiations eased: the deal was virtually complete. The war was not just about effort and conflict; bills had to be paid. Housekeeping matters came to a head and by late 1940 the pip was beginning to squeak.

On 23rd November 1940, Lord Lothian told of the impending exhaustion of the British store of US dollars. Yet all the time there could be no let-up in the war effort. With no ability to pay in ready cash – nearly all the available dollars had gone – Britain was quite illiquid. But war contracts were necessary and the country was encouraged to proceed with military orders it could not afford to pay for. The barrel was being scraped. On 28th November 1940 Lord Lothian referred to illusions of vast undisclosed resources in a mythic barrel yet to be emptied. Scraping the barrel did take place. British manufacturing interests were sold to the US and in payment for aid some $150 million of gold was shipped to the US on board the *Louisville*.

Bearing in mind the extent of U-boat activity in the Atlantic, the Louisville's role is more significant than being merely a ferry boat for bullion. Leaving Long Beach and cruising southwards to the Panama Canal before entry to the Caribbean and Atlantic Ocean, her destination had been the eastern coast of South America. Whilst at Bahia, Brazil, her captain received orders to proceed to Simonstown, South Africa, picked up her cargo and traversed the dangerous Atlantic for New York. The US had not entered the war and neutrality pre-Pearl Harbor meant that a US ship on the high seas was probably best protected by a prominently displayed *Stars and Stripes*, at night under spotlight. Quite how the ship managed to undertake the journey is credit to the captain and whatever intelligence there was at the time.

History is only history after the event, and even then only if the 'event' is known about. My father would not be in the least bit interested in speculating on Britain's perilous financial position, even if it was reported as current affairs.

The momentum of war, the detailed planning and politicing of it, advances in technology and the need for flyers in what was perceived by some leading military minds to be a significant air war, created the most potent circumstances for an ambitious and restless eighteen year old in 1941.

The sheer scale of the war effort is staggering as the British Isles seemed to become fully engaged with the single objective of winning a war. The need for personnel and resources meant that planning and management of production was vital. So-called 'shadow factories' emerged, usually production capacity from the automotive industry, leading to major increases in numbers of home-built aircraft:

> *"It was necessary to take over every available factory space to build planes — fighters, light, medium and heavy bombers, flying boats for coastal command and training aircraft for future air crews. Throughout 1941 a tremendous programme was introduced based on the assembly lines of the US car industry and once the initial designs were accepted, production increased. But the planes need aircrew. A bomber requires eight to ten men. We needed pilots, gunners, navigators, radio experts."*

By 1941 and into 1942, the war was changing, it was intensifying, its pace had quickened as the entire nation was mobilised into concerted action. He might have been self-effacing, but he could easily recognise his own luck. Strangely, war was providing this luck, for as far back as 1940 my father realised that the combination of the withdrawal that was Dunkirk, and a country obviously ill-prepared, would need both aircraft production and trained aircrew. After the Phoney War, Dunkirk, The Blitz and the Battle of Britain, the Royal Air Force, for all it struggle for survival in the 20s and 30s seemed to be able to justify itself in wartime. With air penetration from mainland Europe being a reality and with *Island Britain* having huge coastline, as well as an umbilicus across the Atlantic, a war that had aerial needs would have to be resourced.

War had a ravenous appetite for people and power and my father was hungry too. Aircraft production was in full swing, the 'war effort' was now a way of life. Circumstances were changing. Conflict drew on resources vastly. Relatively small, certainly elite and obviously effective, the Royal Air Force had been able to demonstrate its validity and credentials. My father wanted to be part of it. But how?

Newspapers and aviation journals confirmed that all the time he had been training in Glasgow, a wartime aviation training programme had been up and running. Aircrew selection centres were now active in examining the health, aptitude and attitude of candidates – the cream of the nation's youth – all of whom had an eye on the coveted prize of 'Wings'. Pushing anger to one side and comforted by still youthful ambition, enquiries were made. If Herr Hitler and Mr Chamberlain created the career opportunity for my father, then the far-sighted planning, and particularly the Empire Air Training Scheme (EATS), warrant more than mere mention. This programme and its commitments changed my father's life completely. The Dominion, or Commonwealth, nations took the lead in 1939. For my father it would be the ancillary Joint Air Training Plan programme that provided the greatest flying opportunity of his life, but more of that later.

Here was the fortune of war for my father: the ability to become a pilot. Not for him the open seas or the itchy khaki. Serge blue and a necktie was for him. And, as noted more than once, there were clean sheets too. Yet it would be a matter of time yet before the ethereal reality of flight could be experienced. There were obstacles in the way.

The realisation of the actions of his own father in interfering with his flying career created in him such anger at this selfish, manipulative and damned despicable behaviour. He was embittered, frustrated and was locked in a situation where although enjoying the work and sending plenty of money back home he was still not satisfying a determined desire to fly. The war had put everything else in place. Why not him?

Caught up in a reserved occupation, he would have to struggle free and so he entered RAF service in 1942, in the RAF Volunteer Reserve (RAFVR), but so long as he was repairing aircraft it seemed he would never be called up. In time, the work at Silloth would be wound down. Persistence and patience were rewarded:

> *"At this time I submitted myself for entry into the RAF as a pilot, but as I was in a reserved occupation the RAF were not interested in calling me up just yet and it took a year of constant badgering before I was finally asked to attend a medical in Edinburgh which lasted three days. Then there was another long wait before my call-up papers arrived."*

He was not fully enlisted until 1943.

8
Twenty Years

Spitfire or Hurricane pilots did not just emerge out of some innate ability to fly. They didn't just appear as seeming middle-aged men. They were what today would be termed teenagers. But then they were young men, and women, who had to be trained. Between 1919 and 1939, accessibility to the service would change as it expanded with the emergence of new political orders and new threats. Changing entrance requirements and the expedience of war would open the door for flight training and, for my father, the prospect of becoming an RAF pilot.

The story of war so often ignores its planning, its lack of planning, and the huge mobilisation of resources to support its myriad theatres and objectives. The real story is of how air war, in all its forms and locations, was resourced. The end of the Great War may have seen the formation of the RAF, and during the 20s and 30s it may have seen, firstly, its survival as a service and, secondly, inconsistent expansion, but by 1939 ominous predictions and sombre outcomes required a significant step-change in training output. What was needed was trained aircrew in vast numbers. Within the twenty year period 1919–1939 the structure and scale of the Royal Air Force would change markedly. The technology available to it would change dramatically and the demands of training would, certainly in 1939, expand greatly.

Fundamentally, Britain simply was not ready for an air war in 1939. For my father, the opportunity of joining the Royal Air Force was certainly frustrated by parental manipulation, but the structure and organisation of training and the access to it presented barriers to a young lad without the knowledge of how the service worked or the necessary funding to even become what would now be called 'ground crew'.

For a period of only twenty years between 1919 and 1939 the structure of the RAF responded to many political and economic forces. The service my father joined in 1942 faced a real enemy, actual conflict and total war. The necessity for aircrew meant that numbers of Pilot Officers would now be augmented by Sergeant Pilots. The single greatest opportunity of my father's life was presented as a result of the desperate desire for pilots in wartime. To understand what my father was facing by 1942 is not just explained in terms of the success over the manipulations of his own corrupt father. It is important to look back at the evolution of the service which emerged from the confusion of the Great War and the recognition that Britain, particularly London, was vulnerable. An organised, well-resourced independent air service was required; and one capable of offensive engagement. Training would be a key component of the service.

After the event, history can be rationalised, sanitised, corrupted, changed, disputed and mistrusted. The iconography of the RAF at war is of the stereotype images of Spitfires and Hurricanes, flying suits and deck chairs, moustaches, refined crisp accents and a dog called 'Ginger'. An elitism combined with professionalism may have stemmed from the culture, attitudes and values of the service. Such elitism also stems from the manner in which the service was perceived immediately after the Great War and the standards of quality it strived to demonstrate in the face of hostility from other services. Having withstood pressures from the army and the navy, both services questioning its role and function, the RAF was, in 1939, still a young service and one which, given the preceding twenty or so years of new technology, government cuts, The Depression and European politics, needed not just skills but numbers: big numbers. However, the wider preparations for war were equally understated if the 1938 advertising is anything to go by. A simple black and white advertisement appeared somewhat modest: 'Candidates are required in large numbers for short service commissions – applications by postcard to the Air Ministry'.

There was a perception that only officers could pilot an aircraft. This is an odd distinction in anthropological terms and perhaps Darwinist: officers and, therefore, pilots were on a different mental, if not evolutionary, strata. There were 'officers' and there were 'men' existing in a belief system that only officers had the mettle and resolve, intelligence and skill to command wonderful flying machines. Even the auxiliary air service had an elitism recorded in the account that No 601 squadron, the so-called, 'Millionaires Squadron', was not founded at RAF Northolt but at White's Club in St James's.

As for the RAF Volunteer Reserve, set up in 1936 with a view to increasing civil intake from sixty a year to a mere eight hundred, this too had the hallmarks of a social get-together. Faced with the rise of the Third Reich and territorial expansion, what seems peculiarly British was the incorporation of a short-term response to this threat, with a very, well, sociable 'weekend flying' scheme. This would be operated through civilian flying clubs! One almost has the impression that a reluctant preparation for war was discussed over cucumber sandwiches and tea at the end of a tennis match! The prospect of war was all so terribly, terribly inconvenient.

For all this, though, the desirous hunger of war meant that recruitment processes would have to change. Flying training is a long-established component of the service and by the late 1930s, unprecedented personnel requirements meant a need for more than just pilot officers. The international efforts in aircrew training post-1939 can be contrasted with matters of homeland defence in the 1920s, with France still being considered a country capable of attacking Britain, and the response to the rise of fascism in the 30s. Although the RAF was now a freestanding service and training requirements had been recognised and developed throughout the 20s and 30s – the RAFVR, and by 1941, the Air Training Corps – there were wider opportunities for the nation's youth to enter the service. The compulsion of war and the need for aircrew was communicated to the nation's school leavers in Monk and Winter's 1938 'The Royal Air Force'. The foreward written by the Secretary of State for Air, the Rt Hon Sir Kingsley Wood includes the following:

> *"The Authors of this book have put into language which everyone can understand, particulars of the requirements of entry, and have given information regarding the kind of life young men lead if they are fortunate enough to get into the Royal Air Force... I would advise both parents and their sons, who are interested in the Air Service, to read this book..."*

The training requirements and standards employed in the second war have their origins in the Great War and the response, albeit a late one, to the threat and actions of Zeppelins around the British coast. Whatever the great naval battles or historic military campaigns that were familiar to Great War Generals, the Royal Flying Corps and, after 1918, the Royal Air Force, was a new service carved out of security in the knowledge that the physics worked and the aircraft were reliable. The step change occurred in the epiphany that aircraft had some value in war, would be needed and that flyers could be sourced and trained. Scouting and reconnaissance were acknowledged roles, engagement with an enemy aircraft would lead to dog-fights. But battles were on the ground. Recognising that aircraft could be an offensive weapon was a quantum leap in tactical thinking.

With the Wright Brothers' ascent into the history books in 1903 and British Army Aeroplane No.1 being piloted by Sam Cody in 1908 it was probably a big ask for pilot skills and technology to mature sufficiently for an effective, durable and reliable aerial fighting machine to have any practical use in war by 1914. If the Great War is remembered for statistics, trench warfare and the degradations of hellish battle and mud, it should also be recognised as the first major conflict to involve not just the dogfight of pistol and machine-gun, but aerial bombing. However, militarily, politically and logistically, what can be revealed is a breathtaking inefficiency in the face of a strident enemy. The battle against inefficiency was not just in relation to skills and technology, but supply, bureaucracy and politics, with a military structure still based on the army and the navy serving imperial territorial needs. It was the response to these issues that would give birth to the Royal Air Force.

Out of the ambitions, tensions and frustrations of the time the Royal Air Force would grow. The aircraft would evolve from the flimsy box-kite contraptions of Farman to reliable purpose-built craft such as the Sopwith Camel or SE5A. The value of training would be realised, particularly in wide-open foreign skies. The reality is that whilst the emergence of the RAF was a response to inefficiency, it was also a result of the enthusiasm of a handful of characters who would shape its form and structure; men who had already vanguarded its role prior to the Great War. Central to the evolution of the service were Churchill, Trenchard, Smuts and Henderson; a handful of far-sighted individuals who recognised the value of technology and the development of aviation skills.

The Royal Flying Corps was established at Upavon, Wiltshire, by Royal Warrant in 1912 under the command of Sir David Henderson. The Royal Naval Air Service already existed and so the Admiralty showed little interest in a separate flying corps. The new service was not well-resourced and as a result it was up to a few intrepid souls to learn to fly. Two leading proponents of flight were David Henderson and Hugh Trenchard. Churchill, though, recognised the import of flight and sought to expand the service.

Trenchard was forty-one years old in 1914 and had only learned to fly some two years earlier with a reported log book comprising of a staggering one hour and fourteen minutes in the air. Nonetheless, in 1912 he became a flying instructor. The following year he was Deputy Commandant of the Central Flying School and was responsible for training and recruitment.

Philip Joubert, a contemporary of Trenchard at the CFS and by 1945 one of the most senior ranking Officers in the RAF, writing in 1955, noted that Trenchard got in the army largely through the back door, having been poor at examinations and concealing, successfully, that he was 'practically blind' in one eye. However, by 1915 he was in command of the Royal Flying Corps in France, having taken over from David Henderson, a Scottish engineering student who became a leading authority in Military Intelligence during the South African War. Later, he would become the Director-General of Military Aeronautics and commander of the Royal Flying Corps at the outbreak of the Great War. By 1911 and aged forty-nine, Henderson was the world's oldest pilot. However, he knew from his experience in information gathering, the value of aerial reconnaissance in establishing enemy movements.

The training requirements of the time were studied and in 1915 there emerged plans for an air service of 30,000 officers and 300,000 men. However, the reality was somewhat different. There was no structure and there were too many different aircraft types. At the same time, the RNAS was expanding its training programme and in the process competing for whatever limited supply of aircraft there was. It is a sobering thought that in 1913 the army's complement of aircraft stood at 101. In 1914 the total number of aircraft sent to France, according to Joubert, was under seventy. Those left comprised 'a miscellaneous collection of crocks'.

David Henderson battled administration, money and resources in 1914. The assorted assembly of poorly made and unreliable airframes, were criticised heavily by the press. Bear in mind the trial and error approach to flying, aeronautics, stability and power, and it is easy to see an air force hardly fit for purpose. New aircraft types were demanded – faster and more stable. The airship was a thing of the past and the monoplane considered unstable. Inherently stable biplanes were the future. With Henderson in charge of Military Aeronautics it was possible: the BE2c emerged from the Royal Aircraft Factory at Farnborough, whilst the navy were still ordered from Shorts, Sopwith and A V Roe.

War saw the need for aircraft, and flying was still considered to be an add-on to the navy and army. There were less than 100 airplanes prior to the Great War and mobilisation of personnel saw officers and ranks scurrying around for parts and buckshee kites, and pilots themselves experimenting with bombs and machine guns. By 1915, the Admiralty sought to define the tactical role of aviation in submarine attack, air reconnaissance and observation of fire and attack on hostile aircraft 'over the sea'. However, the scourge of the Zeppelin appeared, reeking aerial havoc over London and the south east. Day and night-time raids ensued between 1916 and 1918. No longer just vast Zeppelins were impregnating the British airspace, but large German bombers: Gotha and Giant aircraft.

In due course, it was realised that supply could not match demand. Trenchard wanted more aerial resource: more and better planes and more and better pilots. General Haig also wanted some fifty-six squadrons by spring 1917; more planes to fight 'The Hun' at the Western Front. But that would mean diverting resources from the RNAS whose later role would be in long-range bombing. It was quickly realised that the organisation and training of aircrew and pilots was being split across two services: RNAS and the RFC. Joubert noted that an 'embodiment' of naval and army aviation – a combined service – had emerged, somewhat organically, but this was short-lived. Inter-service rivalry continued alongside a division of resources which saw naval air training taking place at Eastchurch, Kent, with army air training taking place at Central Flying School, initially at Farnborough, Hampshire. But quite where aviation sat within defence finance and defence policy was an area of debate.

The difficulties presented by bureaucracy and poorly-organised supply is exemplified in Joubert's noting that army observation balloons were being demanded, but had to be sourced from limited naval supplies. Supplies of hardware were limited and at times being diverted. Procurement was shambolic. Joubert noted that guns intended for home defence were installed on merchant ships. Evidently, there was plane confusion: engines and airframes were being competed for, two different air defence services were in operation, defence finance was weak and defence policy was at best evolving. What was the relative split of function between army and navy? It was not a matter of choice, of 'either' and 'or', but of 'both'. Effective and unified aerial defence and attack would yet be realised.

Whilst other towns such as Hartlepool, Great Yarmouth and Derby had experienced aerial bombing, the June and July 1917 daylight raids on London led to huge public outcry with 219 civilian deaths and 625 injured. These attacks led to new approaches to aerial defence involving policemen looking up to the skies. More sophisticated measures followed involving aircraft and guns combing bands of airspace outwards from London: thirteen miles, sixty miles and eighty miles. This homeland defence enabled a concentration of supplies which would otherwise have stretched the RNAS. This sounded great, but by 1917 it was clear that the scale of war and the opportunity for aerial combat and strategic bombing rendered the RNAS and RFC unable to cope with submarine/coastal activity, the Western Front and home defence and the prospect of long range strategic bombing emerged as a serious and deliverable part of aerial operations.

Unification of effort and resources was called for, but was nothing new. Co-ordination had been advanced by previous Government bodies. A Joint War Air Committee under Lord Derby convened in 1916 but was weakened, with no apparent authority or technical knowledge. A further attempt to galvanise an air plan was made under Lord Curzon the same year. Whilst this led to some progress in relation to supply and distribution of aircraft, there was a lack of political clout in there being no ministerial authority to drive home measures to unify the flying functions of the RFC corps and the navy. Some further success came under the stewardship of Lord Cowdray in 1917. This led to a direct link between the workings of the Committee and the command of a Cabinet Minister.

The Air Committee became the Air Board and, in turn, an Air Ministry would follow, but it was the 1917 Imperial Conference organised in London that crystallised the future of air defences. This was attended by the premiers and senior aides from Canada, Australia, South Africa, New Zealand and India, together with representatives of other Dominion nations, and set about co-ordinating Empire military policy. What emerges is the significance of one man to that conference; someone who wasn't expected to be there in the first place!

Jan Christian Smuts – who would emerge as the architect of the Royal Air Force – was born in rural South West Africa in 1870. Southern Africa was a fragmented and fragile agglomeration of States. He would become a brilliant law student, studying at Cambridge, and by 1895 would return home to become an advocate, lecturer and later State Attorney. In the Boer War he would emerge as a brilliant tactician soldier – by 1916 a Lieutenant General in the British Army – later General and Commander-in-Chief, and afterwards, politician, contributing greatly to the shape of South Africa that we see today. It was in 1917 that he was requested to attend what was the first Imperial Conference in London, upon arrival being described by Winston Churchill as a new and altogether extraordinary man; "a man of unswerving loyalty and unfailing shrewdness with a cool far-reaching comprehension". Smuts now had a valuable role in the end-game of the Great War, being introduced to the Imperial War Cabinet and establishing the basis for a cessation of hostilities, examining the minimum demands of Germany over France and Belgium.

His role fulfilled, Smuts contemplated a return to his native home, but his military experience and cerebral, measured approach added incisive thinking. The risk of losing this man was too much to contemplate. Churchill's praise, if not awe is summed up: "the only unwounded statesman of outstanding ability in the Empire". Instead of returning to South Africa, Smuts stayed on in a post as member of the War Cabinet. Lloyd George was Chairman, and together with luminaries Curzon, Milner, Carson, Bonar Law and Barnes, there comprised the brains and visioning to deal with military planning. According to his son, Smuts was without portfolio, but with equal power.

Smuts dealt with two aspects: reorganisation and strategy. To say that Smuts headed a committee may be to suggest that many people were involved. Truth to tell, the committee comprised of only two people; himself and the Prime Minister. Together, Smuts and Lloyd George shaped the Bill that would lead to the establishment of the RAF; independent of the Navy and the Army, though regard must be made to Sir David Henderson, who is acknowledged as having drafted the Smuts Report. Smuts would report formally on 19th July 1917 and again, one month later, on 17th August. By contrast, Trenchard may have been entranced by human beings looking like ants from the air, but Smuts saw in air power the ability to strike offensively:

> '... the devastation of enemy lands and destruction of industries and populous centres on a vast scale.'

Timing and justification were on his side. Smuts tactical response to the Zeppelin raids on the civil population of London was based in attacking enemy air bases and eliminating their ability to attack, and the unification of a fighting force. In November 1918, six months after the formation of the Royal Air Force, air fighting had recorded significant German losses with ninety-four aircraft brought down or out of control against forty-three RAF losses. Long range bombing raids had struck at Dusseldorf, Frankfurt, Cologne and Mannheim.

Hindsight is most clear and informed, but Great Britain at the outset of the Great War was ill-prepared for aerial conflict or the use of aerial machines in battle situations. Which service should control the air, where the aircraft should come from and a belief that all they were useful for was reconnaissance, created institutional failure. Smuts corrected this.

Smuts was a man of such diverse talent and ability, service and achievement that he would later be regarded as the 'handyman of the Empire'. His son, also J C Smuts, honoured his career and widespread contributions in three simple words: simplicity, integrity and consistency. To see the establishment of the RAF purely in terms of Trenchard as father-figure is to mis-state history, though his 1919 paper on the future structure and size of the RAF must be credited with establishing the service as we now see it.

Soldier, lawyer, politician, strategist, diplomat, administrator, Government Minister and Prime Minister, and Commander-in-Chief, Smuts was a man of formidable breadth and depth. His role in the formation of the Royal Air Force is seen in two functions. Firstly, his role as Chairman of the War Priorities Committee in 1917/18 in which he addressed the in-fighting and inefficiency between services over supply and logistics. Secondly, he realised the importance of aerial war, being alarmed both by the audacity and destruction of German attacks on London. He was astonished by the backwardness of certain thinking. Smuts saw aircraft as being offensive and this set the tone for the birth of the Royal Air Force. Fellow War Cabinet member Milner, at the time, is noted to have remarked that:

> "..the soldiers and sailors at the War Office and Admiralty do not yet grasp the fact that there is a new kind of warfare before us and that, besides the help they have to give the army and navy, the airmen will have to fight battles of their own... it may be a better arrangement to have you in the Cabinet with a special obligation to keep, as Minister, the supervision of Air Departments."

Out of Jan Christian Smuts' analysis of the war effort, its organisation and priorities and the important role of aircraft, two reports were filed, dealing firstly with the defence of London and, secondly, with the more fundamental questions of service structure and organisation. As Chairman of the Committee charged with establishing an Air Ministry, in August and October 1917, a draft Bill was prepared. From this the Air Force Act received Royal Assent on 29th November 1917. Twenty years later Smuts would become Prime Minister of South Africa and would have a further key role in contributing to the service efficiency of the RAF.

The Royal Air Force would be born on 1st April 1918 under the command, very briefly, of Major General Hugh Trenchard who resigned from his new post of Chief of the Air Staff less than two weeks later. This short-lived spell as Chief of Air Staff stemmed from a personality clash with Lord Rothermere, then Secretary of State for Air. Brigadier General Sykes took over, but only until April 1919 when Trenchard resumed his duties upon the invitation of Winston Churchill, being given the ability to map out the future of the RAF as he and his advisors saw it.

The role of the fledgling RAF would be formalised by Trenchard's report to the then Secretary of State for War and Air Winston Churchill in the form of a White Paper: *An Outline of the Scheme for the Permanent Organisation of the Royal Air Force.* This was published in 1919, with an emphasis on the quality of crew and growth of the service. However, during the 1920s and 30s, economic restraint would inhibit growth of the Royal Air Force. Combine this with events in mainland Europe and the arms build-up in Germany, and it is easy to see just how poorly equipped Britain would be by 1939.

Although after the Great War the structure of the RAF was being mapped out, there was little mood for militarisation in the 1920s. Despite the unification of air services and the birth of the Royal Air Force, the inter-war period was a time of major contraction, restructuring and expedient growth. If, at the end of the Great War, Britain had the greatest air defence force in the world with 291,000 personnel and 700 aerodromes worldwide, there followed a disarmament programme that would see that claim decimated. The RAF of 1918 had 188 squadrons. In 1919 there were twenty-eight squadrons. By 1920, there were only twenty-five squadrons. The confidence of the growing service suffered a setback in 1921 arising from a government committee chaired by Sir Eric Geddes. What later become known as the 'Geddes Axe' was an unnerving time of economies and savings. By 1922 the Government considered that to dismantle the RAF, returning to the order of army and navy air services would be a retrograde step, though the total personnel at the time would be less than ten per cent of the 1918 figure.

Some moderate expansion had been announced in 1923 with the objective to create a defence force of sufficient strength to protect from attack by the strongest air force within striking distance of the country. Based on the technology of the time, the enemy, according to that rule of thumb, could only be regarded as France. As for the aircraft, many of these were ill-designed and ill-equipped, with neither the speed nor the range to get further. Seemingly, and despite the war to end all wars, military thinking still focussed on early nineteenth century threats. An expansion programme looked to the creation of thirty-four new squadrons with Prime Minister Stanley Baldwin urging this with as little delay as possible. This expansion faltered in the midst of economic and pacifist pressures to the point where, but ten years later, in 1933 the actual expansion was ten per cent short of the target.

Trenchard was determined to consolidate the Royal Air Force's position as a single, independent service. However, in 1919, the immediate requirements of this new service would be rank, order, resources and a training establishment. Oh, and there had to be a band behind which each 'Wing' would march between its accommodation and workshops, the 'Schools' or the airfield. Major General Trenchard looked to the creation of a Cadet Flying School at Cranwell, Lincolnshire, with aircraft servicing being dealt with through mechanical apprenticeship training at Halton Park near Aylesbury, Buckinghamshire.

Cranwell's origins are in the needs of the Royal Naval Air Service to establish shore defences as far back as 1915. This called for a training facility where crews could be trained to fly airplanes, balloons and airships. The choice of location is rumoured to lie in the briefing of a pilot to find a piece of land big enough and flat enough to land. Huts and hangers were built later on what was then the requisitioned property of the Duke of Bristol. The facility was commissioned on 1st April 1916 and later, under the overall direction of Trenchard, the objectives of this RAF training facility were clear:

> *"We have to learn by experience how to organise and administer a great Service, both in peace and war, and you, who are present at the College in its first year, will, in future, be at the helm.*
>
> *"Therefore, you will have to work your hardest, both as cadets at the College and subsequently as officers, in order to be capable of guiding this great Service through its early days and maintaining its traditions and efficiency in the years to come."*

Aside from flying suitability, Cranwell was appropriately remote:

> *"Marooned in the wilderness, cut off from pastimes they could not organise for themselves, the cadets would find life cheaper, healthier and more wholesome."*

Cranwell is synonymous with the RAF. By 1934 the distinctive classical buildings would be the home for the first Military Air Academy in the world, having officially opened on 5th February 1920. In addition, there was the creation of an auxiliary air force and university air squadrons. Where the *survivability* of the RAF may have been rooted in quality, its elitism can be detected in the distinction between privileged middle-class cadets being sent to college for £215 in 1920 and the so-called 'boy apprentices'.

These young adolescents, in their mid-teens, would be trained to look after the aircraft. Boy Apprentices were the *stable lads* of the air, contrasting with the better educated, middle class, preferably public school background of Pilot Officers.

The effect of the Trenchard Paper of 1919 was to provide a formalised and structured role for Boy Apprentices at Halton Park, which was purchased by the then Air Council and soon to be the home of No. 1 School of Technical Training. This training facility has its formal origins in a muddy field in Buckinghamshire, but not just any muddy field, though. It happened to be owned by Mr Alfred Rothschild and was in the grounds of his fine Victorian chateau-style mansion; his weekend retreat. At the time of the Great War, the house was still relatively young, having been completed in 1883. This thirty year old detached residence in extensive grounds was in close proximity to London, closer yet to Wendover, and had the benefit of its own railway line.

Lord Trenchard recognised the need for quality training and quality skills and the three-year Aircraft Apprentice Scheme was introduced in 1920. In the remote, country house setting of Halton Park, young students would develop academic and practical skills which would translate not only into military, but civil fields. Athletic skills were developed too and history and military tactical education could be pursued through study trips. The recurring theme of RAF training – quality – would lead to some of the so-called 'Trenchard's Brats' reaching the higher ranks. Halton's role continued and twenty years later another conflict would lead to more maintenance crews being required.

British politics in the 1930s was complex; anxious under Stanley Baldwin to save money and balance the books following the Wall Street Crash and Depression, anxious, under Neville Chamberlain, to address domestic and social problems. The domestic agenda was one thing, but the European dimension could not be ignored. If the Great War had left Britain with a beleaguered economy and colossal debt, aggravated by The Depression, then the rise of fascism, the Spanish Civil War and the marching beat and territorial expansion of Germany and Italy commanded much attention. Clearly concerned as to military rearmament and expansion in Germany, the rise of the Luftwaffe and Britain's potential inferiority, Ramsey MacDonald announced steps for further acceleration and expansion of the RAF. From a defence perspective, a tipping point was being reached where German air forces would match, then exceed, Britain's. This created a dichotomy: the government could see what was happening politically in continental Europe with the rise of the Third Reich and militarisation on a threatening scale, but as 1939 drew nearer it wished to avoid war at all costs.

In his speech to the Commons on 30th July 1934, Baldwin spoke of the defence of England not by reference to the Dover Cliffs, but the Rhine. This echoed Smuts' strategic thinking in 1917. Baldwin announced in 1934 an increase from fifty-two new squadrons to seventy-five. The Marquess of Londonderry announced planned expansion of a further forty-nine squadrons additional to the previous figure. In 1935 the Metropolitan Air Force was created. Air power would grow from 844 planes to 1,304 planes by 1939. Based on a combination of Great War politics and 1930s political and economic circumstances, by 1935 politicians realised that intervention was required to further expand the RAF aircraft, boost aircraft production and increase pilot output. The years 1935–1939 saw waves of investment in the RAF as Great Britain recognised potent threats from Germany. Not until territorial expansion in mainland

Europe and North Africa took place in 1936 would there be a dawning reality. The threat of future aerial war was all too apparent. By 1937, bombs were being dropped by Germany and Italy on Guernica and Barcelona. Compelling circumstances required urgent action.

The RAF's measured growth required 2,550 new pilots by 1937, together with some 22,000 other personnel. In support of this, the emphasis was on officer training and short-service commissions were offered. Advertisements would be placed in newspapers encouraging applications to the Air Ministry. Less numerous, though still significant, the title 'Airman Pilot' would be offered to those not qualifying for a commission. To train these new pilots new flying training schools were established with by 1936, a total of eleven schools. By 1938, the total complement was 4,850 officers and 51,000 airmen.

RAF training would be a critical part of the response to the changing European and World order. Without pilots, the planned aerodrome, squadron and aircraft expansion programme was meaningless. Though, although the RAF was now a military unit in its own right, the emphasis on aircrew training seemed curiously limited. Logistically, the concern was that forecast pilot numbers were too few, that squadron expansion was necessary and that quality training should be introduced. What was happening in Germany justified an intensification of this training.

If the Treaty of Versailles resulted in the unfinished business that was the years 1939-1945, the Hitler had a gift for irony: he asserted 'Living Peace' – lebensraum. Who was Mr Hitler kidding? He had, by now, re-crafted the dynamics of mainland Europe and North Africa. Following rearmament and militarisation, Hitler motioned over the continent with Grand Master ease over a chequer board. By the Spring of 1939 Moravia, Bohemia and Ruthenia, places which sound like they were borne from a Marx Brothers' script, would be hopped over and captured. The

Rhineland was taken and union was effected between Germany and Austria; Ethiopia was all of a sudden 'Italian' by 1939, and so was Albania; the Spanish Civil war continued. Appeasement came and went. Finally, Hitler got to the other side of the board. The Czech peoples were let down and Poland fell. To show for this, we had a piece of paper in our time.

The imminence of war and its implications were perhaps not fully realised, but the need for training and the key role of an air defence service had been long-recognised and long-debated.

Between the wars, Europe had seen an instability and unrest economically and politically. Whether it was civil war in Ireland, the French occupation of the Ruhr, the Spanish Civil War or the tearing up of the Treaty of Versailles, tensions simmered and embers – still burning since 1918 – could so easily turn into major conflagration. These events would be unknown to my father, but with leaving school not so far away and, in 1937, the pre-tensions of war being palpably obvious in the news, he would be entering a period, for him, of substantial change. My father was growing up. Whatever sorry childhood there had been there was certainly no such thing as 'teenage years'. Short trousers gave way to long trousers overnight and school was now work; yesterday a child, today a worker.

The outbreak of war required a scale of response unprecedented and one which required massive international mobilisation. Britain could not do it alone. The reality was that Britain needed aircrew. The Great War had proven the threat; the Spanish Civil War had demonstrated horrific effect; a new war would have scale and loss. Air war would present challenges in replenishing the stock of aircrew. The greatest international conflict ever, and one which saw mass aerial warfare for the first time, raised issues of lives, losses and logistics: how big could an aircrew training programme become and how quickly could it be deployed? How many would die? Pragmatic steps to address the situation would begin with the recognition that only international agreement could provide the resources. Without this, the future was grave.

RAF training structures meant my father could never be a pilot during the 1930s and even if he had some of the necessary funding, he would not have wanted to become merely a 'boy apprentice'. For all the efforts of Trenchard after the Great War, despite the aviation technology and defence policy changes of the 1930s, despite the elitism of the service, it was the international and egalitarian response to aircrew training that gave my father the opportunity to bypass what until December 1939 had been a preserve for the privileged.

9

Anyone for EATS?

oundations for my father's flying career were laid by a
group of like-minded and determined men who, with
government-backed authority, met in Ottawa, Canada, in
the autumn of 1939. In a matter of weeks, the group would
sign the Riverdale Agreement; a backbone of war effort and an
opportunity for far more than The Few.

The Riverdale Agreement was named for Lord Riverdale,
otherwise Arthur Balfour, steel manufacturer and Chairman of
Arthur Balfour & Co, C Meadows and Co, and in 1939 Chairman
of the Advisory Council for Scientific and Industrial Research.
Knighted in 1923, becoming Sir Arthur Balfour and, by 1935,
Baron Riverdale of Sheffield and the County of York, he was
described at the time as bold, bald and bluff. Under Arthur
Balfour, the mission sought categoric support from Dominion
states for a programme of concerted effort: an air training
programme. The British delegation also included Air Chief
Marshall Sir Robert Brooke-Popham and Air Vice-Marshal
Sir Christopher Courtney. Also travelling was F T Hearle, the
Managing Director of the De Havilland Aircraft Company, so
the prospect for them to gain from additional business may have
been clear at the outset.

The objective for Britain was speedy agreement by the Dominion governments with the draft plan being to train 29,000 aircrew a year, requiring some 5,000 aircraft. Despite RAF expansion and the significant regard for pilot training dating back to the Great War, the resourcing of WWII – as an *aerial* conflict – would not commence until fourteen weeks after the Prime Minister's solemn statement on 3rd September 1939 that unless by eleven o'clock Germany withdrew its troops from Poland, a state of war would exist 'between us': Britain could 'consider' itself in 'a state of war' with Germany. At such a moment as that, the so-called assurances of support inferred, assumed or received from The Empire may well have been a source of profound encouragement. What the Prime Minister did not confirm was that such encouragement fell short of any agreement.

That a tactical conference should be convened following the start of hostilities, during the months of October, November and December, is a peculiar beginning. Morally, spiritually and practically the will to co-operate was there. Financially, the mission brief was simple: meet with your counterparts and get the best deal you can. No one knows the value of money more than a Yorkshireman. However, politically, The Dominions, as a young brood, would assert independence of mind in key areas of negotiation over a British Government naively hopeful of unquestioning loyalty to the Crown. Britain would certainly be fighting against what the Prime Minister had described as *"brute force, bad faith, injustice, oppression and persecution"*. Right would prevail, but only with the support of the Dominions.

The intensification of aircrew training has a complicated history and the irony is that the actual steps towards producing more aircrew were taken only once the war had started. The ramping-up of training would require agreement between the governments of Britain, Canada, Australia, New Zealand and Rhodesia. The Ottawa Conference would carve out an agreement that would put in place a vast wartime aircrew training programme capable of supporting an air war and withstanding significant loss of life.

The actual programme would become known under different names. Initially conceived as 'The Imperial Air Training Scheme', it became the 'Empire Air Training Scheme' and, after 1942, more widely termed the 'British Commonwealth Air Training Plan'. In all it lasted some six years and would, with effort and cost, produce some 170,000 aircrew. My father was one of them.

The EATS appears not to be given sufficient credit in twentieth century British history. But for the research and authorship of a few the efforts in mobilising international co-operation in defeating a common enemy are under-recorded. If an official account, *What Britain Has Done, 1939 –1945* is to be believed in giving a 1945 perspective (a 'general understanding') on British wartime out-turn performance and suffering, then it does rather play down the significance of how aerial war was resourced. Come to think of it, it does not play it down at all; it is virtually ignored. There is but one brief reference to what would emerge in 1939 as the Empire Air Training Scheme, but even then it is hidden behind the immense significance of the Battle of Britain. The figures speak for themselves. The so much owed to so few is evident in the Battle of Britain tally of 2,375 enemy aircraft destroyed against 733 RAF planes lost and 375 RAF pilot losses. But there is more to six years of conflict than one very busy summer.

Commenting on the achievements of the Royal Air Force, the Battle of Britain was won on the basis of technique and foresight, similar foresight being shown in the initiation of the EATS/BCATP to provide the crews to man the bombers, with operational units *leading the way to new heights of land-air cooperation*. The account, justifiably, portrays effort, human achievement, skill and suffering across the three commands: Bomber, Coastal and

Fighter. But still no real acknowledgement of the international scale of the EATS/BCATP programme and its significance to enabling the 700,000 sorties or 20,000 plus planes destroyed.

Politically and logistically, economically and internationally the EATS/BCATP programme was a vast undertaking set up in the context of international negotiations and with vast resource. It was far from a British initiative since it involved principally the government of Canada, supported by, Australia and New Zealand. In time, Rhodesia, South Africa, India and other countries would offer training facilities. It was also about more than just aircrew training. As Time Magazine reported in November 1939, the British intention was to turn out 3,000 new RAF officers every month. This sounded like a noble effort, particularly where the cramped, foggy British Isles were deemed no place to train fliers. But faced with the demands of the European theatre, it foretold of 36,000 a year being none too many for replacement.

It is the Canadian contribution to the 'war effort' that warrants particular mention in terms of scale of response, that country's physical attributes, its location and, in September 1939, the unequivocal political support of its Prime Minister, Mackenzie King. In his first term of office he had, at a 1926 Imperial conference, suggested transatlantic cooperation on the creation of a reserve of airmen. It was he who, thirteen years later in December 1939, would pronounce the Empire Air Training Scheme as a *"co-operative undertaking of great magnitude"*.

Mackenzie King was far-sighted, he also knew of the risks to the North American continent. Using the term 'Northern Bridge', made up of relatively short hops via Newfoundland and Labrador and Iceland, he knew only too well that North America was only a night away. This 'air bridge' across the Atlantic was vital to resourcing a European war, but with the appropriate meteorological and aviation know-how, North American targets could also be in range from Europe.

Canada offered more than the ability to turn out what Time Magazine described as 12,000 pilots every twenty-eight weeks; in wartime the training programmes would be expedited. Canada's key role is measured in its natural resources. In the early stages of war, what Canada offered in terms of air and land mass, flying conditions, manufacturing capabilities, and anchorage was clearly recognised. Wider measures were anticipated or speculated, including large-scale redeployment of British shipbuilding capability. Speculation saw a prolonged war and damage to British ports leading to the de-centralisation of British shipbuilding. Larger and stronger ships, together with new port facilities were contemplated. Here, the paradox of proximity (a week's passage) and distance (out of range of many aircraft at the time), and yet still latent, perturbing feelings of vulnerability from sea or air.

The inception of the training programme may have been relatively logical – the necessity for a scale of response. However, behind the practicality lay serious bargaining and negotiation. The actual fusing together of multi-national air training commitment was neither simple nor easy. Negotiations struck at the heart of Anglo-Canadian affairs and raised serious constitutional questions. Putting aside these constitutional questions the need was for Britain to benefit from Dominion, Empire or Commonwealth resources in personnel, hardware and airspace. But not without compromise on the part of Britain, its dominions and its allies would a united, international, defence be deployed.

Various individuals have been noted as being instrumental to the setting up of the EATS. Trenchard's service vision was compromised by inter-service rivalry; the navy and army saw no unique role for an air service other than one tied-in with their own structures. Twin forces of economic difficulty caused by the Great War and then Depression were combined with poor rearmament programmes, resulting in a poorly-equipped and limited fighting resource. That said, the RAF had appointed Air Commodore Arthur Tedder as Director of Training in 1934 and his reporting of pilot training needs created the momentum to address this vitally important issue. This was the era of peace in our time, a Britain which wanted to avoid war at all costs and was struggling with the aftermath of the Depression. This was also the era which saw massive build up of military armament and ordnance on the back of fascism in Germany.

Tedder, in reality, had an experienced staff member in the form of a Canadian, Group Captain Robert Leckie, who had presented a proposal as far back as 1936 involving the training of pilots in Canada and elsewhere. Amidst the politics of the time, this simple idea did not gather any momentum until the combined resources of Canada, Australia, New Zealand and Rhodesia were marshalled. The actual establishment of the Empire Air Training Scheme would date to reconnaissance visits to Canada as far back as 1937. Cooperation with Commonwealth – *Dominion* – governments was essential and as a result of shuttle diplomacy, cost analysis and detailed planning the EATS was established under the Riverdale Agreement dated 17th December 1939.

Whatever historic ties between Britain and Canada there may have been, the lingering question of neutrality arose. By 1936, Canada had agreed to send limited numbers of officer cadets to Britain for training. Australia and New Zealand did similarly. Rhodesia had plans afoot in 1937, with Charles Meredith offering London the opportunity of organised training involving Rhodesian aircrew within the RAF. However, timing was against him. His one man mission arrived in London in October 1939. However, as a result, Rhodesia got more than it bargained for and was up and running in air training before Canada's contribution could be effected. The Antipodes have claimed that the first definite proposals for the Empire Air Training Plan were made in September 1939 by the High Commissioner for Australia in the United Kingdom, Viscount Stanley Bruce, whose proposals were discussed the following month at the Ottawa conference which led to the Riverdale Agreement.

In May 1938 a British delegation had been sent to Canada to evaluate aircraft manufacturing potential. Group Captain J M Robb of the Central Flying School visited the following year to examine training possibilities. By autumn 1939 Air Chief Marshall Cyril Newall foresaw the need for air training with the Dominion nations, and Canada in particular, making a major contribution. If Group Captain Robb's 1939 visit had been disappointing and frustrating in the host's concern with future requirements, then this was a foretaste of things to come later, at the specially-convened Dominion conference held in Ottawa in October–December 1939.

This conference would deal with issues of air training in the face of conflict in the European theatre. Ever diplomatic, the British Foreign Minister Anthony Eden wanted Canada to 'sympathetically' consider the proposals for the conference, the simple act of a personal invitation from Anthony Eden to Mackenzie King securing this. In hindsight, the move itself seems cynical and ingratiating, but it worked. It seemed to draw out a pivotal role for Canada and there was the comfort of the home stage for the Canadian Premier, Mackenzie King.

Whatever the personal exchanges between senior officers, mandarins and diplomats this culminated in telegrams being sent to Dominion governments, with a personal message from Chamberlain to Mackenzie King. With leverage and flattery, soon Mackenzie King accepted the proposition in principle and the role of the host for the imminent Dominion governments' conference in December 1939. It was this that would lead to the so-called Riverdale Agreement, named after the aforementioned

Lord Riverdale who had accepted the role of Director General of the 'Imperial Air Training Scheme'. He accepted this post only after Sir Hugh Trenchard had turned it down.

Writing in 1941, Mackenzie King confirmed that when war came, "Canada did not hesitate", resulting in the transformation of "one of the least military peoples into a nation organised for modern war", supplying ships, aircraft, guns and other essentials. He knew of the tactical importance of training to military objectives: decisive supremacy in the air. Although Canada was regarded as storehouse and granary, with huge pride, Mackenzie King overcame internal tensions, putting Canada very much at the forefront of the war effort. The political complexion of Canada was just that: complex. There were 'old country' tensions and the fear of casualties arising from conscription was a legacy of the Great War, and there was the French-Canadian component who would want nothing to do with a European war. He would affirm Canada's part in the British Commonwealth Air Training Plan as the greatest concentration of air training in the world and the greatest single contribution to the common cause.

If the actual conference had been racked with these contextual tensions and Mackenzie King had been skilful enough to placate homeland concerns and reach agreement, there were many practical questions to which answers would have to be negotiated.

Any expectations of and optimism for easy negotiations based on harmony between the Dominions are probably ill-founded. For all the portents of doom, for all the intelligence and for all the cohesion of commonwealth, there appeared a fragile spirit amongst the British, Canadian, Australian, New Zealand and Rhodesian representatives in Ottawa in 1939. The pre-planning of negotiations, personality conflicts, desperation of Britain and the dynamic of Canadian politics conspired to agitate very delicate proceedings. Prime Minister Chamberlain was, in 1939, so uncertain of the outcome that he considered personal intervention to steer Canada towards agreement. There was no easy passage for the tense negotiations and it cannot be taken for granted that, at best, paternalism favoured unquestioning obedience from a young brood. At worst, imperious negotiating stances tested the loyalty between nations far from a European war. In the process this precipitated a constitutional crisis. Various senior officers and politicians recognised the problems yet support did eventually emerge for a training scheme focussing on a pivotal role for Canada.

The announcement of war clearly altered the overall mindset between the Dominions, expediting major Canadian contributions. A complete North American aid package would follow in 1940 and not until December 1941 would the United States enter the war. However, in the Ontarian Fall of 1939, positions were fought hard and individual characteristics of obstinate, unyielding arrogance and sheer anger preceded commitments: who would run the programme and who would administer it, and would there be a supply of Canadian pilots or merely the training of Dominion pilots? Assertions were made. Was Canadian authority being undermined in the process? Was there overbearing Whitehall control? What way would Canada go? Was the country being isolationist and anti-British or was Mackenzie King merely safeguarding his country's interests?

William Lyon Mackenzie King was in his late twenties when the Wright Brothers saw through their achievements in North Carolina. At age forty-seven in 1921 he would begin the first of three terms in Office as Prime Minister, the last being a remarkable thirteen years from 1935 to 1948. He had seen the development of his country through the early years of the twentieth century, had seen technological and industrial change. In a new world far from Europe he had experienced how the tensions of conflagration manifested amongst his own people, arising out of Great War conscription and losses. Resting independence from Britain in the 1920s and experiencing issues of French-Canadian partition, here he was in 1939 answering the 'King's Call'. In his speech of 4th September 1939 he stated :

> *"This morning, the King, speaking to his peoples at home and across the seas, appealed to all to make their own the cause of freedom, which Britain again has taken up. Canada has already answered that call."*

At the very outbreak of war, Mackenzie King addressed the Canadian people and spoke of the shadow of impending conflict and the patient search for peace. Control, aggressive designs, deception, terrorism and violence had spawned from a 'pagan conception of social order' which contrasted with Christian conceptions and the sacredness of the human personality. He echoed President Roosevelt's speech to Congress on 4th January 1939 in defending religion, democracy and good faith.

The Canadian government looked to its Parliament, recommending measures for 'effective cooperation' with Britain. Even before the final agreement was achieved on 17th December 1939, Mackenzie King was heralding unequivocal support. The text of his speech on 10th October 1939, as reported in the Hamilton Spectator the following day, confirmed agreement in *principle* of a development of great importance between the United Kingdom, Australia, New Zealand and Canada. These were the arrangements for rapid expansion of air training required for the enlargement and maintenance on an enlarged air force and increased aircraft production. The objective of that undertaking, within the language of partnering, cooperation, mutuality and morality, was clear: air forces of overwhelming strength. Mackenzie King reported the British government's warm words that Canada's co-operative effort *'may prove to be of the most essential and decisive character'*.

At the time of the speech, the British government representatives, headed by Lord Riverdale, were on their way to Ottawa to discuss and agree the detail of how the agreement would be put into action: aircraft, airfields, instructors, and ground staff. Curiously, though perhaps shrewdly, matters of cost were absent from Mackenzie King's speech. Unanimity of purpose was one thing, the hard-fought negotiations on how, when, where and, particularly, how much, would dominate the remaining weeks leading up to the announcement of Great Magnitude.

The contribution of Canada was about more than just politics and morality, it was about practical steps. The EATS was born and would become the British Commonwealth Air Training Plan – combining purpose and group effort shared under the Commonwealth banner, rather than the apparent sub-ordinacy within what was seen as a 'British' Empire.

Between June 1940 and September 1945, Canada was in business turning out aircrew in Ontario, Quebec, Alberta, Manitoba, Saskatchewan, Nova Scotia in the east and British Columbia in the west: twenty-five schools in all. Dominion support was crucial in producing men, women, infrastructure, organization and tools. The demands of war meant not just mobilising countries, but their capabilities. Even before war had started, in 1938, preparations were taking place. The aircraft manufacturing potential of Canada was small in comparison with the United States, but was configured to increase production; a critical move in the face of US neutrality in the early years of war.

Pre-war initiatives included establishing Canadian Associated Aircraft Ltd (CAA), originally set up in 1938 as an amalgam of six different companies (Canadian Vickers, Canadian Car and Foundry, Fairchild, National Steel Car Corp, Fleet, and Ottawa Car and Aircraft). Involved in manufacturing the Handley Page Hampden, the group later built the Lancaster.

Time Magazine on 4th December 1939 reported the role of CAA in coordinating aircraft orders from Britain, the initial 'educational' order, shortly after it was set up, was for eighty Handley Page Hampdens – a not inconsiderable US$10 million contract. During the Riverdale discussions an order was mooted of US$20 million worth of bombers and 'plenty more later'. By 1942 the company had been wound up.

The sheer magnitude of the Canadian contribution is impressive. Some 131,000 flying personnel were processed through the EATS, with almost seventy-five per cent of these being trained at Canadian training facilities. Clearly it delivered on "the training of pilots and aircrew on a vast scale". Brief reference is made in some texts to this vast scale, but in the main the Canadian, Australian and New Zealand accounts have more pride and recognition of their respective contributions and the overall achievement. However, the story is as much about the size of the practical undertaking, as it is the political, diplomatic and economic factors in its negotiation.

Although the process of discussion and agreement appears, with hindsight, to be incredibly swift, over the months October-December 1939, it reflected expectations of mutual co-operation in the face of a common enemy, but seemed to magnify 'old world' paternalistic, imperious attitudes bearing down on 'youthful' Canada. Did Canada want to be associated with a European war? Would it want to threaten the lives of Canadian citizens through conscription? Was it being hoodwinked and could it afford to pay for the programme? Who would run the programme? Personality, too, had a major part in the often heated discussions. Although of similar age to the Canadian Premier, Mackenzie King, an apparent disdain emerges. Noted historian Andrew Stewart identified the look, demeanour and anachronistic nature of Lord Riverdale as a factor in the difficult, tortuous route to agreement. To Mackenzie King, Lord Riverdale, with all the characteristics of a Yorkshire Industrialist was – *"all that he perceived to be wrong with the British Empire"*.

It was the scale of Canada's acceptance of the programme, following bitter political wrangling over financial and political points, that secured success. That Canada's airspace should be used, that its personnel and facilities should make contributions might have been broadly accepted, but imagine the tensions of a deal where you have to pay substantially for something, whilst another party manages it.

Elementary training would be shared across the Dominion nations, with advanced training taking place solely in Canada. The bitterly contested area was money – who would pay for this undertaking? Senior officials were taken aback with the costs involved and Whitehall's stance seems hopelessly optimistic and naïve in the expectation that Canada would assume the bulk of the financial costs. At the time Canada summed up an estimated billion dollar expenditure in return for $140 million. Negotiations were hard fought, but it was the expedient thing to do in the autumn of 1939. The cost of training was to be split Canada forty-eight per cent, Australia forty per cent and New Zealand twelve per cent.

In the initial stages, Canada had vast airspace but limited resources of planes and engines, pilots, instructors and production. Capacity would have to be expanded. The country's role and huge contribution is summed up in the actual figures of numbers trained. Of the total numbers of Dominion-sourced pilots and aircrew processed during 1939–1944, some seventy per cent of the total figure of 168,662 would be trained in Canada. Figures for other Dominion nations are: Australia (23,262), New Zealand (3,891), South Africa (16,857), Southern Rhodesia (8,235).

The Empire Air Training Scheme and its South African counterpart Joint Air Training Plan (in the United States, the

Arnold and Towers Scheme) was well under way in the early 40s, and a major logistical operation which required pre-planning, resourcing and massive political cooperation from the so-called Dominion nations, and others too. Canada, Australia, Rhodesia, South Africa, and India all played a part. In due course pilots from Czeckoslovakia and Poland, France, Norway and Denmark found their way in to this truly marvellous operation. Facilities, instructors, personnel and aircraft were all needed.

In 1939 some forty-four flying training schools, reducing to thirty wartime schools, had been established in the British Isles. Overseas schools numbered as follows: Canada (twenty-five), Australia (twelve), New Zealand (four), Rhodesia (five), South Africa (eight), India (two). Eighty-six schools in total. By 1942, the EATS programme had developed momentum, with dozens of flying schools around the globe. In 1939, and without an adequate RAF structure to procure training, the deficiency of pilots stood at 1,000, but by 1942 Canada would be training over 14,000 pilots in that single year.

It is a sobering thought that against the economic troubles of the 1930s and Chamberlain's reluctance to arm, the war got off to such a faltering start. Yet pragmatism prevailed and it was the expedience of doing the right thing that probably triumphed. In the midst of the turmoil, posturing and inter-personal conflict, serious constitutional issues – the threat to the Commonwealth – would also be raised. Statesman-like Mackenzie King and his Parliament committed Canada to becoming the greatest contributor to flying training during the war. It is this, maybe this, that veils our recognition of this period of British history.

If the pre-war recruitment advertising had been understated in looking for large numbers of personnel, by 1941 the copywriters were actively selling the RAF lifestyle and short-service commissions. The RAF life was 'interesting and informative', pay was good and company was 'congenial'; leave was on a generous scale. The gratuity in 1938 was £300. By 1941, it had risen to £500. Candidates with 'the makings of a first-class pilot' were teased in advertisements that queried motives and tenacity, pandered to physical fitness and instinctively knowing "how much to ask from his machine". Elsewhere, *"You're in your element in a scrap – all the more so when it's against odds".*

War was presenting life and death chances and the Air Ministry knew it. *"Never before have the young men of our country had so great an opportunity to attain distinction"* ran one advert. It followed with an allusion to the greatness of conflict and the calibre of RAF pilots distinguished by their Wings, spirit and self-reliance, who would be desirous for action and adventure, keen to hit back for Britain and hammer the enemy. The prospect of international travel was presented in curious strap-lines such as "Book your seat for Berlin". As the demands of war increased, the pre-war age limit for pilot recruits, twenty-five years, was increased first to thirty-one, then thirty-two and later anyone under the age of thirty-three.

Volunteers were no longer being lured by short-service commissions; the working man was being targeted – if you wore dungarees then you too could be off to fly with the RAF. By 1941, the recruitment drive contained a clear route for my father. Reserved men could now volunteer as pilot or observer:

> *"To win the war, Britain needs thousands of young men for flying duties in the RAF. This is the only fighting job open to 'reserved' men. Go after it."*

By this time my father was just beginning to see the light of day. By 1942 he was in the RAFVR.

10
Clean Sheets and Cocoa

nitial examinations for the RAF Volunteer Reserve were held in Edinburgh in June 1942. The selection process involved interviews, oral tests, aptitude tests in English, mental reactions, colour recognition and aircraft classification. The assessment of virtually every physical and cerebral faculty was tiresome and the ever-increasing forensic nature of their examination resulted in the ignominy and embarrassment of medical examinations and 'coughs'.

A long and hopeful train journey back to Dundee followed, and then a long and hopeful wait for the result. A seemingly interminable eleven months passed by before final written confirmation of acceptance for RAF service arrived by post in May 1943.

> "I was at home when the brown envelope arrived marked OHMS. Inside was all relevant documents and a travel voucher to attend the induction centre at St John's Wood, London. My heart was lifted beyond description."

A railway warrant enabled travel to London, a postal order and full instructions on getting to St John's Wood on a certain date were also issued. The man was exhilarated:

"No words can describe my complete elation at this news. Hurriedly packing my few necessary belongings, preparing for the grand departure and excitedly counting the hours to a fond farewell to all the drudgery of factory work."

Training Command was growing. The logistical needs of the air force, in the midst of actuarial conclusions, were manifest. What was required was massive numbers, dozens of facilities to handle the men, women, aircraft and hopes of our youth. There were elementary flying schools, advanced schools, ground instructor schools, gliding schools, refresher schools, and staff pilot schools; schools for air gunners, observers, gunnery, navigation and, above all, flying instructors. Across the country, from the North Sea to the Irish Sea, from the Channel and West to far north Scotland there were new training establishments required.

Following the air force expansion programmes of the 1930s, additional commitments to UK-based training were being made during the early war years. What emerged by 1939 was a process for training the vast numbers of aircrew which was fundamentally unchanged since the end of the Great War. However, the scale of training had to grow and its organisation would have to adapt.

The entire RAF training structure grew from the pivotal role of Cranwell and Halton to an almost franchised, *build-it-big*, approach to producing huge numbers. Within this vast structure No.54 (Training) Group would be established in 1939, its HQ being at Sunningdale, Berkshire. In this very *Home Counties* set-up was a form of preliminary training, otherwise Initial Training, which would draw the nation's youth together and ring them through the mangle that was No.54.

By 1943, the Empire Air Training Scheme was in full swing and a long train journey saw my father leave Dundee for London. As for the grand departure, there were no flags, no bunting, and no party. Dundee Tay Bridge Station with its steam engines, the smell of oil and coal, soot and cigarette smoke was not the stuff of soap opera or matinee drama. No Trevor Howard and Celia Johnston here. George Duncan all gruff pragmatism and no sentiment; Jeanie Duncan, tearful, safe journey and haste ye back.

Whistles and the slow drag, chuff and strain of steam pressure and cylinders up the long ramp to get to bridge height and the splendour of the Tay; rural Fife spread out to the south, Perthshire far to the west, and the industrious Dundee, all chimneys and smokestacks, being left behind. Railway travel in wartime, an economic necessity, but uncomfortable to the last. Ahead of him lay fourteen long hours of stop-start-stop-start.

The rhythmic journey, past stations with names removed or painted over for security reasons, was quite unlike any journey before; the longest in his life and with the ever-present thought, however unlikely, of German fighters strafing the carriages. And in the midst of this mix of danger and excitement, boredom and sleep, there were dreams and nervous anticipation. So the scale of wartime pilot training, my father's successful application and rail warrant drew him southwards for initiation into the Royal Air Force.

Pulling into London King's Cross, the window pushed down to greet the sights and sounds of the capital, his head would peer forward to the platform. Hand held out and turning the outer door handle of the carriage door he stepped onto the platform and greeted London for the first time. Hoards, hustle, bustle, jostling, an array of platforms, cacophony, different voices and the ironic loneliness of not being alone: he had left home, and probably for good. Where the war would take him was a mystery, but his dreams would manifest only through studying instructions that would lead him to the bus stop. Next destination? – St John's Wood and the efficiently named ACRC. What more acronyms and abbreviations would he have to master? But first, and most importantly, was the need for tea.

Arriving in London for assessment and processing, the young men would then be spread around the country to be indoctrinated into ways military and the dangerous delight of flight. My father would first report, like thousands of others, to No.1 Air Crew Reception Centre (ACRC) at Lord's Cricket Ground.

The poverty of the 1930s would never be described as *art deco*. This adjective was reserved for art, architecture and style. No such exposure in the provinces. For my father, it was darkness, factory work or the engineering workshop, and nineteenth century living conditions. Even when away from home, it was the remote, rural backwater of Westmoreland and the faded splendour of Silloth that was just too close to the qualities of 1930's Carnoustie. There was no exposure to grand modern living. However, to the north of Regents Park and between Primrose Hill and Lord's Cricket Ground were situated modern apartment blocks, such as Abbey Lodge, Viceroy Court and Grove Court. London was the rallying point, with the Regents Park area chosen in particular because there were many flats available and, according to the then Head of Training, Alfred Critchley, everyone knew where Lord's Cricket Ground was.

Art deco was in the capital and apartment blocks no longer resembled houses; they were now looking like ocean liners – clean lines and efficient with what looked like railings and a deck on the top floor. Brick built and massive, these were vast modern mansions far-removed from the cold stone of his upbringing. So vast was Viceroy Court, it had three front doors! Grove Court was bigger still. The main apartments above the entrance portico had enclosed balconies within earshot, if not, *smellshot* of London Zoo. Beyond the portico was a wide double door giving way to a reception hall, a small elevator and stairs and passages leading to the many rooms. Large south-facing windows, some with curved glass, imported huge quantities of light. These were the latest lightweight steel windows from

Crittall. Alas, in wartime, the apartments had been stripped bare of many of their fittings and offered comfortable, but not luxurious, accommodation for trainee aircrew. Better than Panbride and 63, he thought. Ten minutes walk away was the Air Crew Reception Centre.

The scale of the pilot training programme and its intensity and discipline need to be appreciated. Hundreds of potential aircrew were accommodated in St John's Wood with what my father called the 'labyrinth of humanity' constantly being under direction and control of senior ranks. The daily routine emerged of kitting-out, inductions, check-ups, interviews, uniforms, parades, drills, barrack inspections, sanitary details, mess duties, drills, drills and more drills. No time for recreation in the conversion of civilian to airman.

This labyrinth, as large and complicated as it was, as daunting and edifying, was but one tiny component of a vast military machine. In so short a history as the RAF's, the import of air war had been realised. No longer was the force configured around the imputed threat of Britain's nearest neighbour, France, as it had been in the 20s. The European Theatre was bigger now and transatlantic flight a reality. The threats were potent and actual. Whatever mistakes or miscalculations had taken place in military planning in the early 1930s, the needs of war were now directed by a scale of response; everything was big: new runways, air force expansion, new aircraft and production facilities, new committees to examine and ensure re-armament.

My father would have to adjust to new discipline and protocol. What he was joining was a leading-edge military service, fit for purpose, fit for war. The command structure alone was huge and complex. The Air Staff comprised the Chief, Vice-Chief, Deputy and four Assistants. Below this was a series of ten directorates dealing with, for example, plans and signals, ground defence and air tactics. Separate to this was the Air Ministry made up of further directors reporting to members of the Ministry. Strata upon strata, rank upon rank. Then, of course, there were the separate commands: bomber, fighter, coastal, etc. Within this body could be found Flying Training Command, responsible, ultimately, for the training of pilots, observers, navigators, and gunners.

To support this structure there were masses of abbreviation, numeric shortening, and slang, much of which has entered common parlance: we 'plug away', have a 'prang', 'get in a flap'. Entering this vast organisation and fitting-in, learning a new language and adjusting to discipline was the dream of thousands; thousands of the nation's youth, tantalised by flying and hungry for what, to them and my father, was the ultimate experience.

Perhaps military discipline was better than the domestic variety. At last he was in. His enthusiasm, ambition, energy and drive were rewarded with little time for pleasure. Aside from the odd bit of socialising in the various apartments, or perhaps a visit to the pub, what else could one do in London in 1943? Regent's Park Zoo held initial curiosity but could hardly sustain interest. In the capital city, even in wartime, the possibilities were endless.

The scale and intensity of London excited, delighted and fascinated. He was far from home and all that he had hoped for and worked towards was before him. So many houses, cars, people. Comfort and uniform were with him now. Not only were his dreams being fulfilled, he was also being paid! Amidst all the drill and parades it was easy to forget that war and its accompanying discipline was remunerated.

The first foray into central London began with pay day. My father, and some new-found pals, had managed to 'escape'; the temptations of life beyond Regent's Park to the south and east being too great. Oxford Street was a comfortable walk away and the West End beyond still drew people in; lots of people, working, playing, enjoying, or just 'getting by' in the stricture of war. No lights at night, shop-fronts boarded, broken or plain lucky, sandbags, statues shrouded and protected by wooden cloaks. Eros had been removed. Yet in the midst of all this war effort there was laughter; the place was teaming. All through the mayhem and doubt of the *Home Front*, the West End was still drawing-in the young, the curious, the hopeful, the everyday people whose need was distraction. People were defiantly congregating in the collective need to keep mum, avoid careless talk and 'get on with it'; to lead as normal a life as possible.

Morale meant that theatres, well some of them, would be open. Here was London after The Blitz and before the cunning silence of the VI flying bomb, the appearance of which the following year, 1944, led to many West End productions closing, though audiences were still willing to take risks. As the editor of *Theatre World* noted: *"the remaining plays have shown increased takings as Londoners accustom themselves to the new form of aerial attack and begin to put on a bolder front"*.

As for my father, there were no such cultural distractions for him and his new-found chums. The objective was to find the beer and the girl. Throwing caution to the wind, they got a cab into Leicester Square. At the risk of playing to the Scottish stereotype, after fifty years my father remembered the 2/6 fare! He tipped the cabby thruppence, only to have this knowingly rejected: "I fink you'll need it more than I will!" He was quite right:

> *"Sneaked into the Café de Paris. What a menu! Could only afford a vol-au-vent by itself, no trimmings. That and a cup of coffee."*

Doubtless short-changed, royally ripped off, probably humiliated and almost certainly still hungry, but what a story.

Life at St John's Wood was comfortable. Here was a thrilling life in London that so few could possibly imagine. It was strange, new and at the end of the first day's turmoil left him utterly bewildered and exhausted. The contrast with home life is summed up in the pleasure of clean bed-linen:

> "What struck me most at that time was the pleasure of going to bed and lying between two nice clean sheets. At home all our sheets were patiently repaired by my mother – they were cut, re-assembled, sewn and patched so much so that their condition made them liable to tear again at any given moment. My bed was both comfortable and warm and I was able to sleep on my own which was so different from sleeping with my brother or sister, or both – we only had one bed."

As for food, well this, in contrast, to life at home was plentiful and there is warm nostalgia for the simple pleasures of cocoa at bedtime:

> "Food, too, was gratefully digested. Three good meals each day with no cooking to do or washing up to be done afterwards – and a cup of tea or cocoa at supper time. This was great. These moments in my life live with me and I was happy at that time to get away from miseries of home with its associated atmosphere of poverty, restriction and control."

London would be home, but this did not rule out journeys home on leave; the contrast between RAF life and the outside world being apparent. In the early days of training in St John's Wood there would be long home-bound train journeys, northwards. At home, the differences between his current and previous lifestyle would be marked. Here, there would be physical and emotional reminders of the poverty and discomfort he had left behind.

By train to Dundee meant a fourteen to sixteen hour overnight journey from King's Cross. A crowded platform would lead to a clamour for space and a journey that was devoid of catering facilities, but full of constant apology as weary travellers disturbed each other as they moved, shifted or were jolted by points. A trip to the toilet ran the risk of losing precious space, finally finding that the toilet was occupied by the sharp cookie who had found that slumber was the more important function of this private space. Overcrowded compartments and narrow passageways were uncomfortable hallmarks of the northbound clickety-click of starts and stops.

The kitbag became seat and bed, and then only if there was space for this. Standing room only was a norm until some passengers got off at, say, Grantham or Peterborough, Doncaster or York. There would be irregular stops during air raids. And all this without a buffet car:

> *"During the course of this journey there were no catering facilities, not even the penny chocolate machines could provide a morsel. No food until the train reached York. Here one could leave the coach to reach the catering trolleys. For 4d one could, after a long queue, get a pie. Still the most luscious pie I have ever tasted and never to be forgotten."*

This memory is tarnished by the meagre allowance of one pie per person. That, and the cup of sooty railway platform tea! Meanwhile, the quality of RAF food had done little to his frame. Not yet twenty years old, he stood at five feet eleven inches and one quarter, with a thirty-four inch chest. Nonetheless, he was declared Medical Category Grade I and was of very good character.

Just months earlier he was an eighteen year old lad, an aero assembly fitter who was disappointed with the inability to do more with instruments. Now, he was somebody. Importantly for him, he was subject to a Ministry of War restriction. Boldly centred and in red print, the instruction was clear:

"Not to be employed other than as pilot or observer"

One month later in June 1943 and with white flash on his cap denoting the coveted 'selected for aircrew training' he would be sent back north. This time to the Yorkshire coast for three months, to No.11 Initial Training Wing, Bramcote Lodge, Scarborough. Bramcote Lodge was a large red stone building and had been appropriated for the war effort. Scarborough, like many seaside resorts, was well-suited to training; clean air away from the main cities, a wealth of hotel and guest-house accommodation and opportunities for leisure in the form of sports facilities, as well as promenades and beaches. The foundations of wartime pilot training lie in buckets and spades.

The Head of No.54 (Training) Group was the aforementioned Alfred Critchley. An unassuming name, but a truly remarkable man. In charge of RAF training 1939–1943, it was he whose foresight would see many a seaside resort converted into RAF training facilities of at least a make do and mend type, appropriate for wartime. No.54 (Training) Group had been set up in 1939 to manage the process of Initial Training, deal with the logistics and somehow find accommodation for tens of thousands of keen, ambitious and curious young men.

At first glance the list of destinations sounds like an RAF-recommended list of notable hostelries for repast and pleasure at His Majesty's expense. RAF bases had expanded in the 1930s, though further expansion was required. Fine hotels were chosen to accommodate a good many of the trainees, in grand towns and, predominantly, still hugely popular coastal resorts. From Cornwall, through Devon and Sussex, thence upwards to Warwickshire and west to Cardiganshire, east again to Cambridgeshire and then *Up North* to the Yorkshire coast and further still to, curiously, Fife. The Northcliffe at Babbacombe, the Bellavista in Torquay; The Arden at Warwick and not one, but three, at Scarborough: The Grand, The Prince of Wales and Belvedere House. There were many others. Scarborough was high on Critchley's list of proposed training establishments; apparently because of the fine hotels and promenades and the beach for sports and PT. Neat, tidy and sedate, facing the North Sea, it was home to many trainee aircrew billeted in the town's hotels. Some 6,000 trainee aircrew passed through the town.

Fife seems to be a peculiar choice. One can speculate on the presence of one of Scotland's leading universities and the flying training school at RAF Leuchars, but the accommodation chosen for the Initial Training Wing at St. Andrews was, in fact, the New Golf Club. It just so happens that the man behind ITW operations was a very keen and competitive golfer!

The general thrust of the training was to prepare students for the aircraft they would fly and also make them fit to fly; physical training was a requisite. Initial Training Wings took pilots and observers and, perversely, had neither runway nor air station. The philosophy of Alfred Critchley was that it was best that they do not see an airplane as this would detract from the main focus which was to get these young men fit through physical training and drill.

However, there was a wider curriculum introducing pupil pilots to navigation, meteorology, airmanship, signals, air force law, aircraft recognition, theory of flight, rules of the air, aircraft engines, and armaments. Study required effort followed by the pressure of examination. This led to my father excelling in creative answering in exam situations. Here was the man who could define 'flutter' as an unstable oscillation due to the interaction of aerodynamic and elastic forces upon the inertia of any structure! But such academic theorising was useless without practical flying. Drill, parades, and inspections were routine, but still no flying at this point.

No sooner had he started on Course No.43 at Bramcote Lodge he succumbed to scarlet fever, was hospitalised for three weeks and sent home for a period of convalescence. He re-entered on Course No.46. This set him back quite a bit, but whilst he made good, there is frustration in retrospect.

If it had not been for this unfortunate episode of bad health he felt, even years later, that his flying training would have been accelerated, with a later five month wait at Heaton Park, Manchester, being avoided. This could have led to flying in *action* with an operational unit. Even in May 1945 and with the Japanese War continuing, he felt that *some* action could be experienced in that theatre. He might progress to flying Typhoons in Burma. These were lofty ambitions, but in 1943 my father had not flown at all and could not foresee events over the next two years.

Critchley was a Great War veteran and deemed well-suited to the role of being in charge of young men undergoing military training. He had, in fact, been in charge of officers' training during the Great War and was a pilot himself. He seems more than capable in influencing, cajoling and seemingly getting people to do what he wanted. What better man than he to be in charge of moulding the lives of young RAF trainees; young men who had joined the greatest fighting force in the world but who would have to wait until they got their hands on a real airplane?

Despite his age at the outbreak of war, by then forty-nine years old, Critchley opted back in to military life following a twenty year hiatus. Having relinquished his commission in 1919, he remained armed with seniority, rank, connections and

Fig 1: 1944 – The Sergeant Pilot   *Fig 2: 1949 – The BEA Steward*

Fig 3: Training in South Africa – Vereeniging, 1944

Fig 4: 'Deanna Durbin'- the pretty, yet skittish, DH82A Tiger Moth

Fig 5: 'Jane Russell' - the full-bodied North American Harvard

Fig 6: The Burnelli-designed Cunliffe-Owen Clyde Clipper
(Picture courtesy The Burnelli Company, Inc./www.burnelli.com)

Fig 7: The Vickers Viking

Fig 8: Passenger handling 1950s style – a Paris-bound Viking.

Fig 9: Tourist class on a Viking.

natural gifts of seemingly innate leadership. He had an ability to manage and was well-suited to the job of RAF training. In May 1939, he wrote personally to the then Secretary of State for Air, Sir Kingsley Wood, outlining a proposal for aircrew training, he heard nothing for a period of months. By August of that year he was summoned to a meeting with Air Marshall Portal.

Demonstrating his credentials and availability, as well as his overall approach to training, he was summoned back to military life. With the rank of Acting Air Commodore, No.54 (Training) Group had its first boss.

Critchley was remarkable for many reasons. Without doubt he appears to have been a charming man, gifted with good fortune and the ability to talk himself into situations and out of them too. He enjoyed gambling and understood how to deal with individuals and large numbers of people. However, there are many discrete veils over much of Mr Critchley's life. The hows, whys and wherefores of an extraordinary life can be surmised from an autobiography that stops short of open vanity, but may reveal some self-regard for his own fortune and how he managed to come by it, lose it and win it back again.

Canadian by birth, he was a man of The Empire who would embed himself in British business, political and military life for over fifty years. Born in 1890, he entered the Canadian military in 1908 and would enjoy a meteoric rise through the ranks of the Canadian and later British military, including transfer from the army to the RFC/RAF. He become a Captain at age twenty-five in the 7th Canadian Infantry Brigade formed in France in 1915. From this dizzying height, he would rise further, becoming a Colonel, in charge of training in France of the Officers of the Canadian Corps. By 1918 he had taken on the command of the officer and cadet training school of the RFC with the rank of Brigadier General (the youngest in the army). This rapid rise actually saw him in command of his father, a junior officer.

By the end of the Great War he took leave from his duties.

Maverick entrepreneurial skills combined with audacious opportunism saw him set up, in 1919, the official-sounding Ex-Officers National Federation where for the princely sum of £250 each (covering travel and accommodation) 100 ex-officers could pioneer the establishment of a colony on the US/Mexican border where farming and forestry would be developed. Mexico's post-revolutionary settling-down presented opportunities to exploit. The Mexican President, Carranza, was happy to sponsor the endeavour, much to the chagrin of the US.

The Secret Service tailed Critchley's movements, press and politicians on both sides of the Atlantic watched intently. Washington was far from pleased with the apparent militarisation close to the border and Whitehall expressed concern that citizens of the Empire were reaching beyond the Dominions. The venture failed and following a further series of very costly investments in oil, Critchley hitched a lift back to Plymouth with £200 in his pocket and the dilemma, upon arrival, of whether to purchase a first class ticket to London, or not!

In the 1920s he would speculate in concrete and build a fortune before laying the foundations of British greyhound racing and then introduce, believe it or not, *cheetah racing*.

Together with Charles Munn, in 1926 he set up the Greyhound Racing Association to front his investments and would own the White City in London as well as Harringay dog track. This was huge business in the 1920s and 30s. In London alone some 6.5 million people were going to the dogs in 1932. Not content with this, he diversified into being a circus promoter, Earl's Court providing the 'big top'. Not satisfied with that, and perhaps as a function of his upbringing (his father ran for public office in late-Victorian Canada), he would flit from one circus to another, becoming a Member of Parliament.

On the back of the Depression and a by-election, he became MP for Twickenham, though by his own admission, evening attendances at his dog tracks kept him away from the House. In time, he would become Chairman of BOAC and would lay claim to finding the site for Heathrow Airport, if reports of frustrations driving from his Sunningdale home to South Coast airfields are to be believed. As for Sunningdale, well, he also happened to be a leading amateur golfer, playing in tournaments, even in Nazi Germany in 1939. This passion for golf may explain his keenness to have the New Club at St. Andrews as a Scottish base for No. 54 (Training) Group.

And the cheetah racing? Well, that was a proposed business venture involving a piece of steak attached to a mechanical hare. Appealing to one cheetah, the other three cheetahs didn't take the bet and were intent on making a killing of a different kind. They turned their sights on the bookmakers.

11
Days of Youth and Things That Fly

Aside from the biplanes above the beach at Carnoustie, maintenance work on airframes, and sitting in a crashed Junkers in a Glasgow street, the actual experience of flying had yet to occur. London and Scarborough provided mere theory. Another long train journey, this time to Carlisle, would be experienced before my father began the actual journey towards getting in the cockpit. The romance of the sky would certainly send him upwards, but not necessarily defying gravity; this time to the county of Westmoreland. Any dreams of getting away seemed hopelessly dashed. Ironically, or conveniently, after the government training scheme in Glasgow he had been posted back to Angus. He was then posted to Silloth and why, oh why, was he now being posted as close as you could possibly get to the Scottish border?

Flying training began in earnest in November 1943 at No.15 Elementary Flight Training School at Kingstown, near Carlisle. Kingstown had been a popular civilian flying school in the 1930s, but in wartime it would be the home of No15 EFTS which had relocated from Redhill, Surrey. By 1943, the training type was the Tiger Moth. His first hours were accumulated in a Moth under the instruction of a chap whom he remembered as a sergeant of the Royal New Zealand Air Force.

The nervous and exciting first experience took place after the many hours of theory and study, but with patience he masters the control and the confidence necessary to defy gravity in what is a very attractive little plane indeed. Of course, a Tiger Moth looks substantial enough if it is your first flying experience: big enough, but not intimidating and room for an instructor behind you. With each hour adding further to confidence, the novel and unfamiliar steadily becomes the routine of stepping onto the wing, climbing ungainly into the snug cockpit, the nose rising high above the wooden control panel, the engine being primed and then that distinctive note. Despite the months of examination and theorising the initial flying was described as a strange and new experience. My father, in his own words, "got the hang of it". After ten hours he had his first solo flight.

If his engineering apprenticeship had denied him a relationship with an aircraft, with the Tiger Moth he met a stranger, became acquainted, and found a friend for whom he had a lifetime's fondness. Pert, robust and taut she may have been on the ground, but taxiing along on the uneven, rutted, grass runway sent every bump and vibration through the airframe until the wheels left the ground and then the constant touch of the stick and rudder to maintain steady control, in the early days, a ham-fisted affair, prone to over-correction: nose level, wings OK, airspeed fine, trim. Skittish, she was, breeze and draught having to be corrected constantly. Each flying experience would bring physiological (that is, the initial queasiness as your innards adjust) and psychological experiences of initial trepidation, if not fear. In time, the stomach adjusts as one anticipates how the plane behaves. Banking and turning, diving and climbing all become second-nature. Fear can subside.

Confidence in flying should stop short of the risks of overconfidence. Defying gravity is a fine and enjoyable experience for some, whilst others like terra firma; the firma the terra the better. However, my father was progressing and enjoying, innately, each and every hour accumulated, even if the routine of circuits and bumps was limiting. Realising this, on one occasion the Kiwi instructor competed against the wind noise and shouted through the Gosport tube: "Have you had any experience of inverted flight?" A confused hesitancy followed. This is a no win situation. Answering 'yes', he would be asked to perform the manoeuvre; 'no' and he would have to experience it! There is an old adage: if you tell the truth, you don't have to remember anything:

> *"I should have lied and said I do it all the time. The next thing I knew was the transition from sitting gravitationally firm on my parachute to hanging by my straps. It would not have been so bad if I had really tightened my straps before take-off. When the aircraft assumed the inverted attitude I suddenly found myself dropping out of my seat and dangling on the straps."*

The initial experience of flying upside-down in an open cockpit airplane was scary to the say the least – and what a surprise it was. In this position he was experiencing the full blast of air hitting him at 100 mph. Rubbish and dirt is falling from the cockpit floor falling past the goggles and flailing hands. His feet are a good twelve inches from the rudder pedals. He was a pilot apart from his machine. Meanwhile the Kiwi instructor is explaining the manoeuvre and inviting some response from the pupil pilot who is struggling against the forces of gravity, is not in control of his aircraft, and cannot reach the mouthpiece to answer the teacher sitting behind him. Here was a fun experience, but never again did my father attempt the manoeuvre, even if Mr Kiwi did think it was a good means of cleaning out the cockpit.

The training programme covered virtually every aspect of flight and whilst the true love was the flying experience, the use of artificial flying equipment, such as the Link Trainer, was not a good experience. This toy-like miniature plane would try to simulate real flying conditions, but was no more than an aid to understanding. An inconvenience if all you really wanted to do was 'get up there'. The cockpit would sometimes be hooded under a larger wooden canopy. Instrument-only flying required concentration and constant observation of the various instruments: rate of climb, artificial horizon, revolutions per minute, altimeter and compass. Getting through the experience was tiring, but a further experience of 'blind flying' – where the pupil pilot would fly the actual airplane with the cockpit under a cloth hood which obscured everything would follow; this time in real flight conditions. Instructions, again, were through the Gosport tube and mercifully did not involve inverted flight or mid-flight lessons in cockpit cleaning. Taxiing out to the runway, my father would strap himself in. The plane was hooded, but the cover was slightly ill-fitting. Production line quality or haste in preparing the plane meant it failed to follow De Havilland's design. This presented opportunity and, ever the resourceful, my father contrived a favourable result from the experience.

There was a slit of light between the hood and fuselage and this enabled some limited vision, certainly enough to inform the pilot, as to landscape and features. Importantly, the horizon could be made out. The throttle was opened and as he ducked to see through the slit, he would fix the line of take-off by reference to a tree, then bringing the tail up, he and the instructor were airborne. Mid-flight, the drift or yaw of the plane would be corrected by feel and by sight. Here is a rare flash of the most false modesty there ever was!

"Of course, much was accomplished in the air with the aid of the instruments, but much too was accomplished with that little opening. In fact, after landing I was complimented by my instructor for showing him the finest piece of blind flying he had ever seen!"

He can fly, well, a little. He is ambitious, has drive and determination. He has struggled to realise a dream. Despite parental intervention and corruption, he has battled out of a reserve occupation. He has passed all the exams. The expectation was that more advanced training would follow. There is a war on, pilots are needed and he has begun the programme. The delays which now ensue must have been excruciatingly uncomfortable.

The events further to the Prime Minister's 'consequently' address to the nation on 3rd September 1939 had originally begun with the piece of paper he had brought back from the German Chancellor. The emergence of a 'phoney war', gas masks and evacuation gave way to foreboding and the realisation that it would not be over by Christmas. On the back of The Depression and a marked reluctance to go to war, Prime Ministers Chamberlain and Churchill had made some pretty bold decisions to build the engineering and military capacity to fight a sea, land and air conflict. Lord Beaverbrook, as Minister for Aircraft Production, then Minister of Supply and Minister of War Production, has been in charge of supplying essential hardware.

The Empire Air Training Scheme/British Commonwealth Air Training Programme (as well as JATP and Arnold and Towers Schemes) have been set up with the clear purpose of creating aircrew, a major part of a fighting machine capable of taking on German military might. Those training schemes, with Dominions offering a critically important role, are a mighty success. Hitler and Chamberlain have given him a chance to fly.

Romantic nostalgia of powdered egg and Lord Haw Haw is one thing, but the early years of war offered an uneasy and interminable disruption to ordinary lives. Lives in underground stations, lives in battered hospitals and lives on the edge, in the balance and in ruins. Tin cans and scrap metal were vital to making ordnance, planes and tanks. Shells were being made in their thousands, aircraft designed, made and delivered. D-Day was some way off. For my father, the early years 1939-1942 were a time of immense frustration as he struggled to get into the RAF.

Following the 'phoney war', the withdrawal through Dunkirk would stiffen resolve. Chamberlain would step down in May 1940, giving way to Churchill. The Battle of Britain was the main show in 1940, allowing the ignominy of Dunkirk to fade. War in and from the air was what technology permitted; new rules emerged. The Blitz ended Hitler's summer offensive of 1940, and not just the London Blitz but the aerial attacks on Coventry, Plymouth, Glasgow and Liverpool. Then would follow the bombing of great German cities, D-Day and the advance through France and then the routes into Germany.

War, by now, had momentum. Having joined the RAFVR in 1942 and, by 1943, ready to move on to advanced training pending operational duty, my father was itching to progress his flying career. The pace of war imposed great demands on the nation and Dominions, but war had to be planned. Resources had to be balanced and the emerging 'bottlenecks' of too many pilots chasing too few training places resulted in delay and frustration. Despite the apparent success of the wartime aircrew training programmes, my father perceived a faltering, stuttering, reluctant bureaucracy holding him back from advanced flying. It was the guys on operational duty who were doing what he wanted to do.

In 1943 the war is changing. Air superiority in Europe was met with the reality that the training programme and its output of qualified pilots would have to be reconciled with advanced training places and the needs of the Operational Training Units. Behind the scenes manipulation of resources was seriously hampering my father's career. By the end of 1943, just as my father was beginning to fly in earnest, it was revealed that supplies of aircrew had caught up with demand. There were adequate supplies of fully trained aircrew as well as those in training and as a result output was gradually reduced by forty per cent. Later, by June 1944, a serious oversupply of pilots had accumulated.

The huge programme of skills expansion created tensions of supply and demand in an unpredictable war. It is impossible to deny the effect of bloody and wicked conflict borne of political doctrine and/or delusion. The scale of destruction inflicted on European cities, and particularly German cities, is vast in terms of areas laid waste or innocents killed. Conflict has to be resourced and the EATS programme was managed to ensure a balance between skilled instructors and aircrew, and airplane production and losses. The vast contribution of the EATS/JATP programme can be put into context. 50,000 blessed and brave flyers were lost over Europe. It was anticipated that some 20,000 pilots would be needed per annum to maintain a flying and defensive capability. The forecast losses were mitigated by air superiority.

If the forefront of war was challenging the top brass, so too my father was facing challenges. Already hacked off with contracting scarlet fever, course set-backs and administrative delays, he is now hungry for flying hours and active service. These issues persisted until 1944 and I suspect this probably explains the months of waiting at Heaton Park, Manchester. At the time, my father was elated with the opportunity provided by conflict; firstly to get away and secondly to fly. However elated my father was in Carlisle in 1943 at the beginning of his flying career, he was well and truly deflated in 1944 as he waited in line for five months at Heaton Park for a place at an advanced flying school. If there were too few pilots in 1939, by 1944 there were too many and my father would be one of them. Training courses were now being extended to re-align supply with demand. Let's face it, why ship men overseas for advanced training if neither the aircraft nor training capacity existed?

Prior to war, Heaton Park was the scene for boating, promenading, playing and sport, a place for tea on Sunday afternoon and brass band music. By the early 1940s its role would be different as it played host to thousands of aircrew. In terms of military abbreviation Heaton Park was 'ACDC': Air Crew Despatch Centre. It was an unlikely rendezvous point, being a large civic park to the north of the centre of Manchester. And whilst Manchester is sufficiently far from fighter penetration in the south-east and readily accessible by train from the rest of the country, it seems odd that so many recruits should concentrate close to a major metropolitan area connected by a ship canal to Liverpool and North Atlantic sea routes. Its function was as a muster station for departing freshly basic trained aircrew. It was, in effect, a depository for disembarking military personnel. A plaque discretely located on the gable wall commemorates the 133,516 aircrew cadets who were stationed there en route to flying training overseas.

Despite the fact that formal structured training had been set up through the EATS since 1940 the actual management of the process created major problems of matching the supply of eager youth with available advanced training capacity within the system.

The boring and seemingly relentless delays at Heaton Park were only interrupted by a three week sojourn to RAF Thorney Island on the south coast. Still no flying, but at least Thorney Island had aircraft in the form of Wellingtons that had been used for towing Airspeed Horsa gliders – massive troop-carrying gliders. This offered some delight in an otherwise unremarkable flying career which, until then, had provided what amounted to a book on aircraft recognition and an association with an airfield in Carlisle.

Going up and down and across the country from one station to another provided a tiring, wearisome and uncomfortable prospect for many servicemen. You are trained in discipline and self-sufficiency: you, your kitbag and whatever else His Majesty had provided was your world. During periods of leave between courses or whilst waiting for a posting, time would be taken to return home on leave. The three shillings and sixpence a day paid fortnightly was good, but at home the allowance of just over £2 meant that this would be handed over to his mother for board and lodging with nothing left over for him. Some things had not changed, however, and he would wear his uniform as his clothes lay in one pawnshop or other.

This peripatetic life during training meant that the RAF bed and a locker would be a comfortable, but only temporary home and as one left the bedding neatly folded and emptied the locker, it would become someone else's roost; again, temporarily. The Air Force life, its routine and the boredom of being permanently ready and always drilled, was broken in 1944. As the Allied Forces marched in on Continental Europe, a journey by train from Manchester to Greenock in June 1944 would lead to a new posting for my father and advanced training on more powerful modern aircraft. The initial solo flight at Carlisle six months previous seemed a lifetime ago. Would he remember his flying skills? But there was a more compelling issue. Like so many other hopefuls he would not know which flying school he would be going to.

From Greenock he would board a ship that would take him south again. One could consider his life as some kind of yo- yo: Dundee, south to London, north to Scarborough, north west to

Carlisle, south to Manchester, south again to Thorney Island, back to Manchester, north to Greenock, south to South Africa... *did someone say South Africa?!*

The EATS as it was known prior to June 1942, would become the British Commonwealth Air Training Plan. Officially it was born on 17th December 1939 and ended on 31st March 1945. War required hurried preparations and if the lateness of the birth of the EATS/BCATP is remarkable, the key role of Canadian airspace and manufacturing and proximity is significant. However, alongside Canada's role, South Africa's also warrants particular mention.

Truth to tell, my father was not formally trained under the actual EATS/BCATP programme, but a separate and parallel initiative involving the South African Air Force (SAAF). The situation with South Africa was somewhat different and a distinct Joint Air Training Plan formed of RAF and SAAF cooperation would emerge. Despite the United Kingdom's faltering preparations for war, lack of foresight, or even naïve tightfistedness after the Depression, the Republic of South Africa had started air force expansion as far back as 1934 and had introduced volunteer training in 1937. Importantly, South Africa had aircraft production facilities. Strategically, South Africa also had ports which, given the dangers of the Straits of Gibraltar and the Mediterranean/Suez routes, gave her a powerful role in bargaining wider benefit from Britain and the US. Strategically, others were interested too.

During the 1930s, the Union of South Africa sought to assert unity and strength amongst its people and politicians. The country was still young and had many internal and border tensions. Politically, and similar to Canada, the social mix would present challenges to neutrality. There were descendents from British, Dutch and German settlers and this created an uneasy social mix when it came to commitments to war. With the emergence of Nazism in Europe, Italian ambitions far to the north and former German colonies closer to home, there were also threats to the fledgling Union; South Africa was awash with German agents and a thin disguise of 'tourists'. Descent and intolerance provided an opportunity for *Greyshirts* and *Blackshirts* to emerge.

Despite being such a young country, South Africa had developed a strong interest in aviation and had established an aviation corps as early as 1913. Air force expansion was aided by an Imperial gift of 100 aircraft in 1918. Steady growth and a commitment to structure and training after the Great War meant that by the 1930s there was in place a commendable infrastructure, if one that lacked the appropriate hardware and weaponry to fight a contemporary war. Whilst the development and growth of the South African Air Force was pretty consistent throughout the 1920s and 30s, 1935 would be a turning point, with the imperial ambitions of Germany and Italy requiring a strategic decision to further expand the air force.

The Imperial gift of 1918 had been a collection of aircraft including SE5As and DH9s. From 1927, the SAAF had been awarding 'Wings' on the back of a curious bag of now distant, long forgotten aircraft: Spartan, Avian, Genet, as well as the more familiar Tiger Moth. In 1938, the British Government had successfully negotiated the sale of 'obsolescent' service aircraft for £200 each. By 1939 the air force relied upon Hartbees, Harts, Wapitis and Tutors; aircraft of the decade, but not of the time, far short of the speed, range and manoeuvrability required in wartime; woefully inadequate in the face of new technology.

The provision of these planes, bought at this knock-down rate, and with free shipping, would contribute to a structure of flying training which provided a basis to continue to grow a national aerial defence force. South African Air Force records show that at the outbreak of war the complement was 160 officers, 1,400 in the ranks and only 35 cadets. As for the kites, well the 'front line' hangers contained six Hawker Hurricanes, a Fairey Battle and a Bristol Blenheim MkI. South African Airways Junkers were also used as transports. But at least it would have some hardware with which to train a fighting force, albeit one with a hand-me-down wardrobe of airframes.

Yet the South African Air Force was a key component of wartime aircrew training. Airframes having been bought, the military structure was moulded, capable of not only defending a strategic point in the oceans and the continent, but also contributing to allied effort.

Fascist interests had been advanced by the Italians southwards from East Africa during the 30s. South Africa had officially declared war on Germany on 6th September 1939, though with many German agents present and a European population in South Africa, there were inevitable political and social divides. Despite air force expansion, South Africa was some way below its fighting weight. The threat was potent and, if not immediate, was realisable. Hardware and structure were required. The South African Air Force would play an important role.

Out of a far-sighted training programme in the 1920s would emerge, by the late 1930s, a fighting force that combined the strengths of land-based combat but with still limited aerial strength. Military expansion was a major component of South African defence policy in the 1930s. Defence plans emerged, though, as ever, politics and personality would conspire to raise questions over certain commitments.

The Hon Mr Oswald Pirow, as South Africa's Minister of Defence, initiated an acceleration of the country's defences in 1934. This was based on an internal agreement involving civilian and state facilities, not dissimilar to efforts in Britain in the 30s involving flying clubs. However, the 1934 expansion plans failed. In 1936, further plans for expansion did not come to fruition at all. These were mere paper without any form of commitment. Jan Christian Smuts, at the time Minister of Justice, was angered and an uncharacteristic rage emerged. His target was Pirow:

> *"I have no objection to the plan itself, I will fulfil it just as I have fulfilled other promises made and broken by Mr Pirow. Mr Pirow's work was more a danger to this country than a protection."*

If Pirow did not want to go to war then why become Defence Minister other than for shaping a defence force as you see it? J C Smuts Junior writing in 1952 saw Pirow's weakness as an inability to grasp the reality of new war and the arsenals and ambitions of Italy and Germany. Pirow's weakness was not in ineptitude but in "an outmoded bushcart conception of guerrilla war...based on a thin line of half-trained troops moving light through the bush and living on the country as far as possible". This, though, appears to veil the wider criticisms of Pirow, his motives and associations. Smuts Junior, with a mix of fact and diplomatic language, went on to offer a powerful summary discredit of Pirow:

> *"Perhaps it would be fairest to say that his term as Minister was notable chiefly for his indiscreet pre-war visits to the Dictators, by whom he had been much impressed."*

The failings of Pirow were corrected by the outcome of the May 1938 election where Smuts' United Party won significant seats. Pirow was subsequently isolated politically and uncharacteristically lambasted by Jan Christian Smuts, as Prime Minister for a second time.

In October 1939 a Peace Expansion Scheme was approved by the then Chief of the General Staff, Sir Pierre Van Ryneveld.

As a result, some 720 aircraft were acquired. Smuts, by now Prime Minister, was about to deliver on his promise. The *One Thousand Pilot Scheme* emerged, so-called because of the target of training 1,000 pilots by 1942. In addition, 700 ground crew would be trained in the same timeframe. South Africa had a training infrastructure in pre-war days and an organised structure in wartime which saw airfields, training, military and political commitment. By 1939, new aviation hardware was beginning to filter through. And how fortunate, with van Ryneveld offering remarkable perception: "this will last for five years".

The immediate response to the declaration of war was coastal defence, but at least the prior establishment of the Central Flying School enabled this to happen. Airpower requirements expanded out of the relocation and restructuring of the Central Flying School into a flying training division and a separate armaments and air observers school. By the end of 1939 the country was able to increase its potential air power with orders being placed for fifty Tiger Moths – the latest DH82A for training purposes – and the Women's Auxiliary Air Force having been established.

Further moves took place in 1940. Virtually all civilian flying ceased and all aircraft in the country were requisitioned by the SAAF and handed out to the new flying schools spread out across the nation. A Training Command emerged with seven flying schools, armament and observers, electrical and wireless and photography. This structure emerged in double-quick time. Between September 1939 and May 1940 a command structure and mobilisation of resources had led to an ability to train major numbers of aircrew.

Whatever was being negotiated in Ottawa in October-December 1939, South Africa was doing unilaterally, and with results. That year, 166 pupil pilots were undergoing ground instruction; 95 were undergoing advanced flying training and 65 had qualified for their 'Wings'. In addition, 54 Air Gunners had qualified and another 205 were under instruction. It was at this stage that the SAAF entered into an agreement that would increase its size to beyond the wildest dreams of all who were connected with it.

Although my father would enter his war and be trained under the umbrella of the EATS/BCATP, it was the separate, but complimentary, initiative of the 'Joint Air Training Plan' that provided him with his opportunity. With many others he waited in line in 1944 for transfer to advanced training school.

The prospects of integrating the war effort with South Africa's capability was noted in Westminster. In 1939 the then British Government Air Minister, Sir Kingsley Wood, reported to the House of Commons that the South African Government did not consider the EATS to be applicable to that country's circumstances. As the momentum of imminent war in Europe grew, the South African Air Force established on 1st August 1940 a Joint Air Training Plan: *The Plan*.

Formal integration of the South African training resource into the wider Dominion initiative that would become the BCATP would follow further negotiations over the next two years. It would not be until 1941 that a 'joint' British-South Africa agreement would emerge. Why not conjoin in the interests of national defence? It may be that with South African independence in 1934 the 'Empire' tag was not well received. Rather than be directed to from London, in December 1939 Field Marshall Smuts *offered* facilities in South Africa for the establishment of Flying Training Schools for the training of both RAF and SAAF pilots and aircrew.

Two stages of agreement followed. As a result of the offer of facilities, it was announced in April 1940 that Smuts' offer had been accepted by the British Government. Air Chief Marshall Sir Robert Brooke-Popham, Head of the British Air Mission and a veteran of the mission to Ottawa in 1939, was despatched to South Africa. Arriving in Cape Town later that month there emerged by June 1940 the so-called 'Van Brookham' Agreement, a foreshortening of the names of the principal architects: Air Chief Marshal Sir Robert Brooke-Popham and Sir Pierre Van Ryneveld. This agreement was in fact more formally titled the *Memorandum on the Expansion of Training Facilities in South Africa*. This would advance the training infrastructure, with Lt Col W T B Tasker being appointed Head of Air Force Training and creating four Elementary Flying Training Schools, four Service Flying Training Schools, and three Air Observers Schools.

An agreement requires two or more parties to commune in common purpose and here was a joint venture arrangement where South Africa would provide the hard infrastructure: airfields, buildings and all facilities; the UK Government would provide additional aircraft, spares and training equipment. In common with the Ottawa experience, the financial arrangements were either not clear, inadequately concluded, or plain one-sided.

It was subsequently determined that this original agreement was inadequate to cope with training requirements. A revised agreement emerged in October 1940 following the appointment of the Air Commodore (later Air Vice Marshal) Matthew Brown Frew, the WWI RFC ace pilot and career airman, as Director of Air Training.

On 23rd June 1941 the 'Joint Air Training Scheme in South Africa, Memorandum of Agreement' was signed, leading to major expansion of training facilities: seven (not four) Elementary Flying Training Schools; seven (not four) Service Flying Training Schools; six (later five) Combined Observer Navigation and Gunnery Schools; a General Reconnaissance School; the Central Flying School and an aircraft testing station. Aside from the establishment of critical mass of training capability, there was the need to populate the system. Units were transferred from Britain to South Africa.

The Joint Air Training Plan established a unified training structure. By July 1941 all air training units in the Union had been brought within the one system. Ultimately, forty-five air schools were created with eighteen air depots, including two in Italy, where South Africa had an important role in the push northwards into mainland Europe. A depot was also established in Kenya. Under the agreement with the British Government several complete flying units were moved to South Africa and a number of training aircraft, already in South Africa and the property of the South African Government, were included in the scheme. Elementary Flying Training Schools (EFTS) and Service Flying Training Schools (SFTS) would function in tandem, with student pilots transferring to new schools once sufficiently competent. Schools were situated a reasonable distance from each other.

Between 1941 and the cessation of hostilities a vast programme of training called for mobilisation of resources and decision-making: where would the new airfields be, could existing facilities be adapted, how would they be designed, how would the infrastructure be laid on, who would do the work and how much would it cost? The location of facilities matched training requirements and the country's weather conditions – the Transvaal and the Orange Free State were the favoured locations. Local economies grew; small towns became larger. Business was good as construction and ongoing training programmes boosted buying power in many otherwise small, remote communities.

Hundreds of training aircraft arrived between 1940 and 1943. South African Air Force records point more factually to the build up to its contribution. South Africa entered the war on 6th September 1939. By 1940 the Joint Air Training Plan –'The Plan' – had arrived and would shut down in 1945. The figure of 131,000 aircrew emerging from the EATS/BCATP programme is often quoted, but appears to exclude the very important contribution from South Africa. By 1945 the South African contribution would number 33,347 aircrew in what came to be known as the 'Battle of Training'. When added to the records held by the Royal Canadian Air Force, the figures are astonishing:

EATS/BCATP:

Royal Canadian Air Force	72,835
Royal Australian Air Force	9,606
Royal New Zealand Air Force	7,002
Royal Air Force	42,110

JATP:

South African Air Force	33,347

TOTAL 1940-1945   164,900

(Source: WAB Douglas quoted in RCAF/BAC records and SAAF records)

As an idea in 1936 it was a tremendous logistical feet to conceive, plan, mobilise and operate, despite matters of cost and opposition from the Treasury. The reality is that without the emphatic support from Canada and South Africa, the deficit in pilots pre-war would not have been corrected. A programme that barely existed in 1939 would be so effective in producing aircrew skills that it could withstand losses; a programme so effective that by 1943, as Germany turned to face the Soviet Union, it would begin to overheat.

Later in life my father pondered the logistics and magnitude of the training programme. A scheme emerged that would train pilots and aircrew: 200,000 aircraft, at an average five personnel per plane soon mounts up. And a secondary, reserve, team is needed too! When hostilities ceased in 1945 there were thousands just like my father whose training and skill, so essential to the war effort, were redundant.

South Africa is a most unlikely WWII posting. Only if you understand the need for aircrew at a critical time is it possible to comprehend the international geography of political support and the role South Africa played in supporting aircrew training. It makes perfect sense that wartime flight training should take place away from climatically challenged British Isles; that flying conditions should maximise the time available to craft pilots' skills. Whatever the war had in prospect, a trip across the equator was not anticipated; the war was east, not south! If the embarkation from Greenock involved a convoy south then this was dangerous stuff in wartime. Quite what route southwards was taken I do not know, but hugging the African coast would be foolhardy if a circuitous route via Brazil could provide deception and cover. And how cynical the potential greeting, with ever-present and always hungry U-boats in the Atlantic. Following the events of 6th June 1944 there was huge diversion of German naval resource; U-boats anxious to get 'home' would be happy to take a pot-shot on the Atlantic coast of Africa or in the Bay of Biscay.

Energetic and enthusiastic, there followed a routine of medical examination, initial assessment, elementary training and a nine week passage to Durban. My father's initial destination was No.6 Elementary Flight Training School, Potchefstroom, for further familiarisation on Tiger Moths and then to No.22 Service Flight Training School, Vereeniging, where the delights of the Harvard awaited him. There were also brief visits to No.7 Kroonstad and No.75 Lyttelton.

South Africa was a safe distance from Europe, its bombs, its baggage and certainly the boredom of Heaton Park. Its blue skies were perfect and in world terms it had strategic importance in a watchful eye over the Atlantic and Indian Oceans. But unlike Canada, New Zealand or Australia, there were no vast oceans of separation. To the north was the expansive land mass of the African continent with historic German interests obvious in German East Africa, otherwise Tanganyika, and German South West Africa (later Namibia).

How my father actually got to this vast and beautiful country was confirmed only briefly in his writings. Putting this story on paper is like buying a jigsaw puzzle at a jumble sale – you have some pieces, but the box and the picture are missing. You build up the picture and you are forced to interpolate the gaps. It is also a bit like driving down a road and being taken by curiosity on to a side-road. This occurs in relation to my father's journey to Durban. It was on a British war transport ship called the 'Nea Hellas'.

The 'Nea Hellas' was originally built as the 'Tuscania', the third bearing that name, in 1919-21 by Fairfield Co Ltd, Glasgow, for the Anchor Line. Not a substantial ship, at around 16,000 tons, she was renamed Nea Hellas following her sale to a Greek shipping company in 1939. Her career as a transatlantic liner with the odd sojourn to Bombay was interrupted between 1941 and 1946 when she was requisitioned and used as a British war transport ship.

The long passage in convoy across the equator would introduce heat the like of which my father had never experienced. Men and boys holed up on board ship with only card games, books and music to relieve the crippling boredom. Entering Durban its sights and smells, food and opportunity contrasted with life back home. The city was 'at war' two continents away; so far from Europe, yet the distance was imperceptible with huge numbers of British military personnel passing through the docks, onto trucks, then trains and then up to the far north of the country and farther still into the then Rhodesia.

There followed a brief stay in a transit camp near Durban and then the long rail journey. I was only ever acquainted with the penultimate stage of the journey, described as a long train ride over the Blue Mountains from Durban up to Johannesburg with nothing more than the carriage door 'literature' for entertainment.

Not a pleasant trip – the *shosholoza meyl* – of today's South African rail service, the journey from Durban to Johannesburg was a claustrophobic and far-from-enjoyable experience, lasting close to twenty-four hours. For 'literature' read 'safety instructions' which in my pidgin Afrikaans is committed to memory as *Moany de dooor oopmak vor de tran still stan knee:* 'Do Not Open The Door Until The Train Stops'. Quite handy in itself but utterly useless on the next leg of the journey. He got the bus to No.6 Elementary Flying Training School, Potchefstroom.

Settling-in to a new climate with new friends and routine was not easy. Like many, the distant shores of South Africa meant that news from back home took some time to filter through. New foods and styles of cooking would either menace the taste-buds or fail to satisfy an appetite.

Walking into a local shop he found a voice recording machine and was able to send a message by way of a small aluminium seventy-eight rpm record to his mother and father. Greetings and best wishes were interspersed with commentary on his new life. A youthful Scots tongue confirmed that the food was not so good at camp. It was OK if it was cold, but to supplement his diet he always popped into Johannesburg for what he called 'real food'. Extracts from newspapers were reaching him in record time and he enjoyed sharing these snippets with 'the lads'. But it wasn't all hard work, and he and his new friends were even able to enjoy a picnic on the Vaal River at Magaliesburg.

Apart from a story involving the theft of a bicycle which he was in charge of, the actual day-to-day recollections of life in South Africa are fragmented. Potchefstroom was a place to develop his flying skills and provided more experience in circuits and bumps, looping, spinning, side-slipping, engine failure after take-off, stalling, emergency landing and procedure, cross country exercises, hood flying and stall turns.

The limited experience at Carlisle where he had his first 'solo' in a Tiger Moth would be augmented over what was only an eighteen month period between November 1943 and May 1945. A year and a half out of a man's life that defined him and was his culmination. The initial ten hours at Carlisle would be added to with eighty hours on Tiger Moths at No.6 and then onto AT-6's, or Harvards, at No.22 Vereeniging. In total some 250 hours of flying was accumulated:

> "I can almost remember every flight in the two years it took to get my 'Wings'. I can recall every occasion when I made mistakes, got lost or defied instructions. All in all, the programme, difficult as it was, provided me with just the right stimulus to satisfy my eagerness and unstinting determination to master the art of flying. Many times, nay, many, many times had I sat in the cockpit unbelieving that it was real – I was here, I was doing it."

'Potch', as Potchefstroom was abbreviated to, was a six month training programme aimed at perfecting flying skills and adaptation to more modern aircraft. By 1944, it was an established air school having opened in June 1941. Training demands grew, relying on an initial ten Tiger Moths and, by August 1941, an additional twenty-five Tiger Moths. Unit strength grew further and by 1943 there were fifty-eight Tiger Moths, two Hornet Moths and one Hawker Hart.

Climatically it was a complete contrast to training in Scarborough and Carlisle: long flying days, infrequent inclement weather, and the thrill of new sights, sounds, and colours.

Crickets at night, Pratt and Witney aircraft engines during the day. Flying conditions in South Africa were near perfect, and his love of aviation blossomed. The affection for both Moth and Harvard shines in his writing. On the Moth:

> *"It was a beautiful plane to fly once one had accustomed to its sensitive reactions......But I can honestly say that once I had mastered the Moth it was the most delightful machine imaginable. Nothing to my mind could compare to its beauty when on an early morning flight — when the air is still and the airplane is trimmed to perfection — just how serene and smooth that little craft is. Looking along the wings and seeing not the slightest tremor or listening to the steady drone of the engine."*

This sensitive beauty is all too familiar to instructor and pupil alike, for the Tiger Moth amplified error and did not forgive. You may call it *breeding*, but the slow beauty could kick. His early training revealed the essence of the Tiger and there would be instances where his ham-fisted approach would result in the instructor jabbing him in the back of the head with the joystick.

By August 1945 Potchefstroom's wartime function was redundant. Course 38 had completed training on 6th October 1945. Courses were subsequently run down and anyone on Course 39 would have been bitterly disappointed for this course, with only five students, was suspended. Training ceased on 10th November 1945. On 8th March 1946 the JATP closed. My father was one of 20,800 trained for the RAF out of a total 33,347 who passed through the scheme. The so-called 'Battle for Training' had been won.

Mercifully for my father, he would see elementary training completed by Christmas 1944. Advanced training would continue on Harvards at the much larger No.22 Service Flying School, Vereeniging, home of a mixed bag of inter-war and contemporary planes. The sheer growth of the SAAF and the Joint Air Training Scheme is exemplified. In 1941, the school had a complement of 21 Hawker Harts and 33 Audaxes, many still in RAF markings and serials. By 1942, 2 Hornet Moths arrived along with 21 Airspeed Oxfords.

By July 1942, unit strength totalled 132 aircraft: 45 Audaxes, 65 Harts, 14 Hinds and 8 Oxfords. However, this assortment of heavy biplanes was ill-matched to the needs of the European or Far East theatres. Fixed wing monoplanes were required, providing a critical bridge between elementary training and those planes used by operational units. Vereeniging would rely substantially on the Harvard between 1943 and 1945, resulting from the gradual withdrawal of the Hawker biplanes and a loss of faith in the Miles Master. This was a period of virtually complete replacement of outmoded flying machines with new fit-for-purpose airplanes. The first Harvards arrived in January 1943.

The initial delivery of 14 planes was supplemented by a further 37. By May 1943, strength stood at 51 Harvards, 107 Hawker Hart Variants and 16 Miles Masters. Harvard deliveries were increased and by January 1944 this was the dominant type used at the base. Out of 109 aircraft, 107 were Harvards; only 2 were Harts.

The excitement in the opportunity to fly led to profound and long-lasting affection for the Tiger Moth. But if the Moth was a first love then emotions matured with the Harvard; the description is all the more emotional and physical. The AT-6 Texan, or Harvard as it became known in Britain, is not so much a petite girl of size 6/8, more a lady, size 16/18. And curved. There are many curves in its stressed steel majesty: the subtle wing tip curve from the leading to the trailing edge, and the bulbed housing for the retractable undercarriage designed into the underbelly. Cockpit cover proud, upright and the neatly formed triangular tail finishing off what begins with a softly formed engine cowling. She was good looking. She was also loud.

It can only be said that this now fuller-bodied machine elicited a sheer delight to my father's eye. Harvards, or AT-6s, were not a new airframe design, but the volume exported from North America was just what the RAF required. Vereeniging was an exciting, grown-up, proper airfield, which would permit the next phase of his flying career.

Having found his way to the base, vast compared with Potchefstroom, a myriad concrete and steel hangers and plane upon plane, he did his first foot-reconnaissance and found the hardware. Where the Moth was the-girl-next-door, the Harvard was the girl-about-town: Deanna Durbin had given way to Jane Russell. Where Howard Hughes had concerned himself with delightful curves that defied gravity in The Outlaw, so my father found himself preoccupied with similar great masses, this time formed in stressed metal:

> *"It was here I came across my first sight of the Harvard and I must confess I was absolutely awestruck with its immensity. It was huge in comparison to the Tiger Moth and as I looked over its lines and flashing finish the all-metal framework seemed to portray a power I could not possibly overcome. It was as if no man could control a thing of such size – an immense engine, long canopied cockpit highly set over a long robust body, then wings that seemed to stretch forever – again, all metal. What a monster! What an impossibility! Even looking at it made me feel I had reached the end of my flying career because no way could I see myself controlling this great mass of metal."*

Trepidation, fear, anxiety, inspiration and fascination. An exciting introduction – he wanted to see this girl again. Over time the scale of the aircraft became more manageable as with every additional hour its handling characteristics were mastered.

The Harvard had 600 horse power, five times that of the Moth. With a top speed of just over 200 miles per hour, it flew twice as fast. It had twice the ceiling, twice the rate of climb and was four times the weight. My father said rather kindly that, with familiarity, its awesomeness assumed more acceptable proportions! The fear of its power disappeared and transformed into a bond of friendship – even love:

> *"It became a part of me, and I a part of it. The blend was a mixture of pleasure and confidence which produced a bond of affection never again experienced with any other modern mechanical device."*

A 1942 report of the Harvard's credentials offers the following description; pin-point observation defines the valuable role of this new, modern airframe:

> *". . . a monoplane embodying all those special pieces of equipment and those accessories which are now found as standard on nearly all operational types, and in consequence it provides an excellent avenue of approach from the elementary trainer to the operational machines."*

And as for the distinctive sound of its Pratt & Whitney radial:

> *". . . known to thousands . . . owing to the peculiarly piercing noise made by its engine and airscrew when the machine comes in a certain arc from the listener."*

The Harvard was, from 1938, a virtually new form of aircraft, fit for the military training demands of a new age. Modern aircraft were required to train pilots in the art of powerful, fast-paced aerial combat. First delivered to the RAF in 1939, with an initial order of 200, some 1,100 of the type were delivered before Lend-Lease and in total some 5,000 were delivered to Commonwealth Air Forces.

The EATS programme required good and safe flying conditions conducive to a quantity of pilots being trained pretty quickly. Volumes were trained far from Europe and these far-off places provided the opportunity to fly in beautiful conditions. The Transvaal was no exception. High above the bundu and the cloud cover beyond that, the ethereal beauty of flying and my father's enjoyment of it is captured in graphic detail:

> "On breaking through a few hundred feet of stratus cloud and emerging into a whole new world of white satin stretching out all over as far as the eye could see. Gorgeous blue skies up above and a great ball of fire showering its warmth, light and colour. Alone in this heaven of beauty seems to me to be the ultimate in flying pleasure."

And so it is that flight can be spiritual as well as an experience in defiance of gravity; the laws of physics toyed. Back at base there were equal and opposite forces: the intoxicating pleasure of flight was balanced with discipline and more learning: the Harvard was, indeed, a *Pilot Maker*.

There was the ever-present need for routine. Flying exercise would have to be performed: spinning, climbing, stall turns, slow rolls, barrel rolls, loops, spins. And after half an hour, back to base, pleased with the work and proud of the machine. With the Harvard additional demands were placed on the pilot. It was no longer a matter of flying, navigation and control of the craft generally, airplanes had a purpose and that purpose was to familiarise the pilot with combat functions.

Low level and high level bombing was practiced; formation take off and landing. Handgun, machine gun and rifle practice was involved. How to throw a grenade. All of this with live ammunition! Additional studies in armaments, pyrotechnics, bombs, signalling and aircraft recognition were assisted by air-to-air and ground-to-air gunnery. There was a war on!

All checked against rigid criteria, and if you passed and showed promise then the student pilot could be awarded a coveted brevet to wear above the left breast pocket. Constant drills every day – precision drill was the objective and final outcome. Marching was always done. There were many planes at the station, some in use, others in the hanger for servicing or repair.

In Major Oliver Stewart's 1942 book on aircraft and training of the RAF there is no reference to the BCATP or EATS, or the scale of international cooperation. Security reasons or politico-national pride may explain this. The impression given is of training taking place at home in Britain, without the help of Canada, South Africa, Rhodesia, Australia and New Zealand, and others too. However, an excellent pictorial section provides an insight to the Air Ministry records of training.

The day was made up of class in the mornings and flying in the afternoon. On alternate days this was reversed. After breakfast, the pupil pilots would open up the large hanger doors and gently manoeuvre the planes into lines ready for flight. A briefing followed. These additional tasks seemed to take away from the task in hand – flying – and my father saw these essentially military activities get in the way of his desire. For my father, the appeal of South Africa – and in large measure – was the relative freedom to fly:

"The atmosphere of learning aviation seemed to override the normal routines associated with [the] military. Certainly

marching in small groups was the norm but as the groups were fragmented, morning parades were unheard of and assemblies of any kind were never encountered. Life was a mixture of schooling to learn aero engines, air navigation, meteorology, flying procedures, airmanship, coupled with sports, physical exercises, good food and plenty of sleep."

Physical fitness was paramount with discipline, obedience and learning being core components of the programme. Flying was taken seriously, with each and every activity filled with apprehension. But the thought of failure never arose. Forgetfulness maybe, but never failure. Forgetfulness because unlike the Tiger Moth, the Harvard had a retractable undercarriage. Oops!

"I was on the verge of the stall for a three pointer. It was so smooth that I felt that this was going to be the best landing I ever made in my life. Flash! — it hit me like a bomb! Full throttle — tail up, nose down, airspeed! airspeed! airspeed!! — no climb yet until I got to the edge of the field, then slowly but ever so slowly edge up to seventy knots, eighty knots — into the safe zone. Phew! — what a close one that was!!"

Formation blind flying may not actually have been on the curriculum. Flying in formation without a field of vision would be ill-advised to say the least, but what happens if your hydromatic propeller fails?

"I was No. 2 on the right of leader. Somehow or other on a part turn I slid way out of position and found myself labouring to regain my rightful place alongside leader's wingtip but the gap seemed to increase. Naturally I opened up to full throttle whilst leader was shouting like hell in my earphones. Then suddenly the engine burst and in seconds day had turned to night!

"*The whole of my canopy was covered in oil and I was blind flying again. Opening the hood I throttled back, told leader what had happened and was advised to return to base.*

"*I tried to slide my hand out with a cloth to clear the windscreen but the wind force was so strong it nearly blew my hand off. After landing, the plane was covered in oil due to a faulty hydromatic propeller for the constant speed control.*"

Formation flying seems to represent a difficulty for my father. Here, after all, was the chap who upon taking his 'Wings' written examination defined 'Close Formation' as being where there was no visible distance between wing tips, and 'Open Formation' as anywhere in the sky! Not without surprise both answers were discredited, but a dubious reputation was earned. This student pilot was both original and imaginative.

My father enjoyed navigation and understood the stars in the heavens as well as the mundane process of dead-reckoning, a combination of the *'triangle of velocities'* using heading and true airspeed, track and groundspeed, and wind speed and wind direction. What is odd, here, is that he enjoyed the subject area so much he actually looked forward to the written exam.

He was supremely confident he would pass, exceeding the seventy per cent mark required, but in the face of such confidence he struck off a wind vector in the wrong direction. Instead of north east, he had drawn it south west. Frustration and recalculation followed, but not once did he check the wording on the exam paper. He never did get the final percentage mark and his 'dismal and disappointing' performance would lead to a re-sit.

One of the difficulties of flying is that air is not static. It moves sideways and up and down. The airplane behaves according to the air mass around it and this has to be factored-in when undergoing cross-country flying. Venturing out on cross-country flights across a beautiful, if unfamiliar, landscape would frequently present difficulty in determining where he was. Above the Veldt there was further difficulty of remoteness, lack of recognisable features and the ever-present prospect of running out of fuel. Here he readily admitted to using guesswork, common sense — even a sixth sense — and good luck. After all, a compass and naïvety was all he had.

He had come a long way from his youth, from the roar of engines in the Angus skies, from the half a crown bike and the riding along the familiar roads of Carnoustie. Here he was traversing the Veldt and on the lookout for a solitary cattle shed, somewhere, and belonging to an Afrikaaner he did not know!

He was one of three selected for a brief cross-country flight and all three having put on their flying suits and carrying their parachutes over their shoulders they received a last minute weather briefing followed by verification of calculations. The actual exercise was to climb to 500 feet then increase the altitude to 1,000 feet, fly back over the airfield and then set course for a turning point some twenty-five minutes away. The turning point was said cattle shed — if found it would be visible over the port wing tip.

He was set and ready to go. Maps and notebook were in his leg pockets, pencil to hand, parachute ready and helmet and goggles fitting nicely. Here is something out of Biggles, out of virtually every stereotypical period flying scene. 'Contact', check the magnetos, wave away the chocks and move off to the take- off point. The take-off is sound, the ascent smooth and flying conditions good. Climb to 500 feet and then 1,000 feet. Turn and set course. After twenty-five minutes no cattle shed in sight, just endless *bundu*. The fearsome possibility was that he was off course, that he had flown passed the shed and was by now five or six miles distant from it. He would never see the other orientation points: the Vaal River and railroad. He was not concerned by the error as lessons were being learned and he was philosophical in his appreciation of the conditions around him. Flying in harmony with nature was essential, with the plane being but one element of a 'grand scenario'.

> *"If the pilot could operate in communion with the natural forces around him so much more would his ability improve."*

These vignettes on my father's life are his own personal experiences which I now discover. The only tale I can ever recall my father telling me was of him being booked to fly a particular aircraft then swapping planes at the last minute. He survived, but the other fella didn't. There are only two actual records of my father's flying experiences. The sad tale of 'Paddy' requires mention and the account is drawn word-for-word.

> *"Casualties in training were few in my experience but in the whole Empire Air Training Scheme I suppose the records will reveal quite a few instances of accidents and fatalities. Only two do I remember. One was a Tiger Moth flying into a hillside at Potchefstroom. He didn't survive. Another was the result of a night flying by a young Irishman. He flew the same plane as I had flown the previous night on a cross-country test."*

The official record intimates that the pilot was short of Elmtree Station, was disorientated, and crashed 'out of control'. In more graphic detail, my father would, years later, add:

> *"The plane was L7813 (I always remember it because of the last two digits) and I had noticed it was difficult to fly 'hands off ' because it had an inherent tendency to bank*

> *slowly to port which would result in a spiral dive if allowed*
> *to continue. It required constant adjustment to hold a*
> *compass course. Because the flights were reasonably long and*
> *lonely in the dark I can only assume that Paddy fell asleep*
> *at the controls and lost his sense of sensation as the spiral*
> *dive developed."*

This event was impressed on memory, but alas the aircraft reference was in fact L7313, flying out of No.22 Flying School, Vereeniging, and assigned to an instrument-only night flying exercise. What cruel fate for Paddy whose routine training had led to premature death. This account is all the more remarkable because of the technical insight some fifty-plus years later. Aircraft behave in odd ways and our natural response to certain conditions needs to be checked against proper flight practice. In a dive situation there would be a natural aversion to putting the stick forward; why make matters worse by pointing the nose to the ground?

> *"Pulling out of a situation like this only increases the tightness*
> *of the spiral and creates a crazy instrumentation. It's like a*
> *half spin and needs a good left rudder kick and stick forward*
> *to pull out and straighten up, by which time, of course, one's*
> *sense of position is completely lost. But anyway, Paddy never*
> *came back. I was a funeral bearer."*

Paddy was not, of course, his real name. It was the universal nick-name for any Irishman, a rationale that would be aptly applied to my father; Jock he would be to many in later years. Paddy was in fact Samuel Hadden, who, at age twenty-two years, was no younger nor older than my father. Such cruel fate that the behaviour of the airplane my father had flown the night before could not be corrected.

Paddy was a very young Belfast man from Ballyhenry, Carnmoney. He died on 8th August 1945 and is buried in Grave 19 of Vereeniging's Old Town Cemetery. The place of death is reported as Standerton. He was nineteen when he joined the RAF following a brief working life with the aircraft manufacturers Short and Harland Ltd and James Boyd and Sons, Carnmoney, a firm of quarrymen.

The real story of the South African phase was that concerning a particular flight where my father wanted additional hours. Now this part of his life is remarkable, if not incredible, and so profound was the brief experience, that a poem was composed reflecting the ethereal qualities of high flight:

> "I had the opportunity to experience a solo flight for a thirty minute aerobatic practice. Reaching just under the cloud base at 10,000 feet I decided to penetrate the cloud with the intention of practising blind flying in uninterrupted cloud."

The experience is graphically recalled:

> "Two or three minutes had elapsed before I broke through the cloud and found myself flying over a carpet of extraordinary brilliance that stretched from horizon to horizon. And above, there appeared a whole range of fantastic colours spread across the skyline – blues, pinks, reds, greens and yellows no doubt created by the ball of fire disappearing slowly below the horizon … It seemed so unbelievably permanent, still and silent."

> "It was this vision of immensity and colour that spurred my emotions, the sanctity of space, the tranquillity of heaven, the presence of God that prompted me to write my version."

He later recollects:

> *"I have tried to recapture my poem from memory but after*
> *sixty years, I can now only recall fragmented phrases and single*
> *words without connection. What I do definitely remember is*
> *that the first three lines of my version went thus:-*
> *'Up, up, the delirious burning blue*
> *I've topped the windswept heights with easy grace*
> *Where never lark or even eagle flew.'"*

These lines are now famous the world over and the complete
poem represents a testament to the man to whom authorship is
attributed, John Gillespie Magee, and also awe in its observation
and enduring comfort in its use. Explaining matters further,
he offers the following:

> *"In 1944/1945 (Dec/Jan) I had no knowledge of other*
> *poets and certainly nothing of Magee: nor did I consider myself*
> *adequately equipped to write poetry. But consider this — how*
> *could I possibly write my opening lines at that time in South*
> *Africa?... Another two lines are somehow coincidental*
> > *'And while with silent lifting mind I've trod*
> > *Put out my hand and touched the face of God.'"*

In further notes, the original poem 'as penned at Flying School
1944' is written in manuscript:

> *I have slipped the surly bonds of earth*
> *With silver'd wings spread wide,*
> *And danced the skies with trembling mirth*
> *To cross the great divide*
> *A vision of beauty unsurpassed*
> *Stretched out before my eyes*
> *Brilliant colours, blinding bright,*
> *Held fast in wondrous skies*

Up, up the delirious burning blue
I've topped the windswept heights with easy grace
Where never lark or even eagle flew
And while with silent lifting mind I've trod
The unsurpassed sanctity of space
I've raised my hand and touched the face of God

My father cross-referred to his 1948 transcription – the copy I treasure – and refers in his letter to a pure, original, un-plagiarised, flash of inspiration in keeping with the emotional feelings he had experienced. But this manuscript post-dates Magee's life. He certainly remembers showing the poem to his father in the front room at 63. The father-son thing echoes that of Magee. As a young boy I committed my father's composition to memory and had no knowledge of the wider popularity of 'High Flight'. What I was aware of from an early age was that on a piece of paper in my father's fair hand was a manuscript rendering of this poem. In time, this poem would become regarded as ranking alongside the work of Rupert Brooke, John McCrae and Joyce Kilmer. But the provenance of my father's memories are clear : the incident, the inspiration and the commitment to memory and, even years later, the clarity of the account.

The clear assertion is that prior to getting his wings, my father composed a poem describing emotions in flight:

> *"My central theme was constructed around leaving the misery of earth, the beauties of cloud formations and the vastness of a wonder."*

My father did not have a title for it, nor did he keep any of the original manuscripts. The original was typewritten on a piece of yellow paper. The last time my father handled it was on a homecoming to Dundee where he showed it to his father. But in his own words, whoever made up 'High Flight' had used his lines. He would ponder:

> *"How did the author of the High Flight poem manage to get his hands on my lines? It is a complete mystery and one to this day I have no answer."*

The actual poem attributed to Magee has itself been proven to be a derivative; it is drawn from classical poetry references elsewhere. This is not to deny any craft or artifice in its execution, but if it is derivative, then it is some massive coincidence that two people in air force service can lay claim to these lines. If my father had been 'guilty' of plagiarism then the actual words would have been published somewhere and there would have been some process, conscious or otherwise, to commit the words to memory or to consign them into some cognitive recess.

The Library of Congress offers evidence that the original Magee manuscript dates to 1941 and had been mailed to his father in December that year. It had also been published in a church newsletter at that time. The manuscript had been donated to the Library of Congress in 1943. Importantly, and according to Helen Zimmerman writing in the Washington Star, January 1944:

> *"It was John [Magee], youthful foe of fascism, who wrote the hauntingly beautiful and widely published poem, 'High Flight', and who later crashed to his death in a routine training flight over England four days after Pearl Harbor."*

Helen Zimmerman went on to say:

> *"As an epitaph to the late Pilot Officer Magee, the Royal Canadian Air Force has issued, to all airfields and training stations in the British Empire, plaques on which are written the words of the sole classic in verse to have appeared to date out of this war."*

The immortality of the poem is reflected in Robert Tate Allan writing in the Washington Post on 26th April 1946, less than five years after it being written, following the dedication of an alter piece at St John's Episcopal Church in Washington DC.

The actual evidence is clearly against any assertion by my father. Moreover, any rebuttal of plagiarism is undermined by the fact that RAF stations around the world would apparently receive commemorative, inspirational plaques bearing the poem. But a number of important questions arise. If Zimmerman and Allan are writing in 1944 and 1946, respectively, were the plaques actually received by all airfields and training stations? Just how popular was the poem in war time? What is the likelihood of someone in the Transvaal in 1944 being aware of Magee? Does the church newsletter actually exist? If it was published in a Service newsletter such as Tee Em, then there is plausible explanation, but bear in mind my father's location in the Transvaal and the likelihood of seeing the poem in print. If so, there is logical and plausible explanation of at least unconscious plagiarism.

The legend is that Magee wrote it aged nineteen whilst flying with the Royal Canadian Air Force. He was in fact an American, born in Shanghai. I say legend because my father was strangely uncomfortable with the notion of flying Spitfires at such a young age, with little apparent training and the inability to accumulate substantial enough flying hours to get onto Spits. To the point of giving up, my father analysed, combed, faulted, reviewed and critiqued what is recorded of the service side of Magee's career. It is a puzzle when one sees an offer of a place at Yale turned down, then shortly thereafter a trip to Canada to join the RCAF. In the space of five months from January 1941 to June 1941 he gets his wings, where it took my father fifteen months and 250 hours? My father trained in South Africa at a different time in the trajectory of war. Maybe Canadian training was more efficient and expedited.

Magee's wings are awarded on 7th June 1941. By July 1941 he is in Liverpool, en route to Wales and an Operational Training Unit at Llandow to fly Spitfires. According to notes, the day after he arrived, he took the day off and flew to visit his girlfriend Eleanor Lyons and friends in Gloucestershire, buzzing Kemerton in Worcestershire along the way. His first flight on the Spit was not until August 1941 with 412 Squadron. A lot of things simply did not tie up. If Messerschmitt Bf 109s could not reach Lincolnshire and return to bases in France, why is there reference to battle skirmishes in November 1941?

The United States entered the war on 7th December 1941. On 11th December 1941 J G Magee's plane had crashed in Lincolnshire. He is buried at Scopwick with a headstone that bears the first two lines of 'High Flight'. What my father saw was 'tongue in cheek' acceptance of the man's achievements; a glorification of his contribution and the emergence of a brand of fiction capturing the admiration of the reader. There is seeming support from tangible evidence. My father offered the following opinion: "It does no harm to believe his biography and it certainly does no good to discredit him. He died doing what he enjoyed most." My father speculated on a heavy heart:

"At that age, his attachment to Eleanor Lyon was quite strong and his feelings for her thread through the poems he wrote. Her rejection of his amours set in motion a heartfelt series of continual disappointment which surfaced in poetic expression."

Why publish the poem in 1941? How widely published and distributed was it up to 1944 when my father said he wrote it? Did Magee exist at all, or was he some Lieutenant Kije character, with an identity created 'posthumously'? I can only speculate and reflect my father's sense of astonishment and incredulity that his poem, years later, would assume a title and popularity.

I have no wider basis to question whether or not J G Magee himself was guilty of plagiarism other than what I have learned over the years. Here is a carefully composed poem, drawing upon classic and pre-recorded inspiration. It is evident from father's writing that he has asserted a genuine claim to what he described as a similar version which he recalls was composed in 1944/45 whilst training with the RAF in Vereeniging. In confirming his recollection of events, my father felt that his explanation could verge upon boredom to the reader. For him, the poem was a private bond which he had established with his maker, fulfilling a richness of intimacy he had never thought possible. His claim to authenticity is weakened by an absence of proof :

"I have no proof. In fact, the original composition did not have a title. High Flight has been included by someone else and certain changes have been made to the original, but in essence it is the very same poem I sat down and wrote in Vereeniging Air School. How that short, well-written piece has surfaced in book form is one of the strangest mysteries of the twentieth century."

But ponder his writings from his later years:

Oh, how I dream of days gone by
Of days, of youth and things that fly
Of happy time too often wasted
On pleasures only slightly tasted
Sweet memories of long ago survive
And seem at once to come alive
Their image lasts, defeating time
Because these memories are truly mine

12
Wings

Events in April 1945 signalled the end of war in Europe. Soviet and American troops had convened at the River Elbe and on 30th April Hitler had committed suicide in his bunker. Between 4th May and 8th May German military surrender unfolded. In less than a year from the D-Day landings and with huge mobilisation of resources, major shift in domestic priority, and massive loss of life, Europe was made safe. The continuum of war, that state of readiness, the attitude of defiance, preparedness for defence and suffering along the way had suddenly, incredulously, stopped.

News of surrender had broken on 8th May 1945 and celebrations erupted across Western Europe, and on 9th May in Russia and Eastern Europe. To paraphrase, all forces under German control were to cease active operations at 2301 hours Central European Time on 8th May 1945, the next day surrendering to Soviet forces. Europe would be demilitarised, de-Nazified and restructured. Lands were returned, airplanes grounded, U-boats reported to base and the seaways were safe. Now what?

Amidst the destruction of great cities, full of confused, wearied and doubtless angry, destitute, masses – the nervous dislocated and dejected surviving passengers of war – was some hope for the future. Britain, in relative terms, had substantially and maybe luckily survived the extreme ravages of conflict. The Channel, North Sea and the massive eastward push after D-Day insulated the islands. Infrastructure and currency (probably just) were intact. The political systems of local and national government were still in place and there was law and order. But the years 1945–1947 were fraught with the weary adjustment to peace: political discomfort, industrial dispute and then unprecedented weather conditions. Mainland Europe was in a far worse state.

The Yalta Conference of February 1945, with the key political decisions on the future of Europe being executed by Roosevelt, Stalin and Churchill, would deal with the carving up of chunks of the continent, but more practically, Europe would have to be bailed out. The whole continent was broken and broke. Economies teetered. Means of manufacture were stricken with resource and manpower problems, there was limited money in circulation, and damaged, incapacitated distribution networks hindered whatever trade could be undertaken.

Recognition of these problems would not be announced by President Truman until 12th March 1947 through the European Recovery Programme or what became more widely known as Marshall Aid. The Marshall in 'Marshall Aid' came from General George Marshall who at the time was President Truman's Secretary of State and had recognised that Europe had not just experienced the ravages of conflict and destruction, but was now in an economic plight. He mobilised President Truman and Congress, putting in place an eventual package of some $12.5 billion. In Marshall's keynote speech of 1947, he reflected on the planned, or expected, outcomes of conflict, stating that the physical loss of life and visible destruction of cities, factories, mines and railroads, was 'correctly estimated'.

However, the effect of such destruction was manifesting in difficult economic conditions affecting every household, and some more than others.

George Marshall was the key figure in galvanising an understanding of the problem. He saw the visible destruction as less serious than the widespread economic damage caused by war. The cessation of hostilities presented a series of major financial, social and physical challenges.

Putting in place the practical steps towards delivering a new economic order for Europe, he looked to the American people to understand the problems and remedies; new approaches were to be free of political passion and prejudice. History, he said, had placed a vast responsibility upon America. This was at a time when the Cold War was emerging and the rehabilitation of the European economy placed a massive burden on the United States. Addressing Harvard in June 1947, Marshall spoke of the serious and enormously complex world situation; that the American people were geographically distant from troubled areas, making it hard to comprehend Europe's suffering. Marshall offered the following perspective on a 'total war':-

> *"In considering the requirements for the rehabilitation of Europe, the physical loss of life, the visible destruction of cities, factories, mines, and railroads was correctly estimated, but it has become obvious during recent months that this visible destruction was probably less serious than the dislocation of the entire fabric of European economy. For the past ten years conditions have been highly abnormal. The feverish preparation for war and the more feverish maintenance of the war effort engulfed all aspects of national economies."*

Marshall saw the need for political stability and assured peace. Policy was directed at hunger, poverty, desperation, and chaos. International cooperation was required, but a unilaterally imposed solution would not be correct without the input of European governments. Anticipating cross-border, if not East- West, tensions, Marshall put down a marker:

> *"Any government that is willing to assist in the task of recovery will find full co-operation, I am sure, on the part of the United States Government … Any government which manoeuvres to block the recovery of other countries cannot expect help from us. Furthermore, governments, political parties, or groups which seek to perpetuate human misery in order to profit there-from, politically or otherwise, will encounter the opposition of the United States."*

Machinery and enterprise were shattered as resources had been stripped bare by the Nazi regime and the indiscriminate ravages of war. The simple composite of economy, of trade, banking support, supply and demand, distribution was in tatters. The 'rehabilitation of the economic structure of Europe' would require time and effort. Trade systems had broken down, manufacturing capacity was eroded and Europe did not have the ability to buy its way out of the ravages of war: what Europe needed and what it could afford were miles apart. Social and economic consequences were hinted at:

> *"Aside from the demoralizing effect on the world at large and the possibilities of disturbances arising as a result of the desperation of the people concerned, the consequences to the economy of the United States should be apparent to all."*

Later, Marshall summed up matters:

> " . . .the rehabilitation of the economic structure of Europe quite evidently will require a much longer time and greater effort than had been foreseen."

Meanwhile, the practicalities and bonhomie of Yalta would be replaced with political scepticism. The Cold War was emerging. Whatever the tensions of the time, the resistance of Communism or plots against the Soviets, Marshall Aid was described by Ernest Bevin as a lifeline to sinking men, bringing hope where there was none. International and personal angst prevailed. For my father in 1945, and through into 1947, these were uncertain times. He was not alone.

In preparing for and resourcing war, the Empire Air Training Scheme/BCATP/Joint Air Training Plan had a raison d'etre: pilot training had purpose and magnitude. There was a logical progression – *(i) Process: dream, study, dream fulfilled; (ii) Means: Moth, or equivalent, then Harvard; (iii) Next: Spits, Typhoons; (iv) Objective: operational duty.*

Some 170,000 from the Commonwealth had been processed; youngsters who had volunteered, enlisted or been conscripted. Some would not be flying airplanes, becoming navigators, bomb-aimers, wireless operators, flight engineers and gunners. Others would. They were trained, examined, provided with experience and decorated. As the programme had given opportunity to serve one's country, so it was that many had flown and so many had died. We bow in honour and respect those who gave their lives for their country.

On a warm May day in 1945 my father was awarded his Wings on the apron at No.22 SFTS Vereeniging by Air Marshall Sir Arthur – later, Lord – Tedder, a not insignificant figure in the planning and execution of World War Two. Tedder worked as Deputy Supreme Commander below General Eisenhower and had responsibility for air planning for D-Day. Tedder attended the ceremony of the German unconditional surrender in May 1945, signing on behalf of General Eisenhower. An honour indeed to have one's Wings presented by him.

Not yet twenty-two years of age, here was the proudest day of his life: the 'Wings Parade'. Three years from joining the RAFVR, prior to that the painful journey from reserved occupation, and the then bad timing of scarlet fever in the early days of training, here he was polished, precise and proud. For weeks there had been meticulous drilling in pursuit of exemplar marching and decorum.

From the pilots' point of view it was about achievement and decoration. It was also about seduction and the sleek, slender, shapely to the point of being tactile, curves of the Spitfire or the hungry, ravenous, capacious Typhoon, all gaping mouth and desirous. Operational Duties occupied a lot of thought, hope and expectation. "We've trained and we're qualified, lads. What next?"

The celebrations on the banks of the Elbe and Hitler's suicide had yet to occur in April and May 1945. Military progress across Europe was being monitored though, and infrequent news sent positive signals to Southern Africa that the end of hostilities was in sight. Months of training and anticipation would not be rewarded.

In the days prior to the ceremony the sergeants' stripes were carefully sewn on, but the dress uniform was still without wings. The parade went perfectly well and each airman was called to the rostrum to be presented with the coveted Wings. As unforgettable as the day was, it is not recalled what Tedder actually said amidst the blur of excitement. "Congratulations, I suppose" was a bare minimum memory. Visitors took photographs:

*"Then when it was all over we went back to our billets and
sewed on the prize possessions to our dress uniforms, afterwards
returning to the tented village to mix and socialise with the
visitors and high ranking officers.*

*"Then in the evening it was up to Jo'burg for a night of
celebration and hilarity with most of the drinks paid for by
our hosts."*

There is sadness in the reflection years later, the realisation
that his flying career was now over. Three years of service
and investment was being acknowledged, but that evening of
reward, relief and revelry in Johannesburg was a shor t-lived
celebration of achievement with huge poignancy and irony.
Four months later my father left South Africa. His unit was
pulling out.

The journey south had begun on 16th May 1943, eleven
months after the four-day selection examination in Edinburgh.
In my father's words this was nearly a year of constant badgering
of the RAF recruitment planners. Days of waiting turned into
weeks and new disappointment.

The reality was that as my father left Greenock, the EFTS/
BCATP/JATP was four years old and the maturation process of
these programmes was leading to huge numbers graduating. Put
into context, at the height of the war, it took eleven months for
call-up papers to arrive and a further six months before any flying
took place. Advanced training did not take place until June 1944.
Distilling this down, eleven months of waiting for call-up and six
months of waiting for an advanced flying school place meant that
flying experience at the time amounted to ten weeks at Carlisle
with the solo experience a far memory. Added together, there was
more time waiting than there were remaining months of the war;
but no one knew that at the time.

The elation of that night in Johannesburg, the camaraderie, the booze and the girls. These lads were something now: they were flyers and they wanted more of it. But with the sudden cessation of hostilities in Europe news reached the Dominion Airfields that training programmes were halted: the war machine no longer needed feeding. The sudden end to the war meant that pilot training stopped dramatically. By September 1945, the official orders came through. Bussed into Jo'burg, then by train to Cape Town, ahead of him lay a four week journey back to England.

Life in South Africa began on the SS Nea Hellas on 9th June 1944 and ended as the SS Mauritania, sister ship to the Lusitania, sunk in 1916 by a German torpedo, docked at Liverpool on 25th September 1945:

> *"I had completed 250 hours of instruction and was ready now to go to OTU for training on Spitfires. Unfortunately, this never transpired as the war drew to a predicted end by the time I had travelled from South Africa to Liverpool. There was no more flying now."*

As for his South African flying 'homes', Potchefstroom remained as an Air Force Station after the war for the SAAF. It remained home to a military flying school, but is today a civil airfield. Vereeniging stopped training in November 1945. It too became a civil airfield with the Air School buildings being used by the army and police. The airfield was relocated to the north of Vereeniging and although many of the original Air School buildings remain, the airfield has largely disappeared, having been developed into an industrial area. No.22 SFTS Vereeniging, established on 11th November 1940, was decommissioned on 27th February 1946, less than one year after the wings ceremony. Waste and memory.

Having been sent to London in 1943 and with a three year period of duty, his time was up in the months following the end of the war. The desperate desire to fly and initial optimism resulted in my father securing a three year extension of engagement in a vain and fruitless hope that transfer to an operational training unit would result.

He was a trained pilot. The logical progression would have been fighters, maybe not Spitfires, but perhaps Typhoons or some other combatant aircraft. At the time *Operation Tiger* was being set up, selecting aircrew for possible flying duties in the Far East. There was the vague possibility that squadron service against the Japanese would satisfy the lust for flight and a role in a combat situation. Herr Hitler and Mr Chamberlain had given the opportunity to fly, whilst the Manhattan Project had helped prevent ongoing conflict in the Far East. The Japanese War crumbled and with the atomic bombs being dropped on Nagasaki and Hiroshima, the war was over. The economy of fision meant that any hope of flying on operational duties was forlorn. The juggernaut of war effort, its institutions and practices stuttered. Everything stopped:

> *"Conditions in Training Command were becoming confused. The Empire Training Scheme was a monumental organisation catering for the needs and wishes of a vast number of aircrew who were not required. Everything seemed to stop suddenly and nobody seemed to know what to do or where to go."*

The initial posting after the cessation of hostilities was No.7 Personnel Reception Centre, Harrogate, where he waited and waited, ever hopeful, for an operational role. And as he waited, my father would see yet more EATS 'graduates' come home with absolutely no hope of finding a fulfilling role within the service. The choice was simple: demobilisation or extended service subject to ground duties.

With the war drawing to an end the training programme carried on producing new pilots. What to do with them? By his own analysis the odds were stacked against him and the dream of seeing flying duty again was fading. In the manner of a bookie working out the percentages, the numbers were stacked against him. He had only three stripes and so the officers took precedence.

The situation at the official ending of the European war was euphoric. The definitive end-of-war bash must have been outside Buckingham Palace where throngs of old and young, civilian and military, would be singing, dancing and making merry. A sea of people partying before His Majesty. Here was the massive relief following six years of conflict and struggle; the nation celebrating freedom from the stress of total war.

Conflict would carry on in the Far East and it would take time for soldiers, airmen and sailors to get home. Some by airplane, twenty-five a time in converted Lancasters, many more by ship. What if you were a prisoner of war in Malaysia? Demobilisation, in logistical terms, was a long process and more than just a new suit. In Japan, the events of August 1945 would spell the end of the war in the Far East and Pacific but actual peace would not be signed up to until, believe it or not, 1951. Behind the partying on VE Day and VJ Day, rationing was still in place and the nation was trying to find its feet. The circumstances of domestic struggle in wartime would carry on. At home, the grim reality was a Great Britain, flat broke, debt-ridden and reliant on America to bolster its economy.

Actual post-war austerity is seen as the aftermath of war and a function of its hardships: a period of mere adjustment. Maybe this is true to many, but hindsight reveals a peculiar combination of economic, political, ideological and meteorological circumstances which may be summed up in three words: bread, blizzards, and bombs. An odd combination, but read on.

We take queuing for granted; it is a standing joke. The British like to stand in line and if there is a queue in wartime it must mean that something is available. And let's face it, whatever you were entitled to, found, got, came by, or plain purloined could well be traded for something that you actually needed, better still something you wanted.

Rationing remained in place, but there would also be periods when even a limited supply would dry up. This was more so if supply lines were interrupted. Simple things like eggs or cotton thread might not be available. Particularly in the period 1939 to 1945 not a lot is available in the shops, unless you had your own distribution network: a friendly butcher or hopefully helpful spiv. Living in the open countryside would bring an ever-available stock of produce within reach, with opportunities for pigeon or rabbit. Having gone through the 'war years' on a meagre but sustaining ration and sixteen coupons – the daily intake being about 1,200 calories – and having the stomach bulked out on a little bread and potatoes, the expectation in 1945 would be that the Nation's begging bowl would have been put to one side. Far from it. The effect of rationing would linger long after the end of the war. But it was not just food that was rationed, it was also clothing, petrol and even furniture. Rationing which began on 8th January 1940 would carry on until 4th July 1954.

The process of de-rationing would not begin until 1948. And so upon his return to Great Britain in September 1945, my father would see a complete contrast to the cosseted, far-from-home, shores of South Africa. Ardua and astra were replaced by harsh reality. Climate had been replaced by weather. Food and comfort were in short supply. The make-do-and-mend era of makeshift dishes – frequently facsimiles of long-lost textures and flavours cunningly recreated in kitchens now given to impersonation – would sustain the nation. Woolton Pie or Mock Duck, curiously formed from lentils, mashed potato and herbs, would intrigue and give some grand illusion of Sunday dinner. But it was wheat and its availability that would be a major factor prior to and during the war. Wheat was a powerful bargaining chip. It would also be a consideration in the peaceful years of adjustment immediately afterwards.

British wheat in the 1930s is a low yield, low gluten product with a high moisture content. Good bread requires good ingredients in the form of better quality imported wheat. This would fortify supplies of the home-grown stuff, but the effect of war is to interfere with North American supplies. In 1939, Drs Elsie Widdowson and Robert McCance began research into the relationship between food rationing and the standard bread loaf. During wartime, bread is basically a grey imitation of its pre-war self. It was a tribute act. The 'National Loaf ' would keep the nation going through war, but here was a more grainy, brown loaf.

Whatever ships were serving Britain at the time would be laden and competition for space meant that there were only limited supplies of imported wheat. Limited supplies in wartime would continue whilst harvests and supply lines re-established themselves after the war. However this process would require annual wheat harvests to be spread over a wide geographic area. After the war there was the realisation that measures had to be put in place that would not only feed Britain, but would also feed France and Germany, as well as parts of Africa. Wheat would have to stretch farther and famine relief measures were required. In an unprecedented move, bread would be rationed in peacetime in 1946.

Meanwhile, life in Harrogate for my father was dull. It was a Personnel Reception Centre, an apt description for a base that received home-coming military staff whilst a final destination was sorted out. It seems that the right posting for my father, with flying, was not high on the list of Air Ministry priorities. There would be periods of leave interspersed with RAF duties, although the impression given is of a system that did not know how to deal with dismantling or reducing the scale of military resource. Perhaps a scheme was in place to create disillusionment and voluntary redundancy. It would be easy to paraphrase Caius Petronius: we trained hard and wonderful method it can be for creating the illusion of progress while producing confusion and demoralisation.

Leave followed his time in Yorkshire and he was then posted to Pembrey Sands near Llanelli in South Wales for a month, which he recalled being No. 1 Gunnery School in its more active days, and then to Burtonwood, Cheshire, for nine long months.

He was first transferred to Burtonwood near Warrington in December 1945. In RAF abbreviation, this was No. 3 MPO (Master Provisions Office), a major logistics depot which ultimately had over 18,000 personnel and a huge American service population. At its height the intensity of this vast facility was, literally, incredible. Aircraft in, aircraft out. Thousands of them were flown-in, converted, repaired and maintained. Those not flown-in arrived as kits. There were cocooned airplanes everywhere by 1946, all brand new and never to see service:

> *"The stuff the Yanks left behind was unbelievable. I had never seen so much waste. I always remember going into a nissen hut and seeing all the furniture strewn about – all good units."*

Burtonwood was a vast depository of unaccounted waste, the ebb and flo of war effort leaving flotsam and jetsom of unwanted military might. In the shadow of huge aircraft and with often silent empty space stretching down the runways and over 360 degrees of sky, there were reflections on the comforts of military life and the discomforts of home life.

If the bedding of his up-bringing was cigarette-burned, holed, patched-up and desperate – and that at St John's Wood had proved memorable – then the availability of good US cotton in abundance in Cheshire was not lost. Serviceable, easily packaged up and, if not used, certainly pawnable; it proved that temptation bed linen could be fitting:

> *"I also remember, too, packing a goodly amount of white bed sheets and sending them to my parents in Dundee. My mother would make good use of them."*

He found himself assigned to the Central Registry for six months where, with a civilian staff of twenty, he was to organise all the incoming and outgoing mail. From there he was placed in charge of the Sergeants' Mess. This meant he was running the bar and apparently controlling the food stores for the entire camp. This bar work was in fact quite a lucrative position. The German Prisoners of War with whom he worked were looked after very well and things were running smoothly.

The bar takings were very high, with an officer taking stock from time to time, "who could not find fault with my supervision which was paying off handsomely." Handsomely, perhaps, to him.

If shoes being pawned in his youth had indicated the entrepreneurial leanings of my father, then fiddling the till carried on that creatively profitable waywardness. But aside from the creative accountancy and pocketed proceeds, he was also getting extended leave, writing out his own travel warrants.

With what he described as 'spoils' from this occupation – and what precisely these are, and how much, is not divulged – he took a month's leave and without telling his parents would use the money and go to such places as Dublin for a holiday, or London.

By the autumn of 1946, and over a year after the war ended, my father began to realise that squadron service and combat duty were elusive dreams; he carried a torch that would be snuffed out by peace. He was out on a limb; an airman listless in the misfortune of peacetime and lost in a RAF system that was clearing out fast. His three years of service was actually drawing to a close. As of 3rd November 1946, he would be formally discharged. Now was a time for reflection and the tough choice of exiting the service, or sticking it out in the vain hope of flying.

It is not clear if my father could see what was happening outside of the RAF world, but in the years since 1939, and despite the popular suffering and hardships of war, not once had he complained of hunger or poor diet. Rather the opposite; the RAF had been good to him: quality bed-linen, comfort and good food. He appears insulated from the hardships of everyday life. This was an unprecedented life of easy comfort: all clean sheets and cocoa.

Faced with the prospect of three years service coming to an abrupt end, I suspect my father took one look at what was happening in the real world and decided to bide his time until things got better. Life in the RAF was comfortable, if limited in its career offer. Outside of the RAF there was much more to Civvy Street than bread rationing.

A landslide Labour victory in the General Election of 1945 would lead to nationalisation of key industries: the power sectors, telecommunications, railways, and aviation would be taken from private to public control. There was a National Health Service and new planning controls would effectively nationalise development rights.

The nationalisation of industry sounded great in principle, if you were a fervent believer in this doctrinal approach, but an almighty cock-up occurred in July 1946 when the Samuel Report commissioned by the Ministry of Labour concluded that the miners are getting paid too much and wages should be cut. Consequences? – strike and dwindling coal stocks.

Dwindling coal stocks would fundamentally affect power supplies. In these fragile years for Britain, bread and now power would be rationed. So much for six years of war.

The adjustments to post-war life are beset by an RAF administration that is not fulfilling a passion to fly. This sounds selfish in the face of bread shortages and the effect of a coal strike, but seemingly my father was not affected by this. The reality beyond service comfort was of dark unheated nights or times of the day when cooking was prohibited. Whatever frustrations there were in the lives of the wider population and whatever the current affairs situation with domestic, foreign and economic policy, life in the RAF was better than what he had seen at home in the 1930s.

Despite post-war reconstruction, there was unrest between the government and the unions and 'progress' and rebuilding would mean somewhat inexplicably that by 1948 there would be 2 million unemployed. But before such progress could be made, Britain would have to see through the last few months of 1946 and a meteorological compounding of all that was wrong with restructuring daily life for millions.

The reality of life outside the service may yet have led to a decision to ride out any storms in Civvy Street. Rightly or wrongly he stayed in the service. My father was, in fact, discharged on 3rd November 1946 and the following day re- enlisted, extending his duties for a further three years. And what a time to do it. To add to the domestic difficulties of everyday life in Britain, the country was heading for a bleak winter. Whatever expectations there were that things would get better before the first snows arrived, would be wiped-out between December 1946 and January 1947. The first snowfalls had arrived and things were far from better. High over Scandinavia was a low pressure system which would draw extremely cold air from the Arctic. This would result in temperatures as low as minus 21°C. Gales and heavy snow storms would persist.

Meteorological history would be made between late January and mid March 1947. The remarkable thing is that whilst the British have plenty weather and love talking about it, not once did my father comment on the biggest winter of the century!

Sounds romantic in retrospect, but with the country recovering from war and with coal strikes and limited food continuing, this was not good timing. Railways were grinding to a halt, roads were closed, harbours frozen. There would be major disruption to the distribution of still-scarce goods around the country.

When the snows arrive in late 1946 my father is based at RAF Bridgnorth, Shropshire but en route back to Burtonwood, Cheshire, where he would re-enlist. More train journeys. There were huge difficulties in keeping train services running. This was a time of snowdrifts and snowploughs, of frozen coal and frozen points.

No reference to snowdrifts. Whilst the south and east of the country were particularly hard hit by the extreme weather, with even the Scilly Isles experiencing snow, it seems quite unlikely that the RAF could insulate him from these conditions. Feelings at the time are much more introspective than observational; more psychological than meteorological. There was despondency and hopelessness, and a forlorn sorrow that the war was over.

For the next two years there would be transfers from station to station with extended periods of leave in between. This was the first indication that the RAF was winding down. Sergeant Pilots had fulfilled their function. If extended leave hid military personnel amongst the masses, then their movement between air bases unsettled careers. The impression is one of not quite constructive dismissal, but of engineering circumstances that would make it very difficult for a career pilot to stay in the service. The lack of purpose and direction within the organisation created profound disillusionment and disinclination. Training had created the impression of progress towards a goal. How unfair that the war was over; the inequity of peace.

Constant movement and each new posting led to ground staff positions and the impression of being no more than nuisance value. He was ill-suited to administrative duties and received derogatory treatment from those whom he felt had genuinely earned their stripes the hard way.

As a member of aircrew trained in the more informal South African setting, the discipline of station routine in Britain was a difficult adjustment. By his own admission, my father had not risen through the ranks. He had status, but recognised that his stripes were a different kind of reward that merely enabled better living standards, better pay and an insurance against what he described as delegation to the performance of normal menial tasks usually performed by 'erks' or AC2s. Others were infinitely more familiar with station routine, activities, chores and management.

Whatever actual job he was doing for the RAF, it certainly did not involve being a pilot. By May 1947 he managed to attach himself to a flying section at Henlow. I suspect he muzzled in, forced his way, or merely blagged, but at least Henlow was a flying station, small and well-equipped. There was a Tiger Moth which delighted my father, as well as a Douglas Dakota and Avro Halifax. These were the last planes he flew in with the RAF: he was reduced to dropping dummy parachutes, weighted with big rubber blocks, to test new nylon fabrics – anything to fly. Henlow was also employing WAAFs to pre-pack the 'chutes. Interesting he should note that.

If, by 1946, he felt metaphorically lost in the disillusion of the RAF system, by 1947 this would happen literally. At Henlow, the RAF Records Office lost track of my father. Officially at the time he was AWOL. They could find no trace of him. For the sake of RAF convenience, he was 'absorbed' into Henlow:

"Signals were sent out all over England searching for my whereabouts until eventually they discovered my presence at Henlow."

Biding his time, for him, life was comfortable. He had his own billet, good food and a sociable sergeant's mess. He was content and in his own words, no one interfered with his daily routine. The weight of rank and discipline had eluded him. That is until one day he was looking at the mail board and found that the duty roster had his name attached to the role of Orderly Sergeant. Ye Gods and little fishes!, I can hear him exclaim. The responsibility of duty. Damn. Panic.

> *"Somehow or other I was one hour astray. Perhaps my watch had stopped or I had mistaken the time, but I was going round the barrack blocks blowing my whistle to get everyone out on to the parade ground. There was no response to this wailing shrill whistle and the strange inactivity made me shudder as I suddenly realised my whistling was just a wee bit late."*

That was mistake number one. Having run around the accommodation blocks in the vain belief of rallying his men, he turned onto the parade ground, where there was assembled the entire station personnel, accompanied by the pomp and circumstance of military rank, authority and tradition; the very sum of RAF decorum. Obviously late, my father ran in between these neatly presented rows. The Duty Officer gave this embarrassed Sergeant Pilot a disdainful glower.

Whereas my father had physically stopped, his heart was still racing as he dutifully saluted. A self-conscious walk up to the flagpole followed.

The flag itself lay folded on the ground. This symbol of a nation's identity he knew would have to be treated reverentially, and as he carefully unfolded it, he checked for the correct way to pin it to the line, remembering something about the broad white band being up in the top left corner:

"The second mistake was pinning the flag on to the two hooks on the pulley. Somehow or other I had chosen the wrong hooks or else the flag was the wrong way round. I don't know. But in my tense moment I quickly did the obvious, put two flag points on two hooks and pulled the pulley coil.

Going up fine, the flag suddenly got stuck. It wouldn't budge. What on earth had gone wrong? I pulled, yanked strained and damn near broke the rope but it wouldn't budge. I could see the knot in the pulley was jammed up against the pulley at the top of the flagpole."

As my father sweated, there was sniggering from the ranks and consternation from senior ranks. "Don't bring the flag down!" was the order barked by the Duty Officer with all the soft-spoken humility of a Regimental Sergeant Major, but ever the tidy type, and anxious to please, down came the flag and my father stood to attention. Meantime the bugler was playing his bars over and over, and apparently with time for an encore.

The Duty Officer, who was by now a very exasperated and embarrassed man, maintained the salute position whilst bellowing what were euphemistically described by my father as 'unmentionable oaths'. Maintaining salute, by now he had no circulation whatsoever in his right arm. The parade was dismissed and the officers disappeared. Never again was my father nominated to perform Orderly Sergeant duties.

In June 1942 my father had enlisted at not quite nineteen years of age and confirmed his civilian occupation as Aero Assembly Fitter. Strange that by today's standards he could achieve this at such a young age. His RAF career was in the ascendancy leading to the rank of Sergeant Pilot in 1945, unfortunately after the cessation of hostilities. The insecurity of the time for my father would be all too apparent. Let's face it, here was a man who was being demoralised and he could not fathom out the reason why.

It was not about the bomb or the Churchill 'Iron Curtain' speech at Fulton, Missouri, 1946. It was not about bread rationing or the winter of 1947. This malaise in the running of the service, which my father perceived, would see reductions in personnel numbers and lingering strain in terms of skills and recruitment. I suppose a wider question would be that with over 1 million in the RAF, what effect was this having on the national economy, already broken by the efforts and strain of war?

The RAF years were drawing to a close. Between 1946 and 1948, my father would drift within an RAF set-up that seemed reluctant to keep these guys on. One would have to question one's motives for staying in the Service. Postings here and postings there, with extended periods of leave in between were all part of the package. The initial three years service ran to 1946 and with some cooperation from the Air Ministry this was extended for a further three years to 1949.

Nationalisation may have been ongoing as part of the new Labour Government's plan, but what my father was succumbing to was the effect of the 1947 Defence White Paper which was a post-war adjustment to the circumstances of the time. Written in the context of a 1945 Air Force complement which had swollen to five times its 1939 size, the White Paper was concerned to maintain the structure and continuity of the force, echoing events after the Great War. However, it was not concerned with growing the service; rather the opposite. This could only mean one thing, well three really: disbanding success, dismantling structures and basically getting rid of people. The penny dropped.

At the close of war the RAF was a huge monolith; a vast purpose-built organisation of pilots, gunners, observers, navigators, fitters, maintenance, administration, rank-upon-rank, skill-upon-skill. Some of these skills would find use in the wide world, but for many, re-training and new career paths would have to be followed.

The service had come a long way from the Audaxes and Hynds of the Thirties; airplanes which owed their construction and dynamic to the faith of a previous generation in the biplane being more stable and reliable. By 1945, aircraft were scientifically and aeronautically designed to fulfil specific or flexible functions. They were faster, lighter, more durable, more efficient, flew longer, carried more payload and were faster, climbed more quickly, turned better. That one of these aircraft would be called 'flying fortress' sums up the aerial power and function of an airborne bastion; a complete contrast to the technology and capabilities of the Great War, reliant upon hand guns and manual bomb-dropping.

Endurance and high altitude flying had enabled pressurised pilot suits to be tested. G-forces were understood. Whittle had studied and proven the principles of jet technology, these having been produced for years by 1945. The jet age was upon us and the first deliveries to squadrons had taken place as far back as June 1944. The following month they were on active duty intercepting V1 flying bombs. War was changing and this, together with new, yet familiar, enemies precipitated major change in how the RAF would be re-structured post-war.

The jet age, combined with the emergence of the Cold War, called for a re-appraisal of the scale and operation of the RAF. Domestic priorities, the restructuring of the economy and paying back vast loans, were equally important factors in the shaping of defence policy. Armitage, writing in 1993, summarises the main features of the Defence White Paper of 1947 being the retention of national service and safeguarding the structure of the RAF. Again, the numbers speak for themselves. By May 1945, the RAF had a complement of 55,469 aircraft, of which 9,200 were front line planes. Staff numbers totalled 1,079,835 personnel.

In the face of the high cost of running the service and reappraising enemies and their perceived intentions, how to deal with the downsizing of the service to suit peacetime priorities was key. Air Staff Plan E emerged in 1947 and suggested a 'right-sizing' of 1,500 aircraft comprised in 51 fighter squadrons, 41 bomber squadrons, 13 maritime squadrons, 42 transport squadrons, and 12 reserve squadrons.

Deliberate war sponsored by an enemy was considered unlikely, with a possible increase in threat after five years. Quite how this measure was arrived at is not clear. However, Armitage saw that expenditure was being deferred in the light of the Soviet threat.

By June 1948, even Air Staff Plan E was vastly in excess of the reality: 25 squadrons in Fighter Command – 207 aircraft; 25 squadrons in Bomber Command – 160 aircraft; 20 squadrons in Transport Command – 160 aircraft; and 11 squadrons in Coastal Command – 87 aircraft. In addition, there were 33 squadrons overseas.

The RAF contracted massively from 1945 to 1950. In 1945, there were 9,200 aircraft and personnel totalling 1,079,835; aircrew numbered 193,313. Figures tumbled: 1946-47 to 760 thousand, 1947-48 to 375 thousand, 1948-49 to 325 thousand. By 1950, 202 thousand. The story is told not just in numbers but the new trades and rank structures. There were over 300 trades in wartime; by 1950, about 100 trades. There emerged new structures and new ranks which really hacked-off many aircrew.

What my father went through was the re-structuring initiated by the Flying, or General Duties, Branch of the RAF which in July 1946 introduced new categories of rank for non-commissioned aircrew : Pilot I (equivalent of flight sergeant) or Pilot II (equivalent of sergeant). No longer a Sergeant Pilot, my father was a pilot second class. In 1943 he was First Class. By 1946 he was second rate. Highly unpopular, this system was abandoned in 1950, but at the time, frustrated and angered, he had the audacity to argue the point with Tedder!

Quality and the class system before the war was now institutionalised by rank. The wartime training plan had created sub-officer cannon fodder – a body capable of addressing predicted dangerous shortfall in 1939, but now a disposable resource. Post-war restructuring of the Air Force established new doctrine and new priorities, new training, new ranks, new aircraft. The service was in a process of change once more. At the outbreak of war my father was 16 years old and with the advent of war would come the opportunity to fly. So if the RAF in the 20s and 30s is struggling to survive, and thanks must go to Churchill and Trenchard for putting in train a structure for the service and political manoeuvres to ensure its independence and survival, then by 1947 that success was devalued by the misfortune of peace.

The cynical view must be that the efficiency drives of the immediate post-war years were calculated to reduce numbers of what was effectively a 'spent force'. It would have created such disillusionment amongst lower ranks that exit from the service was a feasible option. And who would stand in your way?

The reality was that modern war would require modern machines and moder n weapons systems. Technological requirements had raced ahead of the simple ability to fly a 1930s airframe.

But for all the recollections and anecdotes, here was a life that, on record, was merely a list of official abbreviations, numbers and cross-references, interspersed with place-names, and meaningful to only the personnel and payroll sections of the Air Force. Just how was it that a training programme could be put in place that would be so successful that the intelligence, aptitude, skills and dedication of thousands would, after the cessation of hostilities in 1945, be virtually redundant?

Final weeks at RAF Henlow were spent issuing demob tickets and train passes for those leaving the Service.

After the recognition that he had what it would take to be a flyer, after the intensity of training, and having stuck it out just that little bit longer than the war itself, it was hurtful for my father to see the enormous number of literally 'fully fledged' aircrew waiting to be kitted out for civilian life. He would be one of them, his services are no longer required:

> "I was posted here there and everywhere and in each new posting I was always placed in ground staff positions for which I was totally unsuitable and generally treated as nuisance value. Feeling out of joint in this category I decided to sever my connections with the RAF."

Always a practical type, probably bored, and seeing an opportunity, my father decided to write out his own demob ticket. On 22nd March 1948, after six years of service, only eighteen months of which involved flying, he took leave of the RAF "at own request" at Kirkham Demob Centre, Freckleton Road, Kirkham, Lancashire, but that is not all he took. Where my father was not suited to ground based duties, he was, at least, one who monitored value in whatever stuff was going spare. He was never a 'spiv', but they would be waiting on the outside:

> "I managed to have two sets of release papers, picked up two sets of civilian clothes and also managed to keep my own flying gear which I later sold to a motor cyclist. Spivs were waiting outside the demob centre to buy the clothing the chaps didn't want and I sold one set of civvy clothes, I think, for £10. The flying gear fetched the same sort of price for I was glad to get rid of all the excess baggage."

As military service drew to a close my father met and struck up a friendship with Ron Ratcliffe, a senior NCO from Kent. Pre-war memories and the home life he had left behind did not reflect in any desire to head north to Dundee. The friendship with Ron led to my father moving to Kent where they would pull together their monies and pave the way for riches. Or so they thought.

From Lancashire the pair travelled south to Ron's home town of Dover to make their way in a wide world of post-war opportunity. There was the prospect of euphoric success in a Britain now keen to rebuild and reshape its economy, but the reality was beset with disappointments. Civilian life held promise, but all too often hopes were to be dashed.

Here was someone, a boy before the war, growing up in a small town, whose dreams actually did come true, and had experienced thrill, privilege and comfort. He was now out 'there' and would have to find his way. He found himself dealing with situations and what to many would be every day occurrences but which he had no real knowledge of, insulated as he was from war, and its effects, by the Air Force. In some way, the Service had denied him certain life skills which would be essential for survival in what would be – post-war – a very different world.

"The urgency led to a succession of various employments, highlighting the unsettled nature of what resettlement really meant."

The legitimate expectation was that the RAF would continue to want flyers, but with limited experience and single engine rating, the prospects were bleak in comparison to those who had twin engine or bomber experience. Still hankering after a flying career, he headed for London and had an interview with the Civil Aviation Authority, but this failed. As a philosophical melancholy descended, my father reflected, "Why didn't I learn to fly twin-engine machines?"

Commercial aviation was beginning to re-establish itself after the hiatus of war. Heathrow Airport represented a vision of future possibilities and there were opportunities for ex-bomber pilots in the emerging airlines. These guys somehow had the advantage, though.

The central RAF administration at Adastral House suggested that my father would stand a better chance if he undertook a six hour conversion course to obtain a Civil Pilots Licence, but the additional training would cost some £300. Severance pay was only £120.

Whitehall, national economics, Government indebtedness and defence policy were ranged against him. He was one of many. Restructuring was on the go in the RAF following the 1947 Defence White Paper, with the rationalisation of rank and skills. In the austerity of the post-war years unless you had 'scrambled egg' on your cap, the prospects were poor. The reality was that there was nothing special about my father's skills set, though this did not diminish his bitter resilience to get back in the cockpit. It got to the point where, in ever-diminishing supplies of possibility, he wrote again to Lord Tedder. One can only speculate on the actual content of the letter, but it would probably begin with a *"Lord Tedder, You may not remember me but you presented me with my Wings in 1945..."* There was a certain 'don't ask, don't get' combined with a polite, personal and impassioned plea for the chance to fly again.

Whatever possibilities he wanted to explore with his plea to Tedder, he tendered the audacious pre-condition that his offer of services to the RAF in peacetime was contingent on personal pride: he wished to retain his rank and his wings. Audacity perhaps, but the man had worked for it and no one was going to take away his prize.

There was a reply, but not from Tedder. It came from a secretary. Alas, the RAF held the upper hand and reciprocated by putting in place their own preconditions: there would be no more flying. In addition, an application to rejoin would be 'limited' to a twenty-one year term of duty. Having served five years already this would net down to sixteen years service in a non-flying role.

Looking ahead, he would be forty-two years old when he left the service. He asked himself the question: would he be better off at age forty-two, than at twenty-six, when his three years expired? Circumstances were being constructed where candidates going back in would have to think long and hard before committing themselves. The reality was that the RAF's own pre-conditions were designed to prevent an already over-swollen service becoming a major drain on the country's limited resources.

What next? Well, it was chickens. The idea that was hatched resulted from the friendship that he had struck up with Ron Ratcliffe. It was apparently Ron's idea, though. This is somewhat odd, for apart from reference to Air Marshall Tedder on the day of the Wings Parade, this is the only named genuine RAF colleague my father referred to.

Together, my father and Ron would start up a chicken farm in Dover. The crude business plan went something like this: the Government at the time subsidised egg production, chickens laid eggs – lots of them – and lots of hens would mean lots and lots of eggs. All Messrs Ratcliffe and Duncan had to do was get hens to produce eggs. This sounded good in theory: a sure fire way to make a living. Here was a proposition so good that my father's severance release money, bounty and everything else was invested.

Neither Ron nor my father were businessmen, let alone farmers. What sounded eminently sensible in principle and what ought to have worked was destined for cataclysmic failure; a triumph of reality over naïvety and hope of easy riches. The figures looked good: hens plus eggs equals multiplication. But supply was strictly controlled, matters which were clearly not fully comprehended by my father and Ron Ratcliffe.

The money situation became desperate until finally there was the realisation that the venture was doomed to failure. Bureaucracy got in the way, with central government only supporting far ms that were operational prior to the war. Materials were hard to come by, feed was obtained subject to licence and there were poultry diseases that my father and Ron knew nothing about. The anticipated simple multiplication towards riches was doomed as their stock dwindled into a handful of gasping, drooping and dying birds:

> *"Getting the chicks was easy, but raising the chicks to productive hens was a different kettle of fish. We couldn't get a licence to buy food unless we had a chicken farm before the war; we couldn't get land, and we couldn't get building materials and we couldn't stop losing chickens all the time because of various illnesses of which I knew nothing."*

The false optimism of the road to 'easy street' gave way to matters of subtraction. From an initial batch of some four-hundred chicks, the estimate is that only twenty survived.

Life was spiralling, nay, nose-diving. Entrepreneurship was against him, the military was against him. The great, so-called, opportunities of post-war adjustment were not there. The war had achieved nothing, well, for him, and the spoils afterwards were at best meagre, certainly desperate; no more than chicken feed.

My father approached the RAF Benevolent Fund, but they could only advise temporary employment. And so it came to pass that my father established a window cleaning business.

The Benevolent Fund did help, though. Perhaps not substantially, but the application to be bailed out led to the supply of a bucket, also, a chamois and a ladder! What would have to be perfected was the necessary skills in negotiating traffic with a ten feet long ladder strapped to a bicycle crossbar! The image requires little imagination, but the approach lies somewhere between Will Hay and George Formby.

In time the window cleaning business picked up and although the income was steady, it was never enough to get by on. A second job was found, this time involving early mornings delivering milk for a local dairy farm.

This balanced out the working day: dairy farm in the morning and window cleaning in the afternoon after a late morning nap. Despite trying to prop up the chicken farm venture, the business plan was never workable. Both Ron and my father must have been completely dejected and frustrated by the trials of moving on but forever facing obstacles: administrative brick walls to scale and financial mountains to climb.

Reflecting on Adastral House's advice, a last ditch attempt was made to secure flying positions. A further approach was made to the Civil Aviation Authority. But the guys were completely broke and would require someone to sponsor their training.

The matter was not pursued. He and Ron went their separate ways, but not before considering offering their services to British European Airways. If an approach had been made to the newly formed BEA then maybe, perhaps, a traineeship on *Vickers Vikings* could have been offered. Unfortunately, it was not to turn out like that.

13
Broke

By the end of 1948, and still only twenty-five years old, my father was flat broke and with nowhere to live. He had been beset by the difficulties of asserting any challenge to get on in Civvy Street. He had tried in his own way, had taken chances and had run the risk of the law. Without the requisite progress, he was humiliated and defeated by civilian life and pervasive, bitter regret.

If there is one characteristic that was displayed throughout his life it was the difficulty in making decisions. Second to that was the angst of making the wrong decision and having to live with it. With hindsight, he could have knuckled-down, becoming an airframe fitter in a reserved occupation. Alternatively, he could have returned to factory work in Dundee immediately after the war. He could also have returned to life in the RAF but he knew full well that the RAF had nothing to offer him: he heartily disliked ground duties. Cleared for take-off in April 1945, the last three years had been an unmitigated disaster culminating in a career nose-dive. There is the old adage that a good landing is one you walk away from. Well, at least he was walking.

There was an additional frustration in not being unique in those circumstances; there were literally thousands like him.

He wanted the RAF, but somehow the RAF did not want him. He was part of the seventy-five per cent of personnel who were *'also rans'* – guys who made up the volumes trained or the numbers dead. How right his arithmetic was. The million strong force of 1945 would be reduced to only 200,000 or so within 5 years.

The Empire Air Training Scheme/BCATP had been a great success, but just how could one feasibly slow down and deconstruct this vast machine without drastic measures?

The policies and plans of 1938 and 1939, of emergency interventions and powers would give way to peacetime corrections: service cuts, the transfer of men and women from the war effort to peacetime commerce, production and trade. Britain was in a mess and the abrupt cessation of transatlantic aide in September 1945 would mean ongoing difficulties. For my father there was emotional turmoil at the time and this translates into more sketchy and cynical reminiscence. This, and the events that unfold, speak volumes.

With financial ruin facing him at Dover and having stuck it out for three post-war years, fighting against authority and raging against the machine, there was but one thing left for him to do: go home. Maybe, just maybe, his father might help him out.

The journey was a seemingly interminable three days and nights combining not just the most inhospitable traits of the English climate, but weathering the indifference of its people. True, there were some offers of assistance, the tractor passing through Teynham, the truck driver's offer of lunch at Sandy, and at Doncaster the seeming uncharacteristic generosity of a Yorkshireman – a farmer – who offered a bed for the night. This sounded too good to be true – just right at the time. And although the accommodation eventually turned out to be a leaky loosebox, it was for the most part weatherproof.

Seven hundred miles of hitchhiking from Folkestone led him home to Dundee and the delightful Silvery Tay. The man is broke and broken, yet there remains the prospect of some form of home life – a roof, at least, at 63 Constitution Road – and a chance of a fresh start. New industry was being set up in the town. My father's sister Jean was working with the American watchmaker, Timex. This growing corporation had established a presence in purpose-built, modern premises. Meanwhile, Ron, his younger brother, later bound for life in Australia, was working in the last vestiges of a jute industry which twenty years later would be virtually non-existent.

There are two routes from the south into Dundee in 1949: across the river from Fife or Edinburgh by train or ferry, or along the low fertile *Carse* road from Perth to Dundee. Either route is pretty and the river setting of Dundee is still one of the most dramatic. At Perth the setting seemed reminiscent enough of the Rhine for a castle folly to be built, and legend has it that when the Romans arrived, the legionnaire in charge exclaimed *"Behold the Tiber!"* To the west of Dundee the river widens and the gentle hills meet the flowing waters famous for salmon the world over. This held little fascination for someone who had seen Table Mountain from a ship astride two oceans, the Atlantic and the Indian, or the Veldt from the air.

Whatever beauty the river had to offer, it was the town itself that still displayed a lack of appeal for the man who seemed to relish wanderlust. He was a changed man in an unchanged town. Home it was, but there were probably no nostalgic or romantic notions of loving comfort. This was rock bottom practicality in a dark, cold, chimney-infested and, for him, parochial town miles from where he wanted to be. He probably did not know where he actually wanted to be, but this was not it. Military service and foreign travel, privilege, and the mere enjoyment of just being away, meant that my father would not settle-in easily to what was otherwise the claustrophobia of the familiar. He wrestled with the uncomfortable practicality of his being back home, for the journey had a pragmatic, if desperate, agenda. Given the servitude of his childhood, contributions through board and lodging and the faltering, corrupted entry into military service, then surely his own father could bail him out? The request was simple and his stay was brief. Pious hope was met with swift retort:

> "It was all jute factories, dirt, grime, poor pay and jute, jute, jute. … I stayed a short period and since I was not contributing to my keep decided to head south again; so I literally walked back to Dover."

A fit of pique maybe, but the bold nature of the insult made him boil, yet freezing with neither the authority nor strength to lash out after the years of torment. Pride could have been swallowed and a settled life with steady employment could have resulted, but why? Dover had presented its hopes and hardships; maybe his English life meant something to him and perhaps he could be somebody without the inexorable draw back home. The return to Dundee had been fruitless. Broke on the northbound journey and with little means southbound, he hitched and on this occasion it took four days. What money he had would have to sustain a long trip made of short hops on trucks and helpful commercial salesmen, travelling about the country.

This was Britain without the motorway network. Towns and cities and the countryside surrounding them would still be insular, self-sustaining communities well before globalisation and the supermarket yet to provide frozen food, let alone baby courgettes from Zambia. The journey would add another 700 miles to what would eventually be a 1,400 mile round trip; a long walk with few lifts along the way. What was the point of hitching to Dover from Dundee? How many people were heading from Dundee, specifically to Dover, in 1948?

The journey was slow and far from steady: from Dundee to Cupar, Cupar to Kirkcaldy, then Edinburgh, Berwick. Not bad for a day. Then on to Alnwick, Newcastle, Spennymoor, and Durham. Luck was on his side with a truck driver heading to Doncaster on day two. Sticking with the A1, by day three he was in Letchworth before noon and at 2am in Covent Garden.

Traders were setting up for the day, deliveries were arriving and the truck driver he was with took him to one side and asked, really, when he had last had a proper breakfast. The truck driver treated him and so my father found himself sleeping in a corner of the flower market. Despite his troubles, he wasn't pushing up daisies, but after four days he was certainly not smelling of roses.

Day four was his own personal D-Day: *Dover Day*. By the time he got there he was reduced to sleeping in bus stations and rail stations. With nowhere to stay, there was little hope of finding a job, unless, of course, a guesthouse and ready money to pay for it could be secured. No such luck.

Ever resourceful, a trip to the Shipping Federation office solved the problem and my father secured a job as a steward on the 'Hampton', a small twin funnel, slab-sided ferry of around 3000 tons plying across the English Channel between Dover and Dunkerque. The Hampton was, in fact, a stern-loading ferry boat built for commercial traffic and passengers. She was also built to take railway carriages. Such an unassuming ship, one that was built for a single role, but by wartime would be adapted to military use and be honoured with the designation 'His Majesty's Ship'. As HMS Hampton she would see much activity. Mine-laying would be one of her roles in wartime, alongside troop and horse carrier, before being re-converted to civilian commercial use in 1947.

A ferry like the Hampton carried trucks, coaches and trains, as well as foot passengers. Passengers needed facilities and hospitality. My father could get along with people and was eager to get on in life. The mess at Burtonwood had served as a catering apprenticeship and his bar and customer skills were put to good use.

Passengers' comfort was important, but then so was his own and old habits do, of course, die hard. Money was tight and he was never one to miss a trick, particularly those learnt at Burtonwood:

> *"Passengers slept all the way unless, by not being able to sleep, came up to the dining salon where we served meals. Tips were good and fiddling the meals was a rewarding racket, all money shared between myself, the head waiter and the chef."*

This was a short-lived occupation, and was followed by transfer to the mail boats – fast passenger ferries. This was described as being both busier and more lucrative with various staff sidelines. However, this was not without incident, as there were risks in the opportunities to supplement one's income!

Some of the ferries carried through-trains from London to Paris; the actual sleeping cars were made up of carriages provided by the *Companie Internationale des Wagons-lits.*

My father recalls this being called the *Silver Arrow* service, but it was in fact the *Golden Arrow.* The train would depart from London Victoria at 11.00am and passengers would arrive in Paris at 5.40pm. There was also a Dover-Calais Motorists Service with the crossing taking some three hours and fifteen minutes. *"I used to work on the 'packy'-boats".* Well, that's what it sounded like to me. Schoolboy French made me think that this was a corruption of 'pacquet', which could have translated into packet or envelope. Mail boats could therefore be termed 'pacquet boats'. Well, this would be sort of true, but the phonetic form has been with me for years. By chance I found the actual form, 'paquebots' did, in fact, mean mail boat.

The Golden Arrow service was interrupted by the war and

restarted in December 1947. How fortunate for my father. For years I marvelled at the *Boat Trains* actually carrying the train and docking at the other side, a train exiting its bow! Amazing how these kindergarten images are established despite obvious problems of different railway gauges and operating systems!

British Rail had been established in 1948 and many schemes of a fraudulent nature were apparently in operation by certain staff. The, at times, *mercantile* side of the British character is somewhere between Dickens' *Fagin* and post-war desperation. Coming to terms with life after the war was far from easy and there were many restrictions on the movement of goods and money.

Rationing remained in place in Britain until well into the 1950s. In France, there was war damage in what is easy to forget was formerly occupied Europe. There were the challenges of re-establishing and stabilising the economy; there were economy measures similar to those in Britain in place and shortages of everyday items. After the ravages of war, German occupation and simply not having enough to eat, there emerged a Black Market in ordinary, but hard-to-come-by, goods and not the rare high-end luxuries.

The demand for everyday goods was certainly there. It was a matter of establishing the supply, the supply chain and the distribution network. In the case of my father the fraudulent activity centred on the smuggling of nothing more sinister than coffee.

There was a simple but very effective distribution infrastructure in place which began with supply – through a shop in Dover, apparently with inexhaustible supplies of the stuff – and then transfer through French boat crews. These crews would take it into France under cover of darkness with the assistance of a spy network who would warn if the French Customs Officers, or Douanes, were active. Despite this clandestine sophistication, there was nothing very discrete about the practice.

The stuff was openly bought in twenty pound bags, with people such as my father, carrying two such bags. It would then be carried to the ferry during a one hour lunch break between 12 noon and 1.00pm, stowed, and then sold-on in the supply chain on the other side of the Channel operating under cover of darkness. There was a routine in operation and generally it ran smoothly. Well, generally.

Below the high cliffs, so symbolic of defiance and national identity and as the road descends to the harbour, the Kent countryside gives up its pastoral loveliness and at Dover becomes a hive of movement, chaos and trade. Amidst the routine confusion of movements it would be a simple matter of my father going to work or finishing a shift. These comings and goings would be filled with effort in lugging extraordinary amounts of coffee beans; there was also tension and risk.

It was one thing being sure about the apparent simplicity of a well-oiled and practiced routine; it was quite another determining the exit strategy if things went belly-up. On one occasion my father was returning to the ferry berthed at Dover with a second load of coffee, again, two twenty pound bags.

This was broad daylight. The time was 12.55pm and only five minutes was to spare before the ship left port. At the time there was a long curved approach between the station and the dock:

> *"As I was coming round the bend I just quickly caught a glimpse of a uniform and two customs men obviously going off duty. The panic was immediate — I couldn't go back, nor could I risk a confrontation with the customs."*

He was in the early stages of being caught. With heart racing, panic in his eyes and Anglo-Saxon monosyllables being muttered, it was quick thinking that saved the day:

"Immediately I looked to my right and there I noticed a gents' lavatory so I dived in not knowing if I had been seen. More panic as I looked at the stone walls, urination section and two toilets. I took out a penny, put it in the brass slot and opened the door. Standing inside and with probably only a minute to spare by this time I stuffed the two bags on top of the cistern, high up on the roof ."

He had relieved himself, well, of the goods anyway. As he came out of the lavatory he tore off a section of a Woodbine cigarette packet and wrote 'Out of Order' on it, stuck it in the slot and ran full ahead to reach the gang plank as it was about to be hauled away. With athletic timing worthy of the 1948 Olympics, he jumped, grabbing the rail to steady himself and caught his breath. Phew!

Not content with consigning this close brush with authority to history, the following day curiosity led him back to check on the contraband. Everything was just as he had left it.

He was delighted to see the holdalls still there, as well as the piece of card in the slot. My father was also relieved to see that the British obeyed instruction and that no one had used the toilet. No one had even opened the door of the cubicle and let's face it, the person who had tried to use it would not have wanted to waste a penny. For all the world, that toilet was broken. Even the cleaning staff had not interfered with the facility. The railway company received a mention in despatches for not keeping the toilets cleaned or repaired. If they had, the valuable coffee would have been found and my father's income from it denied.

The financial benefits to my father of being a *coffee runner* were two-fold. The regular supply from the shop would mean that daily runs across the Channel would mean selling the stuff for twice the price paid in England. In addition, the restrictions on the amount of pounds sterling that the British could take abroad meant that this could be supplemented on board.

My father would sell his French currency to passengers who welcomed it as the ceiling on money leaving the country was restricted to something like £10 per passenger. This was routine racketeering which had its upside as well as downside. The rewards were good.

Forty pounds of coffee at two bob a pound would provide an income of £4, the equivalent of $16 at the time. But that amount of coffee was also a liability and there were times, of course, when the routine distribution would not go smoothly, particularly if the customs people were close:

> *"Many a time we had to throw the coffee through the nearest porthole into the harbour only to find it next morning floating about like the actions at the Boston Tea Party. What a waste!"*

Sometimes greed kicked in and on one occasion my father found out that coffee was fetching four times its British price. He was buying at two shillings a pound, selling it on for four shillings a pound, but the porters on the other side were getting eight shillings a pound!

Fuming with the injustice, he refused to sell his supply through the porters. With a reliable framework of individuals involved in the distribution of the coffee, it was a question of these individuals taking their 'fair mark-up' – everybody is making something and everyone in the chain is happy. To break ranks would be risky, but there was a huge lack of fairness, or so my father thought, in the French guys getting four times the Kent price.

The injustice continued to be pondered and a plan was put into action. He did break ranks, a different approach was deployed and my father sought to circumvent the middle man. He declined to go through the local 'agents', instead ordering a taxi to be at the foot of the gangway at midnight:

"It arrived OK and I sneaked the two bags of coffee into the back seat. Not more than 200 yards down the quayside a Douane Officer held his hand up in the glare of the headlights and I was caught. They confiscated the coffee, I was arrested, so was the taxi driver and he had his cab impounded."

Placed in a cell overnight, the risk of breaking ranks had become abundantly clear. He had assumed too much risk and had been royally caught. Whatever petit dejeuner he had in the morning, I wonder whether a dismissive, gruff, French jail officer had opened the cell door and mocked the inmate: *"Café, monsieur?"*. Worse still if the raw material had been contraband!.

Later in the day he was before a French Magistrate answering to the court through an interpreter. There was no point in disputing the charge. Guilt was admitted. The taxi driver had not been directly involved in any crime and was released. His cab was returned to him.

Meantime, the culprit has to explain that he has no money to pay the £100 fine. *Pas d'argent; non monnaie.* But the sentence requires him to source and pay the money to the court within forty-eight hours. Curiously, as some form of surety, the solicitor representing my father would have been sent to jail in his place if the money had not been paid. There must have been some huge trust between the solicitor and my father!

The chicken farm has cost my father his service bounty. The £120 has gone. How on earth is he going to raise the £100 to cover the fine? Within forty-eight hours he had been back to Dover and sold every single thing he owned, raising £65 in the process. He borrows the £35 from the ferry captain, paid back at £5 a week. The solicitor is set free following the money being paid into the Calais Court. There is now a strange twist.

You would think that having lost everything once and now for a second time, my father would see that coffee smuggling through increasingly patrolled French ports presented a risk too far. In future it might not be matter of a fine: it could be a custodial sentence. These risks are not countenanced. The principal concern on his mind was how to recover the £100 from the French court!

There was perhaps a disregard for dockside protocol, and maybe because he had side-stepped the middle man someone had blown the whistle: he had been set up, peut etre. This ineptitude and greed has cost him dearly. He was angry, but he remained greedy:

> "...so I therefore went about carrying twice as much coffee over until I was able to recover that £100 out of the French coffers. This I did, and managed to make a substantial profit while I was still employed on the Cross Channel Ferries."

The misfortune of hostilities ending and being one of thousands sucked in and spat out of the War Machine created hardships. Yet because Civvy Street was not paved with gold, the years immediately after military service were unbelievably rich in experience; the hard work, risk and sheer balls, the effort just to get by, is admirable. The contrast between the young boy of pre-war Scotland and the roguish guile of a twenty-five year old involved in petty international crime and sentenced before the French courts is there to see.

Somehow history portrays a rational series of events in chronological order which form an equation leading to certain outcomes. History tells us you knuckled down and got on with it, living life through rationing and rebuilding, massive national debt and US aid.

At the time, the consequences of conflict were being lived through rather than being looked back upon. If anything, this period was one of desperate survival. Amidst all this adjustment and disappointment there was a desperation and hard graft amidst a life which strived to be normal, but which was tinged with danger in the uncertainties of the time. It was all about survival. On the boats, in the kitchen, or in the mess at Burtonwood there lay the ability to supplement an income. The chicken farm had failed. The window cleaning round had folded. My father was down on his luck, was just about getting by, but wanted, desperately, to move on. The alternative to knuckling down was to take risks: fiddles were commonplace and the black economy blossomed.

Although life in Kent seemed to provide a basis for a settled life, supported by the risky financial supplements secured through contraband, my father knew full well that boats were not what interested him. He wanted to fly and by the spring of 1949 he joined the fledgling British European Airways, little realising that this would lead him into Berlin seeing out the last months of the civil side of the Airlift.

14

Midwifery, Jugged Hare & the Archbishop of Canterbury

Kent had seemed so vulnerable during the conflict. Not a brief spell or tumultuous interlude, but six long years where the White Cliffs offered national strength and perpendicular defiance against an enemy beyond calm millpond or raging divide. This was where England began and for an enemy, it was temptingly close. Only twenty-two miles away was occupied France. Yet amidst golden cornfields set in a verdant garden of hops, ripe and tall, above, the streaks, swirls and swoops of dog-fights and the drone of formations of military aircraft was a county at war. By 1945 the uncertainty and insecurity of war had stopped, replaced with the uncertainty and insecurity of peacetime: a process of personal adjustments affecting each and every citizen.

There was unfolding a return to normality in many forms. Pre-war everyday life was slowly coming back, but inevitably the Britain of that 1945 summer would be different to that in 1939. War had presented restriction, innovation, adjustment, fear and sacrifice for many; the giving up of simple pleasures and the uncertainty of their return. Peace would foster new opportunity and be accompanied by displeasure and disappointment for many.

Whatever efforts had gone into resourcing a war, there were also resources planning a 'peace'. The expedient necessity of the 'war effort' would need to give way; no longer the acceptance of central control. Social and economic infrastructure was re-establishing itself and in this transition my father crossed the Garden of England to take advantage of what he knew, what he loved and what he felt he was born to do. In the process he moved to West London.

In digs in Dover in January 1949, he was twenty-five years old. He had crammed so much into the short months working on the *paquebots*, though his exploits owed more to opportunism and petty crime than continuing professional development and customer care. Yet he was still restless, merely knowing what he didn't want to do – if he had wanted the sea he would have joined the navy.

The desire to fly led to an application to join British European Airways and something of a settled period of paid work based in Harrow and Uxbridge, Middlesex. The timing was pretty much perfect. Non-military flying had ceased during the period of hostilities and much of the emerging airline industry pre-war had declined. The joy-riding, barnstorming days of the 20s and 30s were distant memories. The simple dreams of childhood had been met by the chance to fly for real, but too many pilots did not necessarily mean no more flying. Rather the opposite; post-war, there would be more of it.

The complex commercial aviation operations that we understand today were cleared for take-off virtually immediately after the war. The possibility of a domestic and European air network had been suggested before the war had ended, but an airline industry borne out of the railway industry is hard to conceive. In reality, though, that is what actually happened.

In October 1944, the Railway Company Association made deputations to government that such a network could evolve as an extension of the rail service. However, it was not until two years later that BEA would be set up in August 1946. With an initial fleet of Douglas DC3 'Dakotas', later augmented with *Vickers Vikings*, the origins of what we now take for granted was effectively born. The prospect of a career in aviation had already crossed my father's mind whilst in partnership with Ron Ratcliffe. At one time they thought they could convince their way into flight deck training based on limited experience with a DC3 Dakota and the belief that this might, just might, lead to piloting twin-engine airplanes. This was not to be, but growth in civil aviation presented an opportunity, if not to be a pilot, at least to be *involved* in flight.

There had been a number of smaller scale airlines established as far back as the 20s. However, civil aviation throughout the twentieth century has been a story of individual endeavour, risk, growth, loss, consolidation and bureaucracy. Even in the 30s, as my father was growing up, the early consolidation of smaller airlines was a memory. In Britain, Imperial Airways is recognised as some iconic, bold provider of passenger transport. Here was an opportunity for an elite and fortunate few to fly in contemporary, if noisy, comfort.

Continental air travel began immediately after the previous war in 1919 with the unimaginatively titled Aircraft Transport and Travel providing its first passenger and parcels service from London to Paris. AT&T had been set up in wartime by George Holt-Thomas and was flying ex-military De Havilland 4A aircraft. The company's other work was a Folkestone to Ghent route for 'relief work' in 1919.

Many other companies followed. Probably the most famous was Handley Page, operating between London and Paris. Daimler Airways offered a service to Berlin; Instone flew to Cologne; British Marine Air Navigation Company from Southampton to the Channel Islands. Cost-base factors combined with political/

colonial considerations led to bureaucratic intervention and a government committee was set up: the Civil Air Transport Subsidies Committee, otherwise the Hambling Committee. This looked to financial support, national pride and practicality in bringing the colonies closer together. The amalgamation of the four existing lines was preconditioned. It would receive a one million pound subsidy over ten years to fly 'nationally required' routes. In return, it would have to 'Buy British' aircraft and engines; it would have to fly 'heavier-than-air' equipment – no airships. The new company was called Imperial Air Transport Company Limited and was born on 31st March 1924.

Further change in the industry was to follow. The explosion of interest in aviation in the 1920s and the developing aeronautics of the time led to many new independent airlines carrying newspapers, mail and passengers. Routes emerged that are inexplicably contrived or plain questionable in terms of why passengers would want to fly such routes. An early player was Hillman's Airways – later swallowed-up into the British Airways conglomerate – believe it or not, flying out of Romford and Clacton-on-Sea with routes via Kent to Brussels and Paris.

Merger and consolidation were hallmarks of the industry through the 1930s, and state intervention was never far away. Ultimately, the long haul of consolidation would go full circle, for the world's favourite airline reverted to the British Airways brand four decades later. However, British Airways was, in fact, a 1930s carrier, one of many whose independence succumbed to merger.

The family tree of British civil aviation is complicated. British Airways had itself grown by acquisition, forming the British Airways Group comprising Hillman's Airways, Spartan Airways, United Airways, British Continental and *Allied* British Airways.

Spartan Airways and United Airways joined forces to become Allied British Airways Ltd, born on 1st October 1935. Shortly afterwards the Allied was dropped and British Airways was born. Another independent carrier, British Continental Airways, is a long-forgotten brand, but formed in April 1935, it emerged to offer sufficient competition to the enlarged British Airways. As a result, it was bought-out warranting its acquisition the following year.

This combined strength pointed to the prospect of a head-to-head between British Airways and Imperial. By 1938, the consolidation forced by the Hambling Committee in 1923 led to further re-structuring with recognition that British Airways was the stronger carrier. A forced merger of Imperial with British Airways operations followed.

My father would come into an airline industry whose foundations lay in the British Overseas Airways Act of 1939. The clue is in the name, for this gave birth to the British Overseas Airways Corporation, or simply BOAC as it became more popularly known.

BEA would follow, being set up by the Civil Aviation Act 1946 *"with a view to providing civil air services in various parts of the world and in particular Europe (including the British Islands)"*. The new carrier would take over routes from 110 Wing RAF Transport Command and add some new ones too.

The immediate post-war years saw a new structure for the airlines. As my father joined the industry, there would be a total of three leading British carriers: British Overseas Airways Corporation (BOAC), British South American Airways (BSAA) and British European Airways (BEA). BSAA as their name suggests would fly Caribbean and South American routes, BOAC would fly long haul routes to the USA and Canada, as well as other Commonwealth destinations.

Though not often realised, these then mighty long haul flights to far off romantic locations in distant continents would start near the Dorset coast, Hurn to be precise, with converted Lancasters carrying only nine or so passengers in noisy, ill-conceived 'comfort'. Hurn is hardly an international sounding name, but then neither is Heathrow or Gatwick or Stansted. Is Newark?

Hurn started as RAF Hurn and would trade hands between the British and US, finally the British, and would see life as a military base, civil airport and post-war aircraft production facility. By 1949 its days as a civil airport were numbered. In relative terms airline travel from Hurn presented opportunities on what is still the fastest mode of travel, to what would now be termed very long haul destinations such as South Africa, the Middle East and Australia.

These far-flung destinations would be reached by a series of 'hops' as distinct to the singular 'flight'. This puts the technology into context. Hindsight is wonderful thing, but a converted-from-the-purposeful air transport or bomber was a cutting edge exploit which spawned a vast industry. Rudimentary, and by today's standards very slow and low flying, the thing was that at least you would get to your destination, well, eventually – and fortified by good home cooking, not warmed or prepared on board, but literally served from a large thermos flask. Staff were still in Royal Air Force uniform!

The other leading airports at the time were Northolt in Middlesex and Croydon, Surrey. More later. Although Heathrow would emerge as the country's foremost air gateway, its role merged only slowly after 1945. Formerly 'Heath Row', 'Harmondsworth' or the 'Great Western Aerodrome', it was requisitioned during wartime, but would open for civilian traffic in 1946. Passenger carrying capability would establish, after the war, a terminal comprising of a tented village only being replaced during the mid-50s by the Frederick Gibberd-designed terminal. These were pioneering times and my father was there, not quite at the beginning, but close to it. Handsome, yet again, this time in double-breasted, brass-buttoned, half-vented, black barathea under a BEA crested hat and single wing brevet. British European Airways would operate the emerging short haul routes. These were domestic, European and North African routes, operating out of another charming, cosmopolitan location: Northolt.

Northolt had also been a Royal Air Force base. Located in outer west London, still very much in the Home Counties, it was loaned by the RAF to the Ministry of Aviation right at the beginning of post-war British commercial aviation. Croydon had been the epicentre of airline operations until then, but the Civil Aviation Act of 1946 would lead to, like-it-or-not, nationalisation, rationalisation and growth. But why Northolt? A principal requirement was a suitable runway.

By the outbreak of war, Croydon had developed into an impressively well-serviced facility: an art deco design displaying the balance and poise of a country mansion, with vast hangers for Handley-Pages strikingly huge before basic concrete aprons and careworn grass. Its weakness was its grass runway. Northolt was concrete and this facility was accompanied by an assortment of buildings, as well as good road and rail access from the West End.

If the post-war origins of civil aviation lie in the amalgamation of different carriers, statute, subsidy and hand-me-downs, Northolt Airport grew out of a long row of what appeared as, at the time, modern pre-fabricated single storey buildings adjacent to the Western Avenue.

The buildings had in fact been the Bourne Junior School, a model of contemporary education standards in 1939, but alas it was deemed to be too close to the runway at the outbreak of war. Four days after the pupils moved in, they were asked to vacate the premises in the interests of the war effort. In use, the rag-bag of a second- hand building, a wartime control tower and an *Aldis lamp,* some men in their old uniforms and a few aircraft are the post-war origins of one of the busiest hub airports in the world. And the passenger experience? Confusing, some would say; confusion arising from Northolt being in Ruislip and passengers alighting at the wrong station. Staff had initial difficulty too. The timetables eventually included travel from central London, the departure point being the Kensington Air Station; within an hour of leaving this West London departure point, passengers would be taking to the skies.

Speed of check-in was assisted by the airport's size. Passengers exited the low flat-roofed buildings with slender Crittal windows, through railings and across thirty yards of concrete to a waiting airplane; a scene so intimate that on a small greensward before the runway, genteel and curious onlookers would have afternoon tea whilst watching the airport as a leisure activity.

By 1st August 1946, British European Airways would be born under the chairmanship of Sir Harold Hartley. The 'continental service' was the first division to come into operation; a bold move, perhaps, given the ravages of war, mangled cities, and an understandable reluctance or inability to travel. Sir Harold's early commentary on post-war air travel, frank and without adornment, referred to 'strenuous' months of difficulties including bad weather and lack of accommodation, as well as "lots of complaints of our shortcomings". But the future of the airline lay in addressing these concerns through teamwork and customer experience.

Travelling by air was an ease which was to be experienced and BEA needed customers. The difficulties faced by the average man (or woman) in the street and the war weary cities of Europe was somehow dismissed by the public relations of the time which pointed to obtaining a visa being a deterrent to the *'average English traveller from percolating much into Europe'*. How very inconvenient. Saying nothing of national unity, this journalism from a British carrier seemed to forget the Scots, Welsh and Irish.

As for the operational side of things, the effect of war on the new airline can be felt in the language of the time and the quality of facilities. Rome was described as a 'station' which had settled down to an efficient existence. Brussels had a 'humbly equipped' airport thanks to the destruction wrought by departing Germans, staff improvising in draughty and inadequate buildings. The customer experience was noticeably influenced by the rationing and aspirations of the time. Paper shortages meant the passengers' in-flight magazine was strictly limited to sixteen pages; a publication which talked of staff on ambassadorial duties and Board members as personalities – a sort of getting-to-know-you, cocktail party mixed with the society pages.

Scheduled services began on 1st September 1946 with a *Vickers Viking* (G-AHOP) en route to Copenhagen. The timetable grew. Twelve flights per day to Paris, eleven flights per day to Amsterdam, daily to Nice by 1948. Hopper flights from London to Munich via Amsterdam-Dusseldorf-Cologne-Frankfurt-Hamburg-Berlin-Munich.

Fares were expensive at the time: Amsterdam and Paris single £8, return £14-8-0; Berlin single £21-17-0, return £39-7-0. Small fortunes making European air travel the preserve of the few. For my father, there was the excitement of travel and airport names now long-forgotten, Lohausen, Wahn, Fuhlsbuttel and Ruzyme, combined with the fatigue of long, relatively low altitude flights: four hours and forty-five minutes to Berlin and nearly twenty-nine hours to Ankara.

The airlines logo – *the flying key* – was opening the door to Europe and by 1947 was looking at doubling its fleet. Passenger numbers speak for themselves, the numbers growing twenty-fold in six years from 1947–1953:

1947	71,177
1948	511,522
1949	577,122
1950	751,512
1951	939,586
1952	1,135,579
1953	1,400,122

BEA had an assortment of inherited and leased Douglas Dakotas, Vickers Vikings, De Havilland Rapides and even former Luftwaffe Junkers (an aircraft the origin and manufacture of which was so potent that its presence on Jersey soil, even in peacetime, was rejected). Pressures on the airline required growth and investment. Staff were needed and so my father would become a cabin steward. I dare say that with some earnest saving and application my father could have been rated for twin engines, but that was not to be. The airline's rapid growth presented an opportunity to fly frequently and whilst not in the cockpit, my father was at the very least back flying again after three years.

Pressures and expectations were huge. This was a period of massive growth in airline operations based on new routes, consolidation, merger, new airplanes and new staff.

In relative terms such numbers are extremely low. Heathrow currently handles some sixty-eight million passengers per annum, with appropriate volumes of aircraft movements to support this. However, passenger movements on small planes carrying maybe thirty people would mean an average of around 2,700 air movements per annum in 1947, the equivalent of over 200 aircraft movements a week. By 1953, the equivalent figures would be over 400 thousand air movements per annum; 8 thousand movements per week.

Consider the daily workload in preparing and turning around twenty-five planes each day in 1947, steadily increasing to 1,200 per day. By 1948 there were growing pains: new planes, routes and services, more timetables, different classes and ticketing, ever-growing numbers of personnel; a future that for my father had prospects.

The exhilaration of flying in civil aviation saw a fresh and professionally-appealing dawn and my father's previous experience at sea and in the air would be put to good use. He had silver service experience, could deal with people, understood airplanes, could take discipline and had good looks and charm. He was lucky too – right place, right time, right credentials – though even to get into cabin crew positions, certain standards were expected. Nothing new here, as the RAF selection process years earlier had provided rigorous experience. You are already intrigued by the chapter title but, believe it or not, these were highly pertinent matters in 1948.

Staff selection procedure was exacting: deportment, speech, manners, knowledge of current affairs and a working knowledge of at least one foreign language. First Aid training included midwifery, which I suspect at the time would have been dealt with somewhat tactfully and carefully. I suppose, too, it was a departure for my father and would have presented quite an anatomical and physiological appreciation of what had otherwise been a rather more entertainingly physical interpretation of the womanly form.

The training was compulsory, but not without a certain Old School Englishness. Pilots were frequently from the middle classes or public school educated. They comprised well-trained officers of the RAF and the credibility they offered – that safe pair of hands at the flight-deck – suited the clientele. Flight was the preserve of those who could afford it. This was an age of romantic flying adventures, limited and exclusive travel opportunities, and passengers who would expect standards of decorum.

And so the questions posed in the qualification examination seem like curios from a finishing school for well-heeled and chinless young gerls from the Home Counties. Questions such as *"What would one serve with Jugged Hare?"* or *"How would one address the Archbishop of Canterbury?"* would be asked. Quite what answers were given one can only speculate.

Medical examination and inoculations would follow, and finally the issue of the tailored Savile Row uniform of raincoat, two grey uniforms, two blue uniforms and two khaki outfits; cap, shoes, socks and tie. Having lost the RAF severance pay on the chicken farm and later been fined by the French judiciary, my father was down £220 at least. He knew the value of money and was well-used to comfort and a certain degree of privilege. The chicken farm had seen him hit virtual bankruptcy, yet now he had a flying career of sorts, with pay and clothing: a free uniform. Well, not just one but six, actually, and tailored too – which was quite, well, necessary in a glamorous age. As my father would sum up, this was all "very impressive and would raise the value of the humble servant".

BEA was the new airline for Britain and it presented an optimism for the future at a time when new types of aircraft were being developed for the Jet Age, such as the de Havilland Comet. Increasingly over the period since then, airliners had increasingly become 'numerative'. Boeing were great, if confusing, with numbers. What was the difference between the 707 and 727? Douglas had the DC3 and the DC4. British aviation companies such as Avro had used a series of regional town names to differentiate their aircraft: Lancaster, Halifax and York. The period civil aircraft in 1949 included adaptations of wartime airframes: for Lancaster, read *Lancastrian*.

The Avro York was a strange plane with a fixed upper wing and an appearance not dissimilar to a gurnet fish. The design language of the passenger carrying aircraft of the latter half of the twentieth century had yet to manifest, though Douglas perhaps stolen a march since the 1930s, with the DC3.

Compared to the Lancastrian and its thermos flask approach to in-flight catering the Avro York, this was an attempt at some drawing room luxury, with polished wood and padded seats. But capacity had improved by thirty per cent, or so. From nine, the capacity had increased to twelve passengers. Elsewhere in the industry there were alliterative names, as in the fantastically proportioned Bristol Brabazon, with its specification including a twenty-five feet diameter fuselage, capable of accommodating two floors of spacious quarters, and a massive 230 feet wingspan.

The plane had been conceived in 1943 as a London to New York express airplane capable of carrying, initially, twenty-five passengers, then fifty and finally one hundred. It is not clear if the designers actually understood the economics of air travel very well. It was a massive airplane for massive wallets.

So huge was the craft that the designers felt that the rich and famous would each require space standards the equivalent of a small room. Seat pitch and leg room statistics, important considerations thirty or forty years later, seem curiously limited criteria when individual passenger space on the Brabazon could accommodate a three piece suite! Designs conceived of, not just in-flight entertainment by way of a cinema, but a restaurant and a promenade! Literally, an Air *Liner*. Only one of them flew and then it was scrapped. Boeing would have the edge on transatlantic travel into the 60s. The 707 could travel more than twice as fast as the Brabazon, and with twice as many passengers.

Under supervision, my father would be on a very British aircraft on his first flight: a Vickers Viking. This was the plane he would have flown if only BEA could have listened to his plea that 250 hours single engine and experience as a second pilot on a DC3 at Henlow was sufficient! The Viking looked the part. The design language of aircraft was changing; no longer did they look like modified military surplus along the lines of "how can we make a Lancaster not look like a Lancaster".

In fairness, the Viking did have its origins in the Vickers Wellington bomber, even borrowing its geodetic construction in early production. It had a contemporary look with well-proportioned, solid engine cowlings, a good area of cockpit glass and a pretty nose. With a range of 1,875 miles and a cruising speed of 210 mph, the aircraft was well-suited to short and medium range European runs. The power-plant was two Bristol radial propeller engines. However, heavily modified and fitted with two Rolls-Royce Nene turbojets in 1948, it can lay claim to being the first jet airliner in the world, capable in 1948 of doing London-Paris run in only thirty-four minutes.

Prior to the larger Viscount coming into service, the Viking was a well-loved, interim, aircraft for BEA. The initial in-flight assessment of new BEA personnel was undertaken on a short flight to Paris or Amsterdam. The Viking carried a crew of four with around thirty, or so, passengers depending on configuration. There was the pilot, co-pilot and radio operator up front and a steward or stewardess at the rear. My father found this a sturdy, reliable aircraft and over the period he spent with BEA he felt it delivered exceptionally good performance. Whilst there were early problems with icing on the wings, a matter which grounded the fleet for a time, on only one occasion did a technical fault lead to my father experiencing a cancelled flight.

The steward's position would be at the back. Close at hand was the securely fixed steel box containing the bar stocked with small bottles of the main brands of spirit, cordials and soft drinks. Soda water was made on board using a compressed air cylinder. Meals were served on a plastic tray and were usually cold meats, maybe chicken or ham, with salad, bread roll, pepper and salt pots, knife and fork and a serviette. This would be his flight deck. With his training and experience of flying, as well as dealing with people from various backgrounds, he got the job and was on BEA's payroll. The hard work was about to begin.

Current expectations of flight reveal our ease at arriving at our destination reasonably quickly, travelling at, say, 350 to 600 miles per hour, depending on the aircraft, altitude and route. But in the 1940s there was much need for careful planning around the aircraft's range and the routes of the time. From the crew's point of view much preparation was required before each flight to ensure that flight times were adhered to. Planning was, and still is, all-important, even if the turn round times now, are significantly reduced. Meals had to be prepared well in advance, baggage handled and checked, loaded. Fuel was required, also maintenance routines and customs checks:

> *"The steward was ultimately responsible for ensuring that all seating was secure, maps and periodicals installed, the drinks bar was strapped in and customs had broken the seal, sufficient food trays were fitted, hot water was available, receipts given for papers and diplomatic mail and landing forms were ready for all proposed foreign destinations en route."*

Whereas longer flights were easier to manage, the short journeys made for intense on-board activity if the full flight service was to be provided, though sometimes this created discomfort - or even mess – for passengers. London to Lisbon contrasts with London to Paris. The Lisbon run reveals the short hops involved in covering that distance:

> *"The longer flights were much easier and could on occasions become quite boring, especially if it was to Lisbon and only perhaps two passengers were going that far, say, from Madrid or Bordeaux."*

As for Paris:

> *"On occasions one would have to do a Paris run twice a day with full loads, each time serving twenty-eight meals and clearing away in a matter of one hour and twenty minutes. Sometimes the food trays were still not collected in when the plane was actually touching down. This would cause some awful mess, especially if it happened to be a bumpy landing. Serving the meals in itself would have been quite a comfortable exercise to perform but added to the meal, of course, was the issue of tea etc, then the serving of drinks, cigarettes etc, from the bar. All in all, it was rushed and pretty hectic. Then it was a return trip from Paris to Northolt with a full load again."*

The Vickers Viking was a small and more intimate plane and one could converse with passengers if the occasion arose. There would be the possibility of conversation with the stars of the time. Not just the routine stuff of "Coffee, madam?"; sometimes they may share aspects of their lives or anecdotes. In the course of his time with BEA my father had occasion to meet Peter Lorre, star of *Casablanca* and *The Maltese Falcon*, whom he thought was "a charming, dapper little man very much like his movie image".

Also, there was Anna Neagle and her husband, Herbert Wilcox, the Prime Minister's wife Mrs Churchill, the charismatic Charles Boyer, and comic Milton Berle who provided some humour on a flight to France where in bumbling, drunken, slapstick style he would exclaim in cod French *"Ou est mon chapeau?"*. As for Trevor Howard, well, according with my father's dislike for the pompous, he was a "supercilious, egotistical, arrogant character".

For all this brief and transient perspective on the lives of stars, the routine work of the cabin crew was considered to be demanding and one of the most frustrating jobs imaginable.

Lamenting the absence of 'nine-to-five' routine or predictable shift patterns of normal civilian life, my father grew weary of flight preparation and overnight stops, an ever-changing routine and an expanding timetable would place some strain on the individual and more so if there was a family back home:

> "Each working week the schedules were different, sometimes operating one day at a time and perhaps a series of longer journeys spread over two to three days in each week. Weekends off work did not exist as the flight plans were worked out over a seven day period. Usually on the longer journeys time off might be one or two days in a fortnight — there just wasn't any rigid format. If no flights were programmed then those days were utilised doing standby duty which involved being at the airport for twelve hours to take the place of any steward who failed to turn up for duty."

Pressures on the airline to build capacity and to develop markets must have been huge. By 1948 BEA departures from Northolt would increase from a dozen or so to some sixty-six daily services. On 17th October 1948 the airline would carry its millionth passenger and the off-peak fare to Paris would be £10. Northolt at the time was the busiest airport in Britain and probably in Europe.

Heathrow was still lagging behind in terms of throughput. The first scheduled service from Heathrow would be to Paris on 16th April 1950. By comparison, Heathrow was carrying 21,000 passengers in 1950 compared with 542,000 at Northolt. The massive popularity of flying has today resulted in a total UK capacity of 180 million passengers per annum from hundreds of thousands of air traffic movements. All of this growth was spawning new mensuration: air traffic movements become 'ATMs' and passengers are measured in millions per annum – 'MPPA'.

However, in 1949, in the midst of all this growth, the pressures on staff are huge and standby duty was severely disliked. Where is the glamour, my father would mourn, in being on standby for your own aircraft, but at the same time checking the preparation for other aircraft, then being perhaps called up for a flight to any particular destination at a moment's notice for an unknown period?

This meant huge disruption to any personal arrangements and effectively doubled the amount of work my father was doing. Standby shifts were of seemingly endless duration and in this period the steward would arrange the kit for the flights:

> "If the 'standby' was not required that was fine, but not so good if suddenly called upon to service a flight which might incur a night stop abroad. This was a frustrating period for any married man, for if he had no telephone communication with his family, it meant anxiety for the wife who might have had other plans. This was really not an occupation for the married man. The airline business was too demanding and uncertain."

The demands of the emerging routes and ever-increasing flight schedules were apparently ill-matched with sufficient new personnel. One was simply a resource to be called upon as necessary. This appears an almost militaristic line which may have suited senior management in these new airlines. After all, until 1948 crews were still wearing RAF uniform.

Whatever working demands there were, domestic or private life was relegated. Based in Paris and on standby, just how could a loved one be told: "I'm not coming home today, darling. Got to be in Lisbon".

In terms of remuneration, my father ridiculed the fixed monthly wage for an ill-defined and often indeterminate workload. But in the absence of a union to represent cabin crew, company policy had an effective free hand in commanding the human resource.

What, of course, the passenger saw was quite removed from the degree of preparation before they had boarded the aircraft. Catering bar stock to check, also supplies of magazines and newspapers, sweets, sickness bags, maps, head covers, seating arrangements, cleanliness, even baggage handling was all undertaken by cabin crew who had to report two hours before take-off.

In due course my father would clock-up hours in flight and would be at, if not quite actually see, the following destinations: Amsterdam, Athens, Berlin, Bordeaux, Brussels, Cologne, Copenhagen, Dusseldorf, Frankfurt, Geneva, Gibraltar, Hamburg, Le Touquet, Lisbon, Madrid, Malta, Marseilles, Munich, Nice, Oslo, Paris, Prague, Rome, Stockholm, Vienna and Zurich. The Latin-titled *Vade Mecum*, otherwise a tourist guide from Rome, is a souvenir and proof that at least some of his time was spent indulging in cultural activities. Of all the work my father was doing at the time it is the frequent flights to Germany that carved a very strong impression.

It simply is not clear if my father knew what he was letting himself in for in 1948 and 1949. For the same reasons that I question the wisdom of him being in Glasgow in 1939, I also question the circumstances that took him to Germany in these immediate post-war years. If the end of the war saw the destruction of my father's flying career, it certainly saw the destruction of many people's livelihoods, in certain cases their liberty, sometimes their lives.

In 1945 the war was over, life and new hardships carried on for many. Work with BEA saw some degree of stability in my father's life, albeit with the challenges of air traffic demands and ever-expanding rosters. Despite the hard work and expectations of the airline, passengers would be greeted with confidence and a winning smile that would mask any individual hard luck.

The first two years of operation led to 1948 being a big year for BEA, with passenger numbers well into six figures. The fleet was expanding and new routes were launched. A milestone was reached when half a million passengers had been carried in one year. New corporate headquarters had been secured at Dorland House, Lower Regent Street. A separate passenger handling facility had been secured at Stafford Court, Kensington: the Kensington Air Station enabled swift transit from central London to Northolt. However, in 1948, BEA's role and function was about to be added to as political tensions in Berlin demanded more aircraft.

If joining BEA had promised the thrill of foreign travel and lots of flying then the company's role in the Berlin Airlift would provide a perspective on the cradle of political tensions that would last a further forty years. By July 1948, the Airlift was in full swing and on 4th August BEA was charged with the management of all British civil companies involved, as well as operating its own daily passenger services from Northolt to Berlin via Hamburg. My father would be a part of it. His base would be Hamburg.

Differing philosophies and objectives were revealed in 1945. The Soviets had got to the Elbe first, they wanted and had secured a piece of Old Germany and had an eye on the prize: Berlin. For America, Britain and the Soviet Union, bombs would be important in 1945. Not just bombs, but 'The Bomb': vulnerability in the stalemate of the 'Cold War'.

During the years 1945 and 1949, four words summarise the domestic situation in Britain: bread, blizzards, Berlin and 'The Bomb'. The domestic significance of bread and blizzards were characteristics of 1946 and 1947. However, in foreign and military terms mistrust would be the key defining characteristic of events in mainland Europe in 1948; part of the fallout of war. The marriage of convenience that brought Churchill, Eisenhower and Stalin together worked: mutual friends getting rid of an evil doctrine. But the two sides turned to face each other immediately afterwards. So much for the fraternal 1944 Royal Albert Hall concert commemorating twenty-five years of the Red Army!

In a Germany under western jurisdiction the objective was reconstruction, repatriation and getting things on an even keel. Social and economic stability were high on the agenda after fifteen years of doctrine, later realised as bigotry, cruelty and shame. The years immediately after the war enabled my father to see Germany in a beleaguered state of recovery teetering, he thought, on the edge of collapse.

Physically, the cities, though not all of them, had been ruined. The Potsdam Agreement of 1945 resulted in what would become the Federal Republic of Germany, but first it would be restructured. Initially it was administered across two zones by America and Britain: the romantic sounding 'Bizonia' gives some sense of place to what was otherwise a framework for bi-governmental administration. Later, a further zone would be administered by France. Imagination stretched to the working title 'Trizonia'.

Meanwhile, the Soviets held on to what would be, until 1990, East Germany. But, the Soviet Union was testing the West's resolve and in June 1948 wanted the French, the British and the Americans out of the island 'city state' of Berlin, far inside the German Democratic Republic. It was their actions that precipitated the crisis and the need for the airlift.

Logistically, Berlin's own French, British and American sectors were served from what was effectively a Soviet road and rail network. This created something of a vulnerable position which was tested by the Soviets who, in retaliation for steps towards an economic unification and the introduction of the Deutschmark, would take radical steps. The Soviets began to systematically interfere with road, rail and river-borne transport serving the western sector of Berlin. In June 1948 they cut off the electricity supply. No power and food dwindling. A city – and The West – being held to ransom. And not even a ransom; it was a case of being squeezed out. Here was the European manifestation of the Cold War; a new relationship.

Being cut off from a supply chain, West Berlin floundered and a major task unfolded in feeding and keeping warm a city of some 2,500,000 souls. This was, to the US, Operation Vittles. In Britain, the code-name was Plainfare. The airlift itself was a mammoth operation to serve the needs of people living in the western sector of Berlin, whose movements and power supply had been deliberately obstructed by the Soviets. Here was a vast stream of aircraft operating with frequency and intensity, forming an 'air bridge' across East Germany, along three air corridors twenty miles wide and 10,000 feet high connecting with Tegal, Gatow and Tempelhof Airports. In the process there were 280,000 flights carrying 2.5 million tons of cargo, over half a million tons of food and over 1.5 million tons of coal. Lives were lost but, apparently, no shots were ever fired.

My father's role was far from critical in terms of keeping the city provided with fuel oil, food, medicine and clothing, but he did play his part. His role was, in fact, much more people orientated. His passengers would be Berliners escaping to the Western Zone:

> *"Our task in those anxious days was to airlift as many Eastern Germans as possible and carry them to the West. The flights were conducted twice a day between Hamburg and Berlin; full loads on DC3 transports and very little in the way of comforts or amenities for the passengers and crew."*

At least two flights a day resulted in an intense relay from the East Zone to the West Zone and carrying NATO personnel to Hamburg or merely to the Berlin West Zone, landing at Tempelhof:

> *"It was a steady flow, backwards and forwards everyday. Catering was comparatively easy; it consisted of a lunch box with black bread, which went down well with the Germans, and a cup of coffee. The flight only lasted one and a half hours, but there were occasions when bad weather at Hamburg would necessitate a diversion to Dusseldorf, where a long wait would be needed before Hamburg weather had cleared."*

There were movements on a large scale which he saw placing great stress on the airlines of the time and also on the local and international administration when social and economic needs were paramount. The safety of passengers was also a concern.

On a return journey from Berlin the Viking – not a DC3 – my father was flying in encountered a fierce and unwelcome thunderstorm. The aircraft hovered over Hamburg in conditions that were vicious, making the flight rough and discomforting for the passengers.

The Viking is not a substantial airplane and as a state of alarm quickly took hold, my father, with limited German, attempted to put the passengers at ease. A fluent *'Sorgen Sie sich nicht, das Flugzeug ist sicher. Wir fliegen durch ein Gewitter'* did not spring easily to the tongue. His knowledge of meteorological and aeronautical German was not sufficient to instil much calm in an electrically and emotionally charged airplane. He did however attempt to convince them that this is what happens in a thunderstorm, nothing to worry about and we will be out of it in no time. All the time the plane is consuming precious fuel and has been refused, for the time being, permission to land.

The choices were not easy for the flight crew: divert to Dusseldorf through a widespread storm; hold out for clearance;

or go back to Berlin. But with the passengers only too glad to get out of Berlin they would not be keen on going back!

The plane circled and held on to its ability, if needed, to land at Hamburg, but as the sky grew darker and darker, there was suddenly a spectacularly vivid blue aura around the cabin completely lighting up the whole of the plane's interior.

This followed by a deafening bang sounding just like an anti-aircraft gun going off nearby:

> "It lasted only a fraction of a second but in that time everyone sensed doom. I was too busy with nervous women and children to feel any concern – we were still flying, the engines were working, and the normal sounds prevailed."

As the drama unfolded, a passenger called my father over 'Entschuldigen Sie mich, die Flügelspitze ist beschädigd'. The passengers drew breath in unison. Explaining the language situation, my father offered 'Bitte, ich nein spreche Deutsch sehr gut'.

Frantic pointing through the rain-splattered window followed. Looking out of the window, he could see the whole of the starboard wingtip was completely curled up like the lid of a tin can. The wing was twisted, but miraculously the control surfaces worked. By now the pilot had no choice. It was no longer a question of permission to land being withheld. He was now at the front of the line. An emergency landing procedure followed. Nervous Berliners were free and their lives intact.

At the time my father was staying in the Atlantic Hotel, usually for a period of seven to ten days. This was a truly splendid looking, elegant, Edwardian hotel. My father recalls The Atlantic Hotel being close to the Hauptbahnhof – the rail station – and overlooking the Great Alster. However, fixing the crippled airplane would lead to a three week stop-over with only the normal meal allowances to get you by.

Hamburg, heavily bombed and with fractured infrastructure, would be a desolate and inhibiting city. BEA's role was unpopular with cabin crew, with little in the way of free time. The suspicion would be perhaps that Hamburg's other notoriety would detract from very important duties.

My father observed that frequent changes of crew, as well as changing shift patterns, denied any opportunity for engagement with others. Without any allowances with which to truly enjoy European cities, my father found that the hotel would be the centre of exploration and a lonely existence it was too. The steward was one of one and where wartime attitudes prevailed, the three up front formed a tight band; a closed shop. The steward was always considered, in some way, 'below stairs'.

The cockpit crew of pilot, co-pilot and radio operator had wartime seniority and experience. The steward would sit at the back of the plane opposite the rear entrance door and adjacent to the toilet. My father had some pretty disparaging comments to make of his cockpit 'colleagues':

> *"Working with the crews was always a difficult task since each trip provided a new set of cockpit crew. There never was any informal relationship with the cockpit crew and each journey was made up of trying to establish some sort of camaraderie, but it was never to be. Even on night stops each member of the crew stuck rigidly to the 'rank' pattern — officers don't mix with other ranks."*

Meal times were far from comfortable. Wartime discipline prevailed:

> *"At meal times the atmosphere was always strained, the silence only broken when the skipper decided to introduce some sort of dialogue whereby it was socially acceptable. Usually the steward*

was completely ignored, which meant I did not enjoy any of their company and tended to eat on my own."

Yet again, rank would lead to the cockpit crew doing their thing whilst the sole steward was left to his own devices. Rank and privilege – class attitudes – meant that cabin stewards were 'a suffering minority':

"It was with a sense of loneliness that made stopovers not well-liked. One never became socially acquainted either with the crews or with other departments connected with the company. Left to my own devices it was a singular exercise to make the most of the situation.

But such conditions usually found relief in local bars, getting pleasantly intoxicated until the money ran out, then returning again to the hotel to suffer again the isolation."

Going to bars and seeing something of everyday life allowed some observations on Germany at a time when the British Army of the Rhine was an occupying force and the Cold War was establishing a currency through the events of the time and Churchill's famous 'Iron Curtain' speech two years previously. How right he was.

In the streets it was clear that the British were not popular with the locals. The feared German army was now a bunch of soldiers returning to civilian life and with little or no employment prospects.

In the Sergeants' Mess at Burtonwood, years before, my father had worked with German Prisoners of War and so was able to see at close hand the human aspect to conflict. This relationship would not have occurred but for the war and there is hint of sympathy when he ponders the similarity of the German and British military personnel adjusting to life in the new world.

He also saw a bitterness in what he described as:

> "An aura of disillusionment at having been reduced from the idyllic master race to one of humble servitude to the British Army of the Rhine. Their attitude toward the occupying powers was one of resentment and tolerance; a mix of insulting behaviour and aggressive opposition."

Based in Hamburg for one, two or three weeks at a time would let him experience the effects of the worst the Allied Forces could inflict on Germany. There were sporadic attacks before and after, but here was unprecedented damage on the city the results of which he would experience in 1949–1952.

Whether or not Arthur Harris actually said "sod 'em" is not known. Certainly "Gomorrah" emerged in the form of the name for the air raid operation which destroyed much of the core of Hamburg in 1943. Where my father was undergoing initial flying training in England, Bomber Command was hammering, pounding and *firestorming* Hamburg.

There is a *tit-for-tat* quality years later which enables us to rationalise our memory or attitude. There is exposed a simple analysis of war: they were doing it to us, we were doing it to them. The instrument that is aerial bombing was not new. Bombing campaigns were launched against German cities in 1918. Indeed, plans were afoot to extend the reach of offensive bombing with an attack on Berlin in 1919, had hostilities prolonged. As a man who found the work of Burns inspirational it is fitting that my father would see man's inhumanity to man. Where the legitimate target may have been the Blohm und Voss shipyards and their U-boat production capacity, it is clear that the majority of destruction was far from the river to the north east and to the north west, some distance beyond the industrial sectors.

The rationale for this conflagration may well have been that if the production facilities were not destroyed then there would be nobody to do the work. This principle was identified by Smuts thirty years previously. The scale of destruction was unprecedented. At the time, it was deemed justified and only history can judge the morality of decisions made in a command centre set in a hillside in High Wycombe. The reality is that bombs were being dropped on residential areas. In these areas would emerge the horror and terror of 45,000 dead in one week, of bomb blast and smoke inhalation of hellish persistent scale.

A combination of dry weather, intense incendiary activity and the structure of Hamburg in 'blocks' resulted in hell on Earth where heat radiation could cook meat, cause buildings to ignite, and melt glass: a *feuersturm* supported by estimated wind speeds of 120–170 mph, creating vacuum and suffocation. A crematorium on a metropolitan scale.

In addition to the death toll, 38,000 were injured, a million plus fled and over half the housing stock was wiped out. A proud city reduced to smoking roofless shells, jagged towers of brick and stone which from the air seemed like stalagmites devoid of any organic activity. A dead zone: the Forbidden Zone. The million who fled went as far as they could into nearby towns where local people were obliged to accommodate them. Some would encamp in woodland. Humanitarian effort led to 786,000 being evacuated in 625 trains.

Strangely, U-boat production would continue. Finally, the city would surrender in 1945, with Allied Forces only then dismantling the dock facilities.

By the time he was staying in the Atlantic Hotel in 1949, with Hitler being dead for less than four years, my father would be overlooking the Alster in an area curiously free of the ravages of the raids and which had not been damaged greatly. But within a quarter of a mile the damage was there to see at close hand:

unemployed, impoverished, disillusioned clinging to the edges of life and dignity. Housed in any shelter and being resentful of an occupying power. What had happened to them?

The contrast between his own comfortable life at the Atlantic Hotel made him reflect on being a bystander in a broken country with a home far to the west, across the North Sea. He had the comfort of a home and an infrastructure around him. For the ordinary German, just getting by presented enough difficulties without the added complications of the emerging Cold War:

> *"All this was happening while we were staying in the best hotels, eating the best food, while thousands were hungry and homeless. It was a pitiful time in our history."*

Across Europe there were unsettled economic conditions which led my father to observe that fiddles and perks were customary and that smuggling was rampant; the limited movement of goods between countries and with limited money in circulation a black market would emerge. And so in these conditions, crew and indeed customs officials, as well as locals saw opportunity to get by a little better than would have otherwise been the case. Inevitably, money would perform a very important diplomatic and practical function.

For my father this meant casual enterprise in the international movement of ordinary duty free goods. He would buy duty free whisky at, say, Copenhagen and it would be sold on in Stockholm. Brandy was also a good seller. But this was just the tip of the iceberg. Changing foreign currency was also lucrative as many passengers would want additional money where fiscal policy would limit the amount taken out of a country. And so it was that, according to my father, the rate of exchange was based on passenger ignorance. There were also vodka cocktails that he would sell to passengers, pocketing the money!

The turmoil and instability of the markets at the time meant a need for paper money to hold value and for escapees to be financially 'liquid'. In this context it was seen that the Swiss franc was especially desirable because, like the dollar, it was a hard currency.

At the time of the occupation, the currency for military or visiting BEA personnel was BAFs for use in the NAAFI. These were British Armed Forces vouchers, or tokens, which looked like currency. Deutschmarks were not issued and were, in fact, a new currency.

The Reichsmark was discontinued in 1948 and the move towards introducing the Deutschmark precipitated the Berlin Blockade.

Through whatever trade they were engaged in, German nationals could secure these BAFs and get access to a greater assortment of goods and essentials than the local shops. In addition, my father, with valuable local currency, was able to purchase goods, foreign goods that were expensive in Britain, but which could be obtained cheaply on the continent.

Articles being cheaper abroad and generally easily obtained would be sought by many customs staff. This provided a steady secondary income. Returning to England laden with goodies meant that the customs officers had been bribed or were receiving European goods and so luggage was never checked. Typically, the customs officer at Northolt would place an order for some foreign goods which my father would purchase with Deutschmarks. And so the scheming, scamming nature of post-war life existed between individuals working across continents.

BAFs put in place a restriction on what you could spend and where you could spend it. Faced with seven to ten day stays or perhaps three week stays, inevitably the lure of the cities' emerging bright lights would tantalise. What does a ten bob BAF get you? Caffeine makes a return appearance here, for

Deutschmarks could be procured in return for coffee which was brought over from Britain. Glee is evident in the comment that "usually forty kilos would bring in plenty of Deutschmarks!!"

> "We mostly carried coffee which was highly prized in Germany where it was non-existent and, from our point of view, was a quick and easy way to get our hands on Deutschmarks. The other way to get local currency was to sell our BAFs to the Germans."

There is something of a recurring theme to my father's post-war existence. The ambition of youth and the fulfilment of a dream has given way to disillusionment, doubtless cynicism and crime: petty crime, opportunistic crime, acceptable crime for the time maybe, but crime nonetheless. Yet even if one examines the fact that criminal activity is taking place, one cannot help but marvel at the audacity, ingenuity and romance of it all!

Just months before, working between Dover and Dunkerque, his supply of caffeine had contributed to French energy levels. Yet despite the lesson before the French courts, the coffee running continued in an almost cavalier fashion. Here was a routine and a very profitable exercise that would now be justified in terms of bringing much-needed coffee to a beleaguered German public. The man is undeterred, and for one who loved flying so much, he had a predilection for a different kind of 'ground' duty:

> "Getting the ground coffee through German customs was usually well-organised. Arrangements were made with the ground staff that coffee was hidden behind the food trays. The trolleys would carry the canisters to the kitchens where the coffee was collected before the trays were washed.

> "The money transacted was paid by the driver of the mini-bus which carried us from the airport to the hotel. I always carried a

small quantity of coffee in my valise for the hotel staff who were
always very grateful for this hard-to-come-by commodity."

The commodity was capable of buying almost anything:

> *"Coffee was more highly prized than gold. I personally carried*
> *two large travel bags of coffee every time I did a run to*
> *Germany — around about twenty kilos…it was rapidly*
> *siphoned off without customs officials knowing anything about*
> *it. And it provided me with a substantial reward of precious*
> *Deutschmarks."*

By now a long-term pattern of smuggling had developed.
What money was gained was most likely frittered away or made
up losses; there were temptations in gambling, drink, prostitutes
in Hamburg, who knows? In the context of late 40s/early 50s
life, one can assume that there was a lot of corrupt activity going
on as the austerity of the period lingered. Back at Northolt, it was
the customs officers who, apparently and allegedly, were guilty of
similar indiscretions:

> *"Always wanting stewards to bring back European goodies was*
> *a regular practice. Usually cigars from Germany, perfume and*
> *lingerie from Paris, watches and clocks from Switzerland.*
>
> *"All items were eagerly purchased by the Customs and Excise*
> *who, in return, would turn a blind eye to whatever goods the*
> *steward brought in for his own personal gain."*

The apparent ease of shifting what were huge quantities
of coffee resulted from the solitary nature of the steward's
position. Teamwork may have been evident on the ground in

doing the work, but airside my father would be on his own. The steward always sat at the rear of the plane. For the steward, such conditions would require good management of the limited space available. Space would be found for two bags. Where the steward was accustomed to taking on board his own hand luggage then this would be stowed beside the bar. If the standby steward was on duty then, similarly, the baggage would be safely placed.

However, momentary lapses in this routine procedure would occur. Flying out from Northolt en route to Hamburg, stopping at Amsterdam, the plane my father was on got to some 500 feet up when he looked and saw that two cases full of coffee were not on board! They had been left behind in the crew room at Northolt.

These bags did not have identity tags and were not locked. Had they been discovered then my father's activities could have become known. Mid-flight he knew that if the contents had been discovered, then he would have to disown the bags and what was in them.

Cool as a cucumber, he disengaged his safety belt and walked to the cockpit and explained to the captain that his overnight bags had been inadvertently left behind. As both planes were scheduled to be on the tarmac at Amsterdam at the same time, there was a chance that steward and baggage would be reunited. Helpful as ever, the captain contacted Northolt by radio and had the two bags airlifted on the next flight to Amsterdam! The bags duly arrived before my father's plane took off for Hamburg. Sheer luck. It was not long before the contents were distributed through the usual channels.

His job expressed many demands as the airlines grew steadily in the years immediately after the war. Yet still he was an opportunist who saw chances to profit from illicit trade borne of uniform and the fact that he could credibly proceed undetected through channels and ports of entry. Obviously he was British and had authority, and who would challenge this in the late 1940s as Europe sought to rebuild itself ? The baggage incident at Amsterdam reminded him of how fortunate he was, but also how lucky and potentially stupid he nearly was. The smuggler's life seemed miles away from the West London life back home at the far end of the Piccadilly line in apparently safe suburbia. It was hard work doing the normal job, but harder still maintaining the conceit of a *contrabandista*.

Despite the strain, the stability of airline work supplemented by other forms of export/import remuneration, provided a good enough income to rent a flat in Harrow, not far from Northolt; not bad for the failed chicken farmer and struggling window cleaner of 1947. Professional and, by 1949, his personal life was beginning to take shape.

In the spring of 1949, whilst passing through the airport at Paris, my father met a young Frenchwoman, Paulette. Who she was, what she did, what she looked like are not recorded, but one can speculate on a good looking French girl with gallic charm to match. The sheer effort of sustaining an international relationship with the demands of a growing airline added further strain, rewarded by limited periods together in Paris. The joy and escapism of this relationship was severely tested in the summer of 1949.

As a life with Paulette was beginning, so another part of his life was closing. The independence of the previous ten years would be shattered in June 1949, when George Duncan dies from a pulmonary embolism, arising from a combination of phlebitis and varicose veins. He was fifty-two years old. This was an event never once talked about, but it transpires that George Duncan died at 9.30am, shortly after arriving at work at the Labour Exchange offices on Dock Street, Dundee. The circumstances of the death warranted a report to the Procurator Fiscal.

Little was mentioned of his demise; my father did not regret his passing. The violent upbringing with servitude was one thing, the corrupt dealings as civil servant and the interference with the dream of flying were disturbing memories of this infuriating relationship. For all the duties as a young boy and for all the sending of money back home, George Duncan not once expressed any gratitude or humility. In desperation my father turned to him for assistance when the chicken farm failed, but he was pissed on.

Where the treatment by him of Jeanie Duncan had, in my father's words, been unforgivable, there is revealed my father's faithful disposition towards his mother that his father did not enjoy. It is difficult to read depths of maternal love, or even affection, but there was always a concern to see that she was 'alright'. Jeanie Duncan was widowed at the age of forty-eight.

Meanwhile, the death has meant hastily arranged journeys back north to Dundee – he signed the death certificate not regretting his passing – balanced with the demands of airline duties in Berlin and Hamburg, further flights to Paris and the pressure of standby duty.

By July 1949, he and Paulette were planning a life together. The fact that he eventually got her over to England suggests some administrative or political difficulty. Perhaps, though, it was simple reluctance on the part of the young girl whose own family were, after all, French and where familial bonds had hardened through the ravages of war. For a young Frenchwoman to simply up sticks and relocate to a different country with different ways would have required some contemplation, but move she did. The civil side of the Berlin Airlift and BEA's involvement in it ceased in September 1949. The following month, my father and Paulette married and settled into something of a domestic life in the Harrow flat.

What an exciting contrast to life in France! Outer West London, the edge of a huge capital city recovering from war, but still coping with post-war austerity. Miles from home and the promise of a better life with the handsome Scotsman who would be working with BEA.

This relationship may have begun with the best of intentions, but was doomed from the start as the absences and time spent apart would contribute to domestic dysfunction and ultimately failure. Ever increasing flight schedules and long periods away from home meant that the anticipated comfort of married life in 1949 was in contrast to how the work demands and personal choices of my father would affect them later. Alas, my father's life at this point was succumbing to so many external pressures.

The uncertainty of airline rosters – standby duty being a particular hell – creating an all-consuming professional life for the aircrew: it was neither part-time, nor full-time. With little or no regularity and the ever-increasing demands of the airlines, this created a 'whole time' occupation of inconvenient hours and hard work. When my father did come home from, say, two or three week stays in Berlin or Hamburg, it was for very short periods. Periods that were short enough to father a daughter. At the time of their marriage in October 1949, Paulette was three months pregnant.

1949 had seen the emergence of a planetary alignment of very evident emotional, psychological and physical strains: marriage and death, fatherhood, hard work and international travel. Striving for stability, trying to make things work and adjusting to a Franco-British way of life in West London contrasted with my father's own upbringing. How could normal family life exist in such extraordinary circumstances? With the absences from the family home necessary with BEA's schedules, Paulette's mother joined the family to support her daughter and grand-daughter in a period of distinct need. A second daughter followed in 1952 and a new, cheaper flat was found.

At the centre of some emotional maelstrom he simply did not know how to deal with domestic and professional pressures. Upbringing and poverty, no parental role model in George Duncan, careers in the RAF and BEA both heavily cosseted from the fear and romantically free of the humdrum of war, and no responsibility. Self-admittedly, years later, he had problems. There seemed to be no way out of the impasse. His self-esteem was haemorrhaged in what is revealed as a solitary and lonely existence, his feelings of failure and the out-and-out rejection of him by establishments, either parental or institutional in the RAF had created a cynical, criminal, dejected, individual.

His emotional state was fragile, even suicidal: money problems, work schedule demands, language difficulties, parental duties and expectations, father's death, mother's plight and his brother and sister also seeing disintegration and looking forward to getting on and moving away. By now he was into a depression described as insidious; an obsession with futility. These feelings – a darkness – seemed to stay with him into his later years. Drinking very heavily fuelled his anger and frustration. Drinking, he said, was a form of escapism that was indulgent and spreading like a disease. He was helpless to control it and actually did not want to control it! He was drinking at home and at work and finally on the airplanes. Following the birth of his second daughter in

1952, the burden of responsibility grew. Money problems meant smuggling coffee was a necessary occupation. This was not a good life for Paulette and their young family.

There is something selfish in the commentary he makes, citing his duties with the airline, but offering no appraisal of his duties as a husband and father. He wrote that he had to 'contend' with a French wife and mother-in-law who would converse in French and with intermittent translations of what they wanted him to hear but, as he says, "that was no excuse either."

*"I did not appreciate what I had but succeeded slowly but surely
to throw it all away. The erosion of my married life was on
a sure course to complete destruction and I simply did nothing
about it. Matters came to a head when I lost my job with the
airlines. I was drunk on duty and was dismissed."*

And yet he says he was relieved, for this was one thing less
to deal with! Yet still he was clinging on to the flying dream,
desperately waiting on tables at the United States Air Force
facility at South Ruislip. He did not fully recall any particular act
that brought about the breakdown of the marriage, but it is all
too clear in terms of location, career, domestic circumstances in
Dundee and the feelings of abject failure. It was a combination
of circumstances. 1949 triggered so much.

Marriage lasted only a short period and his failings preyed
on his conscience for years afterwards. For Paulette, the situation
was too much: no longer the handsome husband, but a dismissed
depressive without uniform, no career, ever-smaller and cheaper
flats, second hand furniture, money and language problems and
two young children, no friends or family and left alone for long
periods, married but with no husband.

For my father, the period 1948–1954 was known as the
'Nightmare Years'. The initial financial setbacks of the chicken
farm and the difficulties of getting back into Civvy Street started
a process that would lead to heavy drinking in an effort to cope
with a tumult of conflicting emotions; he was close to breakdown.
He had a new family structure with a wife, mother-in-law and
children, there were money problems, his own mother's health
and loneliness preyed on him.

Life had been too much, too quickly and although my
father tried to shrug off the life-stage difficulties as phases
or problems that would resolve themselves, no solutions were
being offered. The actual reasons for the breakdown were not

fully understood by my father. He presumed a combination of circumstances and various pressures. For Paulette, she was the one left to cope with the meagre amounts of money he could give her, not knowing when he would be coming home or what frame of mind he would be in.

Recollections were vague and confusing. There is clarity, though, in his returning from a continental trip only to find the flat empty and devoid of life. The flat was rented unfurnished and Paulette's presence and that of the children was gone. Personal effects had been completely removed. Paulette and her mother, the two children, left and stayed in West Drayton. The marital home, the flat where a family was being raised, was transferred to an American serviceman who was stationed nearby. In time, Paulette would meet someone else and applied for a divorce. In my father's words:

> "The damage had been done. Paulette had met someone else − I never found out who it was − and she decided to apply for a divorce. I was drinking a lot at this time which didn't help matters. So it came to an end ... I am prepared to accept the blame for what happened, but at the time I could not seem to marshal sufficient disciplined actions to relieve or improve the relationship.

> "It is only now on reflection that I realise a lot of the trouble lay with me. It was a lifestyle of devil-may-care because I could not see how to stabilise the circumstances and settle down. I did not appreciate what I had, but succeeded slowly but surely to throw it all away. The erosion of my married life was on a sure course to complete destruction and I simply did nothing about it."

By 1953 my father would be living in Greenford and back to a life of factory working, as if it was still 1939. Despite aptitude and attainment with the RAF, despite the adventure of wartime and pilot training, the immediate post-war years were not characterised by resettlement. Rather the opposite: unsettlement.

He wound up waiting on tables at London Airport. They were looking for a waiter with experience of silver service and with his years of airline passenger service, he had the *bona fides* and was suited to the post. Travelling by bicycle to and from London Airport added some time to the working day. One hour each way. The money was reasonable, but otherwise the job was boring. He says though, that the meals were very substantial and very good. Again, some evidence that he liked his grub and maybe did not care for rationing. From there he found work in a pub.

The Red Lion was a very pleasant looking, very traditional looking sixteenth century pub overlooking the green at Hillingdon; a quaint-looking English hostelry in the manner of a chocolate box coaching inn on the road to Oxford.

This part of outer London is now a sprawling mass of urbanisation, fuelled by road, rail and airport expansion. In the early 50s there was still something of a parochial quality to the community of Hillingdon. Little would be known of the scale of London's future growth in the subsequent post-war years.

I have vague recollections of my father singing a 'jingle' about *Watney's Keg Red Barrel*. And I can only assume it dates from this period. It is ironic, though, that my father should end up in bar work.

There is a steady decline in fortunes and here he is in casual and very insecure work, ill-suited to his frame of mind at the time. This work as a barman lasted for about four weeks and was a job that, with long hours, would occupy his mind and provide some steadying routine in an otherwise wayward life.

There was risk, though. The hours were 8am to 3pm and then from 4pm until midnight. Hard work and long laborious hours were balanced with a degree of will to impress and maybe even a desire to turn a corner. Dependability and trust with his employer were being built. He was the head barman and this trust led him to be in charge when the publican and his wife went to a licensed victuallers' meeting. My father was in charge with one female assistant.

Bars tend to run in patterns. Waves of intense activity around lunchtime and again in the early evening after work, another lull and then busy again from 8 or 9pm onwards until last orders.

Unusually, from around 6pm things were getting busy and as is often the case the customer would tip the barman – "have a drink yourself ". The equivalent in money might go into the tips glass. Some discipline is shown; a restraint from 6pm until 9pm:

> *"Of course I declined their offers but put the money in an empty glass which we later shared between us. But from nine o'clock onwards I started to sip a couple of drinks and this got steadily worse as the night went on. I mean I was giving drinks to people who should have paid but didn't."*

The place was now heading for a party atmosphere, the barman a garrulous, ebullient celebrity, lauded by a wealth of new-found friends. Jokes, laughter, camaraderie all fuelled by free beer and spirits. By now the female assistant is getting more than a little concerned.

She has never seen the place like this and knows full well that the landlord is not going to be happy. My father was becoming a nuisance and, in his own words, was "pissed out of his mind". When the landlord returned he was formally dismissed:

> *"An inevitable outcome to a hilarious evening as bar boss."*

Where to next? By now living in shared accommodation in Greenford, my father found thoroughly uninteresting work in the ornate art deco Hoover factory on the Great Western Road as a machine operator, armature shaft balancing to be precise. Behind the beautiful lines of this now listed building, interestingly and years later part-occupied by a major retail store, he was part of the post-war recovery in manufacturing and in a life far removed from the glamour of flight.

The desire, as a young man, was to set himself free from the drudgery and lack of space, light and freedom of factory life. Yet here he was, enslaved by circumstances. What on earth was he playing at? What interest did he have in vacuum cleaners? The answer is he had no interest whatsoever. Assembly processes for vacuum cleaners provided an income; a means to get by. Life did, indeed, suck.

From there he found rather more interesting work with Aladdin Heaters as a process operator. One can only assume that this was better paid, but still mind-numbingly dull for my father. But, in all, Aladdin and Hoover were but temporary occupations. Finally, there was a desperate effort to get back into aviation as a process operator with Fairey, working out of their factory in Hayes. At least he was involved in the manufacturing of something he had an affinity with. The time spent in Springburn in 1939 was something of an investment and at least Cunliffe-Owen had trained him up to become an airframe fitter. He knew airplanes. Work with Fairey would provide an income and keep him afloat. The last post.

15

Contemplating the Naval

L ife in West London was over. My father left Uxbridge. It is 1954. Professional and personal failure lay heavy in the weakened soul that my father became. The adventure and fortune of the war years was now a memory far distant from what was now the selfish, self-absorbed emptiness and drunken loneliness of depression and dejection.

The King is dead and a new Elizabethan era has begun: the end of rationing and the winding-down of Marshall Aid, increased productivity and the new Queen Elizabeth on the thrown. The country was looking forward and the monochrome of the war years were fading in memory. This was a confident age of gay colours and the *contemporary* look. Music was different. No longer the swing bands of Miller and Dorsey. No, this was the time for solo vocalists and new names like Eddie Calvert and David Whitfield. My father went solo as well, as low as he could possibly get.

He had now jacked-in the absolute dullness that was work with Hoover, Aladdin and, finally, Fairey Aviation. There was nothing that manufacturing vacuum cleaners or paraffin heaters could fulfil. The bit part in an aircraft factory was the last vestigial association with a flying career. Engineering training had been something of a fall-back position at least, but he was struggling with the adjustment to what he felt should be normative family life – so lacking in his own upbringing – and facing up to the personal responsibility necessary in peacetime.

He was in a tailspin and had to summon the energy to pull out. The freedom he craved had been supplanted by the production-line routine of *Modern Times*, the film made famous by Charlie Chaplin. Routine was one thing, domestic pressures were another. His mother was a widow recovering from surgery; brother and sister were doing their own thing and respectively bound for new lives in Australia and the United States. Suddenly, it was just him; his desire, if not necessity, was to go home.

On the platform at King's Cross Station, ticket in his pocket, he would shuffle through the crowd, past the hugs and kisses, the carts, the newspaper sellers, through the smoke and the steam. More space than in wartime, but still the same incessant and relentless clickety-click, clickety-click of a northbound steam train following the wearisome, but by now nationalised British Rail, East Coast route, perhaps this time getting more than a pie and cup of sooty tea.

A long train journey is a good time for introspection and soul-searching. A life that had been so rich was now gone. With his possessions now carried over his shoulder, he would also be carrying emotional baggage. He left home at sixteen years of age to train in Glasgow. He was independent of his parents but sending money back home when he could. There were intermittent visits back home in the intervening years, but the RAF had given him a kit bag and postings and a long lost dream of flight. Only in Kent did he have the beginning of a place to stay, and later with Paulette he had the basis for a happy settled life. The failed chicken farm brought him home, the death of his father brought him home.

Kent and Uxbridge were only yesterday and a million miles away from the gloomy memories he was now saddled with. In such dire circumstances, home was yet again the default position. The saddened, dejected and morose character contrasted with the beaming enthusiasm of the young student pilot, resplendent and confident, in St John's Wood in 1943. Such confidence was buoyed by his classification: AI pilot material. Self-esteem was now shot and the prospects were far from certain. Strange what ten years could do to a man.

He was saying goodbye to his international life. Despite growing up in the green fields of Angus and the mills and foundries of Dundee, my father's life blood had, in fact, been very English and South African, European and certainly French. The geographic and professional as well as, shall we say, unprofessional, romance of his varied life and what had been a love for Paulette, would result in that northbound journey. Past Home County, East Midlands, Yorkshire and North East, he would find a border across which he would be home. My father returned to Dundee and for all the recollections of life as a young boy and as an adolescent, the family life at '63' had, in fact, provided a home, well, of sorts. It would be a place to return to in 1954. Here was a base that might enable him to turn his back on the misadventure of the last six years and maybe look to the future. He is thirty years old.

The rail bridge over the River Tay has not the impressive iconography of the Forth Bridge or even the Brooklyn or Golden Gate Bridges. However, it does have history as the second rail bridge to have been built across the river, the first having been blown down in the gale of December 1879. The new bridge was stronger yet maintained some of the idiosyncrasies of its predecessor. The bridge is not straight and this small matter of engineering bends the final stages of the journey affording passengers looking eastwards a prospect towards Dundee and the mouth of the river.

The bridge is also elevated from platform level, and here a metaphor for the state of his life. As the train pulled around the wide sweep of the north side of the Tay Bridge it would meet a long downward slope, grinding its wheels to a complete stop. How appropriate.

The journey home in 1954 was prophetic and practical and as my father settled-in as best he could and, desperate for work, he realised this was a changed town. Despite the war to end all wars, the great leveller of class, and now with a Welfare State in place, personal progress was still being restrained. The pre-war poverty had given way to conflict, thence to rationing and the emergence of the Cold War. The economy was taking years to stabilise and his emotional state was equally far from steady. When would this cycle end? Self-defeat, a life thwarted, were now hallmarks. The reality is that for fifteen years since 1939 he had been insulated from just that: reality and its responsibilities. Devil-may-care wanderlust had sustained him so far. As for the future, well, the prospect of factory work was there and consumer-led growth was everywhere. But did he really want to stay in Dundee?

His mother, my grandmother, was in her mid-fifties and coping, post eye surgery, as a widow with a meagre pension and grown-up family. Seemingly life had not moved on. 63 was even more cold and austere. It was always old-fashioned, but by now it was dated and would stay that way for a further fifteen years. All in all it would be home to my grandmother for thirty-five years, from 1935 to 1970. On my father's return home in 1954 he would realise that this was the home of an adolescent, a boy, who had left to enter the big wide world in 1939. So much had gone on in his life, and the world, in these fifteen short years.

He was now man and had seen foreign travel and opportunity. 63 represented claustrophobia, history and failure. If it badly needed maintenance in 1935, it certainly did in 1954. For Jeanie Duncan, there were financial problems of rent not paid, medical bills and whatever limited income there was meant that my father would have to support his mother; here the cruel irony that after the years of servility and beatings, he was still bailing out the family and, in a way, continuing to patch-up the failure of his father's ways.

Settling a few domestic problems, getting things in order and seeing that his mother was comfortable enough would be priorities, but the return home was fraught with difficulty. The *papier mâché* was still in the wall and the range was still in the kitchen. What was there in childhood, was still there in the mid-50s.

Perhaps he was a beggar being choosy, and it was certainly wrong to be so particular after his own failings, but the absolute constraint of 63 compared with the freedom of the likes of Hamburg, Lisbon or Paris was hard to take. His mother was now older and more dependent. Kent and Uxbridge had been a hard experience, but home was now testing his ability to settle. Would nothing change? Was there terminal decline at every turn?

The retur n to Dundee may have resulted from loyalty and feelings of obligation to look after his mother, yet the inability to settle down and lure of an easy passage seem to be overpowering factors. There is restlessness and the inability to settle. There is a new family order; just him and a widowed mother. Dundee could not fulfil that innate desire to be free. It seems strange in hindsight to see a man who was not averse to hard work, who could have had more focus and direction, who could have saved and pursued a flying career, but didn't.

Fear of a working life in a factory focussed his attention in altogether different areas. He liked the thrill and honour of being an RAF pilot, but why appear content later to wait on people? Was servility a characteristic borne of his childhood experiences of domestic cruelty? Here in Dundee the choices, and the scope to make those choices, were limited. He was grounded, but always he wanted to fly. He liked the freedom it provided. The choices now were more fundamental, though, than what type of factory work. A harsh decision had to be made: stay or move on?

Walking downhill from 63 Constitution Road takes you south towards the town centre; across Bell Street and its rather stately well-to-do tenements of homes, offices and meeting rooms, over Ward Road and into the part of town where the print district places its mark on the medieval past of the city. The offices of D C Thomson – *The Courier Building* – watch over the sixteenth century cemetery – *The Howff.*

Farther still and you reach the commercial heart of the old Overgate, its dark and seemingly ancient pattern of rows and narrow streets giving way to the dock area beyond. Not just one, but lots of docks with ships from India and Pakistan carrying unprocessed jute, those from the Baltic carrying wood. And farther down river, shipyards. There were still shipyards.

Ten years later, much of this would be razed to make way for the road bridge landfall. Docks would be filled-in, the trains seemingly going down the middle of the street, carrying goods to the dock area, would be gone and, curiously, this would explain why the town has a lighthouse 300 feet inland from the river. Years later the remnant Camperdown and Victoria Docks would seem tucked away to one side but at the time they stretched right into the heart of the city. Town and dock meeting at the Grassmarket, at the time a bus terminus.

At the bottom of Union Street is the West Station. The beautiful Victoria Arch, now long since demolished, welcomes and farewells trade, crew and passenger. There is a beauty in the neo-gothic splendour of so much that is now gone. Only historic photographs make apparent such shame. The quayside gave way to cranes, then wharves and storage sheds smelling of timber, tar and the faint whiff of whisky bonds. Sinister beyond that was the gasworks and refinery, huge expanses of the smelliest, foulest and most dangerous industries congregated either side of the imaginatively-named Dock Street and, parallel with it, the Dundee to Aberdeen rail line.

At the bottom of Trades Lane, and at the heart of this, is the East Station, a simple arched building with a large fanlight window at either end, seemingly fighting a losing battle, darkened by the build up of decades of soot. This is another building long gone, but at the time, a devilish hall of steam, whistles and smoke.

Across the wide cobbled street with its rail lines and tramlines running sinuously and in the midst of the warehouses and sheds is moored a most imperious and splendid three storey, stone-built, double-fronted Georgian mansion, with a high central portico of Ionic pillars and carved pediments. Probably more at home in Edinburgh's New Town or Bath, this richly decorated edifice comprised the offices of the Harbour Board and sat immediately opposite the very humble, but comforting for many, seamen's mission.

In 1954 this area was still where the seafaring trades met within the commercial heart of the town. It was where modes of transport congregated and it presented four choices for my father: head north by train, head south by train, go to sea, or stay. In the midst of this industrious and busy part of town lay a decision. A stark choice it was: stay and work in a factory or take advantage of the prospect of the closest thing to the freedom of flight, a chance to be free of dry land and rid of emotional baggage.

The choice of staying in Dundee or moving on was made a little easier by the fact that his mother was coping after the succession of eye operations and the death of her husband five years previously.

Between the Harbour Board building and the East Station was a small, easily disregarded, stone building, but one which would provide an escape route for my father: the Shipping

Federation office. Years before, in 1948, he had travelled back to Dundee expecting some good fortune when the chicken farm failed. The long journey back to Dover led him to the Shipping Federation office there. Here in Dundee, the same institution would bail him out. It would also provide income, a roof, and no obvious responsibility. By now, this building had greater emotional significance: the Labour Exchange building at 54 Dock Street was practically opposite. The spectre of George Duncan, who had died there in 1949, may well have expedited my father's departure.

Standing in line with other hopefuls, his demeanour was different, more worldly, yet common denominators prevailed. All were desperate. My father was ever-willing to please and oblige, he would want to impress upon the clerks his military experience, knowledge of language and how to deal with demanding customers. This would have placed him in a different category to the stevedore or deckhand. I don't suppose at the time he was fussy, though, more relieved at the prospect of these skills being of value to him and his employer. Experience was his passport. Luck was on his side and having stood in line he would leave content in the knowledge that he would not be staying in Dundee for too much longer.

Suffice it to say his success with the Shipping Federation would see him appointed to the SS Oronsay. Experience of silver service was doing him proud; a passport, which with whatever airs and graces he could muster from his foreign travels, would see him through a career befitting of the Orient Line's (later P&O's) investment in what was, at the time, the pride of Orient's fleet. And what a ship it was!

The Oronsay was a magnificent, virtually brand-new, £4.3 million vessel with over 600 crew, the latest furnishings and interior designs. At 28,000 tons and over 700 feet long this ship was, for her time, a colossus, or so my father thought. She was also excitingly modern, having been launched and completed in 1951. Perhaps not so handsome as current cruise ships, with cranes and winch gear as well as tropical open balconies, she was designed for freight and passengers, was very well appointed and strongly handsome, with a beautifully designed curved stern:

> *"My first impression of the Oronsay was its immensity. I hadn't seen a ship as big since I sailed in the Mauritania from Cape Town after leaving South Africa."*

The interior was contemporary: all clean lines and mahogany or sapele wood; very glamorous for the age and, in the true sense of the word as used in the 1950s, it was gay. The design was a break from the utility of wartime troop ships or the earlier cruising ships of the Edwardian era and in view of her Hebridean name was given a most Scottish interior branding – The Tam O'Shanter Lounge, the Duke of Edinburgh Suite. This was a purpose-built, post-war ocean-going cruise liner, designed especially for the long haul of the Indian Ocean and the Pacific Ocean: an Elizabethan ship and always Scottish. What my father hadn't realised was that even this ship had its own hard luck story; the drama of having suffered a major fire before being launched.

In 1950, whilst being built at Barrow-on-Furness, a fire had taken hold in her cork insulation whilst in the shipyard. As a result of the amount of water used to quell the slow burning, but intense, fire she lay on her side at something of a twenty degree angle. Think about it, though: a ship filled with water? Ships are meant to be waterproof. How do you let the water out? In the case of the *Oronsay*, you cut a huge hole. Patched-up and finally launched, her role was to cross not just water or seas, but vast oceans.

And so apparently within days of returning 'home', he was southward bound, clickety-click, clickety-click; Dundee to King's Cross, and on to Canning Street Station. Eastwards into Essex, across a war-damaged, pock-marked, yet expanding 'East End': a *Far* East End where council housing programmes were extending into Essex. Parts of Poplar, Silvertown and Beckton conjoining with Stratford, Dagenham and Hornchurch in the outward spread of the capital. The River Thames, as a complete series of ports all doing different things, was alive with the buoyancy of the time and the massive Ford plant was an icon of economic prosperity, the future and a celebration of life and work on the river.

As the expansion of urban London gave way to green fields at South Ockendon and Grays, the low, sinister, fog-bound flatlands of the Thames came into view, together with the sheer scale and industry of Tilbury Docks: the unromantic point of embarkation set within fleets and marshes of the lower reaches of the Thames, down-river of the Isle of Dogs and the City of London. Here was an opportunity to get away. For ten years, England had been his base. Various parts of England, in fact, and a little bit of Wales, and now Essex. The opportunism of that trip to the Shipping Federation office was now providing free food, not a care in the world, income, and foreign travel. Thirty-one years old and no obvious responsibilities.

One minute in Dundee, the next sailing out of the Thames Estuary towards the English Channel, Essex to port and Kent to starboard and in the distance the lights of Canvey Island and Southend. Only the previous year, in 1953, had this area, and others around the east coast, been affected by the biggest flood disaster in recent times.

Under the command of Captain Blake, all would enjoy the Orient Line experience. Balconies, promenade decks, sports facilities and first class lounge and dining room facilities would greet the passengers and provide an antidote to the years of austerity and lingering hardships of the time. With all the certainty the Orient Line could provide, this would be comfortable passage for the many whom would be emigrating or visiting far off family.

Gay it may have appeared, but the daytime entertainment seems rather staid and limited. This was a large ship for the time, but relatively small by today's standards: about a quarter of the size. No sign here of the purpose-built cinemas and show theatres, multiple bars and fine dining experiences. Throughout the cruise one could enjoy card games such as contract bridge or canasta. There was also *housie housie*, or bingo as we term it today, and a race meeting which was probably newsreel footage of horse racing backed with limited betting.

For the more active, one could enter the deck quoits competition or table tennis singles. Light music, provided by the ship's orchestra, was played daily in the lounge, and in the evening fancy dress cocktail parties and, the highlight – the Gala Dance. The atmosphere would be one of polite, genteel couples and families seeing something of the world and maybe moving overseas. In Australia, passengers would disembark at Queensland or Victoria. All very 50s, all very British, my father would be awestruck by the contrast of life on board and the life that had greeted him post-RAF. Here was no sign of struggle, or hardship or rationing. This was luxury on a scale which he had not seen, probably ever. Amidst the greyness of a Tilbury morning, this gleaming white and corn-gold coloured ship must have seemed like a floating palace. He would go to the ball!

He reported initially to the purser and was then sent to get his first steward's uniform. He was now beginning a career as a First Class Dining Room Steward. He then went to his cabin, shared with three others.

The first cruise was a short Mediterranean trip to Gibraltar, Marseilles, Naples, Malta, returning via Sardinia, the Balearic Islands, through Gibraltar and back to London. Two weeks leave and a trip back home to Dundee where the limited pay, but good tips, would help to clear his mother's debts which lingered following George Duncan's passing, plus medical bills and poor housekeeping.

Here he was, still looking after things at home, very much in the manner he had when he was a boy. Following the two weeks leave and another train south, he was again assigned to the Oronsay, but this cruise was a little longer. In fact it was to last six months: Gibraltar, Port Said, Port Suez, Colombo, Papua New Guinea, Perth, Adelaide, Melbourne, Sydney, Tasmania, Auckland, Fiji Islands, Hawaii, San Francisco, Los Angeles. No one I know has been to Port Moresby in Papua New Guinea, but my father made it on his second voyage with the Orient Line. And I know nothing about this, other than the fact he was there. No indication of passing through the Panama Canal and so my father describes the return to London, dismissively and without importance, as being pretty much by the same route.

The expectation would be that excitement and curiosity would drive some fascination with these wonderfully romantic, far-off, destinations. The journey through the Suez Canal would surely elicit some emotional response, crossing the vast Indian Ocean was a complete contrast to the packet boats of the English Channel. What thrill in docking at Colombo, there the strange sights and sounds of orient emerging as Ceylon (at the time) floats amidst the trading routes from Malaysia and China. Then southwards, crossing the Equator, where captains would present passengers with commemorative cer tificates authenticated by Neptune!

The bowels of a ship and shift work would compromise these experiences, after all, this wasn't a holiday. But curious to me is the absence of recollection. Sunsets, heat, language, scenery, sounds, smells and camaraderie would gel, normally, into memories of being there. But no, and there was a reason for this.

Given the hardships that had been experienced both as a child and later as an adult, he had, at least, survived. There a tenacity, gall and brass neck in his approach. The proceeds of petty crime had supplemented his lifestyle. Through chance or design, life had kicked him and class and education had effectively barred progress in the RAF. It may come as no surprise that working on a luxury cruise liner far from the bleakness of his life, he would now see how the other half lived.

Yet he still had a melancholy about him and was bitter and disappointed with his lot, self-inflicted or not. He was more than envious. He openly admits jealousy. He was a *voyeur* of a middle class life, a comfortable life lived by others. They were not troubled by setbacks, were comfortable and had stability. They had moved on; he had simply moved from place-to-place.

In the RAF he had seen privilege and had been marked down by, he felt, background. With BEA he had seen how the well-heeled lived and behaved. On the Oronsay, he continued to see luxury and privilege. Not unnaturally, he wanted to be part of it, not some working class bystander eager for the morsel or the leftover crust. He had seen life and could tell a story; he could walk with these kings and hold his own. And so a plan was put together.

Being part of a ship's company of 600 plus, from all parts of Britain and overseas, required skills in getting to know colleagues, working closely with them and respecting their privacy. Over a long cruise, the new teams would get to know each other, friendships would be forged, character traits picked on and nicknames given. With a discrete distance between crew and passengers and a rigid staff hierarchy in place, the ship's company was tightly packed on a floating village. However, on day one of the Pan Indian-Pan Pacific Ocean cruise and with the benefit of different cabin mates working different shifts – he was in a cabin of four – my father's new colleagues did not know him and he barely knew them. He was virtually anonymous and this could be an advantage.

It seems incredible now, but pre-planning must have gone into what is recorded as whim; a sudden thought process it certainly was not. My father considered the shift pattern and worked out who was who and who did what within his cabin. Based on this my father knew that there was a fair possibility that he could be invisible.

The passengers themselves were meeting new people and fellow passengers day in, day out. He was an unknown and took advantage of what he described as his nonentity to savour a little of the indulgent lifestyle of the rich. The incredible thing is that this scheme had been put together with only the limited experience of one Mediterranean cruise.

Here he was, about to put the plan into action. Put simply, he had cooked-up some zany scheme whereby he could conceal his identity in the throngs of passengers and pass himself off as one of them!

Typically, passengers on the first day of cruising are excited by their surroundings, confused about the layout of the ship or merely exploring the 'feel' of the ship. Some are passive and some hold court. There is a leisurely approach to the day and then in the evening, the finely tailored gowns and dinner suits appear.

Dinner finished at nine o'clock and the passengers continued to indulge in cocktails, refined good humour and dancing. Conversation would be liberally filled with anecdote, enunciation and vowels. This was quite a party, and so possessed was my father by a pervasive jealousy which was all-consuming and compulsive, that he was driven to join in. He was to venture into their midst and enjoy some of the delights of living it up on board a luxury liner. Yet again, he was operating on his own, but this time in a quite ridiculous, far from sublime, massive risk, bravado with the return of that devil-may-care we had seen before with BEA and the French court.

> *"My civvies were quite presentable and so was my conduct —*
> *up to a point. As the hours slipped by, I enjoyed the dancing,*
> *conversations with total strangers, the music and I even enjoyed*
> *the swimming pool."*

With the atmosphere and story-telling in full swing, and the alcohol consumption increasing as the evening went on, dancing would ensue, an opportunity to operate at close quarters with the passengers. Quite what happened next is not clear. His behaviour was getting quite rascally and some 'idiot' passengers had reported this to the Purser. Whether he had insulted or offended someone, spilled a drink, or even placed a hand inappropriately whilst dancing is not known. The complaint was made and it was requested he should leave the area and go to his cabin.

At this point, even the crew had not twigged who he was. He was not a passenger and as for 'his cabin':

> *"I didn't have one. Nor did I have any identity and what is*
> *more I wasn't even on the passenger list!"*

The bar had been his downfall. Drinks were duty free and he had taken far too much, allowing his conduct to slip and his guard to fall.

He had enjoyed himself, but now after the telling off he was drunk and shamed. He shuffled and staggered his way back to his bunk. But so inebriated was he that he had lost track of time. Not having a bloody clue, he went to bed, and there was a rude awakening one hour after getting into his bunk. The alarm went off. He was back on duty.

Towards late morning the dining room is being set up for lunch. Once the passengers start arriving and service is in full swing there is wave after wave of serving and clearing. Meanwhile his head is throbbing and his hands are less than steady. He has flashbacks and embarrassing recollections they are too. If only he could get through the day and back to his bunk, he may be able to put a sorry and regretful incident behind him.

There is limited contact with the small group of dining and kitchen staff and shift work means that a degree of anonymity is maintained. Although a dinner table with the ship's captain present is aspired to by certain cruise passengers today, on the Oronsay in the 50s, it was customary for each table in the First Class dining room to have one of the ship's officers present.

The timing and coincidence could not have been better as with huge misfortune it transpired that the officer sitting at the table my father was waiting on was the very one who had reprimanded him the night before.

Immediately standing up, and offering his excuses to passengers, the officer's gritted jaw, cocked head and raised finger spelled danger and imminent threat. He was fuming, but decorum before passengers prevented a full blast of his furnaces. Cornered, my father's later recollection was summed up:

"Oh, he knew me all right!"

"Steward, a word! Now!", the officer barked and then exclaimed "I recognise you!", his voice rasping with all the emphasis required of someone in the process of apprehending a criminal.

In a dining room at sea, my father had nowhere to run. The officer's rant followed in the 'privacy' beyond the kitchen door. "Never in my career, have I witnessed a member of crew trying to socialise with passengers. And worse than that, trying to hoodwink me into thinking you were a passenger! You've been a bloody embarrassment to the line and me in particular." The officer informed the Maitre D' and ordered that he be withdrawn from First Class dining room service for the rest of the day. House arrest at sea was his punishment. The following morning he was escorted to the bridge to face a severe dressing down from Captain Blake who heard the officer's undisputed account of events. The truth was out. This was no mere dispute between passengers.

My father had no excuses and the previous night's high jinx, which had gone too far, would lead to disciplinary action. With no excuse, he accepted the punishment that was to be bestowed on him:

> "...which was to be allocated a very special type of work in the bowels of the ship – namely the refrigerators. These were large units for the holding of all vegetables, fish, frozen foods of infinite variety and all the meats. It was a very cold job but I didn't suffer too much as there were occasional breaks to the food stores. But there was plenty of cleaning and scrubbing."

The incident occurred on the evening of day one. The ship was not yet out of the English Channel. He could cope with the hard work, but resented the stupidity of his actions. He had missed out on the first and second legs of voyage, crossing the Mediterranean and through the Suez Canal before crossing the vast Indian Ocean.

So as a result of jealousy and rage there is no recollection of events associated with Gibraltar, Port Said, Port Suez, and Colombo and the myriad other ports of call across the Indian Ocean.

It was not until the ship reached Perth, Australia, six weeks later that he was once again to put on the waiter's uniform and resume duties in the First Class Dining Room. Ahead of him lay Adelaide, Melbourne, Sydney, Tasmania, Auckland, the Fiji Islands, Hawaii, San Francisco, Los Angeles.

"God, what a long trip that was! Without so much as one day off to enjoy the scenery. I was able to make contact with my father's brother (Uncle Bob) who had made his way in Auckland for some considerable time. He was delighted and surprised at my calling and was proud to show me the Austin Ruby his father had bequeathed him."

Tilbury was a distant shore indeed. There is something of a rationalisation of memory or mere indifference to the wonders of the Indian Ocean or the Pacific for it is absolutely perplexing that no recollection of sites and sounds exists. Arriving in San Francisco, what memory was there of the 'Heaven on a Half-shell', the wide bay, Alcatraz, of streetcars and what would, in 1954, be the biggest engineering structure my father would ever see? No stories exist of greeting San Francisco Bay or of seeing the still striking and bold Gateway Bridge, no hint of cold, foggy, July days. And Los Angeles, home of Hollywood and his much-loved movie-stars? Again, nothing. Hawaii? – nothing. The long return? – nothing.

Maybe ships and their confinement and hard work were not for my father. If you take one step back, his commentary on and affection for flying sticks out; not boats. The Merchant Navy life was another consignment to history and shame and lack of esteem may have been the reasons for this. I never did have a conversation with father about the navy days.

Years later, at the age of seventy, and elderly in the way of someone of that age some thirty-five years ago, is a frail grandmother with feeble vision, sitting by a television, and close up to the screen. A shawl provides a throw-back not just around her shoulders, but to an era of long skirts, petticoats, bodices and broad hats. In the hallway is a photograph of the Oronsay entering Sydney Harbour. Only now, as I write this, is the significance of that long-since-destroyed photograph realised.

In 1955 a kitbag was thrown over the shoulder and my father boarded a train. Kings Cross. Northbound. Again. Clickety-click, clickety-click.

It was a single ticket.

16
Real and Wonderful

The train stops in what appears as the stone-clad trench that is Dundee Tay Bridge Station. My father reaches forward and wearily draws his hands down his face, cupping them over his mouth and nose, exhaling wearily. What next?

Pausing whilst fellow passengers collect their belongings, he swiftly reaches up and lifts down his suitcase from the rack above. He exhales again with a certain philosophical sense of 'well, here we go', as he looks down to the seat beside him.

Grabbing his overcoat, he places it over his arm. The train door is open and the whistles, steam and smoke and accent so familiar, yet different to what he was used to, is something of a nonsense. In London, whilst fixing a car, he had asked for a pair of pliers. The local thought he was mimicking his accent: "Players? Sorry, but I don't smoke," came the reply. The thought and memory raced through his head as he rearranged his hands and luggage and reached for the cigarette packet. Here in Dundee the voices restored his hearing to the distinctively throaty accent. He was now back home and the sights and sounds of the world were yesterday. The platform was well-ordered and calm by London standards. An emptiness echoed as his ears and eyes adjusted to the familiar. The train moved on northwards.

Picking up his suitcase he walked up the stairs from the tracks to the street above, then out of the station and up Union Street. It wasn't Kent and it certainly wasn't San Francisco or Sydney, their harbour settings now replaced by the Tay Estuary. Crossing the Overgate and retracing the route that took him to the Shipping Federation Office two years previously, he was walking through a town where he could not settle then, nor four years prior to that when his own father had died suddenly.

His was a reluctant association with a town; at arm's length and wanting not to get too close. He so desperately wanted to get away, to move on, to make a life. Yet home exerted a huge draw. In 1955 there is irony: the town that drove him away was now pulling him back. He had put off re-settlement long enough and, like it or not, circumstances pulled him back to 63 Constitution Road: a vile pile of lack of maintenance, with a mother just about coping in the premature old age of her mid-fifties.

Conditions had improved in his hometown – certainly so far as work was concerned. New international firms had taken up residency in the efficiency and optimism of post-war growth. Jute was no longer the main staple of everyday life or the product under every factory chimney. New opportunities had opened up in engineering and Sir Stafford Cripps had applauded the visionary 'neotechnic' industries supporting the British economy. Many were American corporations, such as NCR, Timex or Veeder Root, riding the back of Marshall Aid and boosting employment and productivity in the New Elizabethen age. If you were going to have economic growth, you may as well measure it! New designs and new products would meet consumer expectations in a vibrant future. NCR had opened up a plant in the city as early as 1946 and expansion continued into the 50s and 60s. A return to lathe operator or process engineer was the immediate prospect for my father. In a factory.

Back at 63 Constitution Road, he is sixteen years old again. A persona defined by wartime, its effects and opportunities, was now laid up. Fundamentally he was a machine operator in 1939. Sixteen years later he would be doing the same thing. The war, its offer, and its hope were irrelevant. All he ever wanted was to fly. All he *never* wanted was life in a factory. Here he was – a caged bird. Fifteen years of wartime exploits, demob failure and continental adventure, cosseted by His Majesty and sustained by BEA, meant nothing now.

No more the fulfilment of dreams flying solo over The Veldt, chicken farming and coffee smuggling, a French romance and the destruction of great European cities. The Indian Ocean and the Pacific were clear blue and not the murky brown of an East Coast estuary. Sixteen years of travel and life – *half his life* – now wasted and already but a fading memory.

Prior to 1939 there was longing and desire to get away from the not *dire* poverty of the age, but the grinding, dysfunctional cruelty of a family. There was hope and future in war. Skills were wanted and my father was Grade One, a resource so precious that Ministerial restrictions applied. For him, he was a pilot and nothing else. In peacetime he was demobbed, de-motivated, demoralised and depressed.

The thrill of aviation remained with him throughout his life. At the age of sixty-five, taking off and landing David Cyster's beautiful Tiger Moth was the last time he piloted a plane. But that, too, was nearly twenty years ago: a fading memory for someone who peaked too early. He was, after all, redundant so far as the RAF was concerned before he celebrated his twenty-second birthday. The wartime training programme had provided the reward in the form of his hard won and proudly worn 'Wings' and the illusion of more flying. But here are the twists and coincidences of his life.

The realisation that air crew surpluses were being created just as he was doing his first solo flying at Carlisle in 1943 severely prejudiced his flying career; the air war supremacy in Europe leading to the D-Day landings of 6th June 1944 and his despatch to South Africa three days later would hold him back. The EATS programme was by then being run down. His 'Wings' parade in May 1945 was days after Hitler's suicide. His Wings were presented to him by Air Marshal Tedder, who was instrumental in RAF training prior to the setting up of the Empire Air Training Scheme in the first place. Bad timing, but who would have known that then?

The hope of youth and the fortune of war saw my father ride a wave of good luck. It may be more appropriate to use a flying simile here, so let us just say that he rose on a thermal. He was good and the military wanted him. The effect of war, and in particular the logistics of war, provided the chance of a lifetime for my father. Ironically, war provided relief from suffering and deprivation. War is discomforting, but the effects of conflict were not experienced by him. He was distant from his family and far from the torture of his upbringing. He was also free from hardship, day-to-day domestic responsibility and far from any theatre of war. The military fed and clothed him and treated him to a simple luxury. And then they did not need him and tens of thousands just like him: a spent force.

The highlight years of my father's life sit between two pieces of paper, and these were not his birth and death certificates, though they may as well have been. His flying career was born under the Riverdale Agreement of 1939 and it died as a result of the Defence White Paper of 1947. My father was enthused and liberated by war. RAF life defined his apotheosis in a child's mind. It also created such enigma.

Put into context, his flying hours were accumulated over two years, 1943–1945, itself such a limited period of time for an octogenarian. The thrill of flight stayed with him throughout that life, but just how was it possible to create so many pilots and a training programme so successful that in the end the skilled pilots were worthless? After all these years, I now understand the cruelly fated misfor tune that my father experienced in having his dreams dashed by peace and the seeming disorganisation within the RAF structure at the time. It was not disorganisation, though. It was de- organisation: an orchestrated restructuring of the military to suit the requirements and needs of the peacetime economy.

This very rational, political and economic response to circumstances at the time affected my father badly for years afterwards. Whatever heartache there was for a wasted career was now compounded by despondency and soul-searching over subsequent decades.

There is a simple expectation that upon demob you get your suit, you go back home and, in time, you get back on your feet. Any consideration that demob would be easy is ill-founded. After the defining conflict of the twentieth century, the ease of adjustment to ordinary life was nowhere to be seen for my father. He did not want to go back. Perhaps ill-equipped after a difficult childhood, or hopelessly optimistic after the fortune of war, disillusionment creeps in at a point in time when his creativity and ability to get by are maturing: he has something to offer – he's a pilot!. Whatever skills had been developed and whatever talent had been nurtured, it was a self-reliance and desperation that brought him to dabble in petty theft and, shall we say, *marketeering*. Cross-Channel coffee smuggling is an utterly romantic affair. Desperate attempts to get up the ladder of life would only lead to the ladder of a window cleaner, but even here there is admiration and humour in these clandestine and, later, comic exploits.

There was failure in the 1950s and his whole life at this point was stressed and further weakened by his father's death and a failed marriage. Loneliness in Hamburg in 1949 was the first sign of this. It was a creeping, pernicious depressive, negativity about his life after leaving the RAF; a loneliness and feelings of abject failure that characterises the period 1948–1954. A pilot one day, but not an officer; a former RAF pilot but relegated to eating alone because the civil aviation cockpit was the preserve of an elite. Rank was perpetuated and attitudes lingered. Despite being fully trained and 'winged' he was inferior, felt inferior, or was made to feel that way. Officers were one thing, sergeant pilots another. Even with BEA, the 'old school' prevailed.

My father was marked down in uniform and not good enough for commercial aviation. Two wars had not seen off the class divide. Maybe 'Colonel' George Duncan was right to remind Major Smythe.

Pressures within his own family back 'home' would result in either a drunken fog that masked the reality of the time, or a veil of shame that years later would hide the reality. Airlines and marriage and the steady decline that would lead to sacking after sacking are what feed into a spiral of decline he could not correct. With the benefit of hindsight, war was just an intervention that interrupted a logical factory-based career. Certainly that is what he would return to in 1955.

There was neglect, he felt, in not pursuing a good education. He never aspired to greatness but did understand the need to add value to his labours as a young man. His main neglect was in not sticking it out and forging a good engineering career. Curiously, later, his skills would lead him to consider that he was the best bevel gear cutter in the business!

But the privilege of life with the RAF and BEA had pampered him, I suspect, and the 'caged bird' experience of factory life was not for him. And so, he felt, with no distinction in society or great wealth, his life was one of drifting from one occupation to another:

"... a floundering mass like the proverbial rolling stone that gathers no moss."

He had not consolidated his life after the war and this lingered malevolently, malignantly, on his mind for years to come. My father wanted, himself, to understand the events of a lifetime, to succeed and be a good parent. He wanted to provide for those around him and be comfortable. He felt that the middle part of one's life should constitute:

"... what one has made for oneself – how one evaluates standing, contribution and how you leave your mark on society."

Childhood poverty can be a romantic and comfortable memory as long as you can get away from it. For my father, cruel beatings and servitude would continue to be uncomfortable memories. He had an ingrained, perhaps even brainwashed desire to please his father. But whatever force there had been in childhood would not be eroded. George Duncan's passing in 1949 defines the moment of justifiable relief, but the process of getting rid of one issue in his life, magnifies other problems. Domestic life and an invalid mother further added to my father's plight, contributing to the circumstances that would warrant his return home in 1955. Even after his death, George Duncan had a lingering influence and cast a long shadow. Family life had created insecurity and a long-restrained revulsion that would persist into final years, without one shred of regret at his passing.

My father's life is recounted in pride in achievement and personal struggle to cope in a Britain that belongs to generations before. It is a life that no one else has lived. Today, we have a relatively strong and resilient economy and we compete on a 'World Stage'. But for all the confidence of the age, I feel we trace our attitudes to a Britain of the 1940s and 50s which is empirical, impoverished, broke, Americanised, European and forgetful. It fought its own weaknesses, probably from the day Queen Victoria died, through the emergence of the middle classes, and through two major conflicts. For perhaps a long time between the 20s and the 50s we appear to have been a quite unsettled nation. VE Day in 1945 was not just about the end of hostilities, but the end of dreams and beginning of nightmares for my father.

The struggles of 1930s poverty and wartime sacrifice and 1950s austerity – *and the detailed causes of it* – shaped a nation and we have such little understanding and such little regard for those who experienced it. This was long time ago, yet for me but one generation ago.

Wartime provided long years of phoniness, doubt, uncertainty, struggle, fear and good humour, national unity and personal pain and loss, all supported by adjustments to doing without or doing with little. Efficiency in the use of gardens, allotments and farmland could only do so much in the face of U-boats and so the country looked to others for support. The war effort was one thing, the national debt another. The perception that Marshall Aid only applied to mainland Europe may yet hide the perilous state that Great Britain was in by 1945.

In the post-war years not only was my father broke, the country was too. It has been a long-held question whether years later we were still paying for the Second World War. The 'stuff ' the yanks left behind at Burtonwood provided a clue. The volumes and quality of materials was little short of the *Marie Celeste*; a sudden departure with no obvious accountability or ownership. By the time hostilities had ceased the cost of conflict would have been massive and payments had continued over subsequent decades in emotional and sentimental terms. On 2nd September 1945, the Lend Lease arrangements with the United States were abruptly terminated and an outstanding value of goods was commuted into a long term loan facility – the Anglo-

American Loan. This was the root of the 'special relationship'. Great Britain was certainly broke and had fulfilled its role as strategic aircraft carrier. But financially, just how much did we owe? And to whom? When was the actual debt paid off – if at all?

The actual scale of WWII debt can be answered in a series of questions raised and answers given in both Houses of Parliament in 2002 and more recently in the Commons in 2006. These are recorded in Hansard. The scale of war effort contribution from the US is estimated as $50.1 billion at 1945 prices. The equivalent of some $700 billion at 2007 prices.

Great Britain was on the receiving end of the equivalent of $434 billion ($34 billion – 1945) which was written down to £1,075 million based on a value of items retained in Britain at the time. Repayments were agreed with an interest rate of two per cent in fifty instalments. Annual payments had in fact been made every New Year's Eve since 1950, except on six occasions when the nation was in financial strife arising from exchange rate conditions and levels of foreign currency and gold reserves. As at 31st March 2001 the principal stood at £243,573,154 ($346,287,953). Final payment, due on 31st December 2006, was in fact paid two days earlier, with formal thanks being expressed to the United States for its support.

Not long after my father's passing, and some sixty years after the events of May 1945, approximately £42.5 million ($83.3 million) was 'wired' from the Bank of England to the US Treasury, the final payment on a multi-billion pound debt racked up during and after the Second World War. A final instalment – £11.6 million – was also paid towards £600 million borrowed from Canada. All through the remaining years of my father's life and beyond, the economic cost of wartime presented a debt.

It is a rare privilege to see into the life of another; an even greater privilege – an honour in fact – to reveal the deeply emotional, perhaps even troubled, side. This story is not just one of memoirs and chronology; it is more than that. This story is one of love and regret. Years later and as a widower in his seventies and eighties he had the time to reflect on his life. The old man in the low door had a story to tell, as many people do. But his was rich in its wealth of tale within tale. Life: a unique formulation of events planned and unplanned, expected and unexpected.

More than that, the handsome young man in the studio photograph was part of history. Yet for all his writings and shared experiences, he had not realised it as it was. There was shame and blame and a blindness to the truth of what he had done, the difficulties of childhood, the opportunity to fly and in a small, and quite unique way, to be part of that marvellous, romantic and dangerous period.

He didn't see it that way. The old man sitting in the chair could only see an unadorned life through feelings of melancholy and deprecation. In the solitude of his final years he would reflect on his inadequacies. There is pathos and humility in his writings and a pain in recounting personal regret. The fear of reading notes and letters was here revealed. Above all, he felt he had let himself down. Here was the confessional:

> *"Self analysis is not always a good thing to write about. It is better, I feel, to leave character criticism to others who may, or may not, wish to express their opinions openly, but as I sit here in the twilight hours of my life, sometimes reflecting on the past, it occurred to me that a void existed in not taking stock of myself ."*

There is guilt, for he felt he had done many bad things, some of them quite unforgivable. Countering this, there may have been many good things which he could not obviously recount.

The magnitude of what tinkering with model airplanes had done for him and what a flying career – even one so short as my father's – had done for him was not fully appreciated. The freedom of flying and beauty of the open skies ahead of him, the distinctive lazy rip of the Moth or the roar of the Harvard's radial, were far distant memories of another age. But what they were was his life-blood.

After the war, the disjointed state of the RAF in peacetime and the removal of flying duties was like an adverse blood transfusion. His body was rejecting it. Despite what has been written and despite the richness of his life, my father felt that for all the effort and struggle, there was little to show for it. But the regret and longing for forgiveness for what he did not make of himself, things he had and had not done were carried to the end. He failed his loved ones in 1952 and this gnawed persistently into the subsequent fifty-four years.

Regret kicks in, not in the fact that actual events created sorrowful recollection, but that more could have been done. Self-esteem suffered. If you forgive the foray into illicit transfers on the European commodities market and the penal effect of this, the strain of work and marriage, and an evil pernicious depression then in the midst of disappointment there are incredible events so familiar to my father – *he was central to the plot* – that he never ever realised them as they were. Persistent cruelty, more than poverty, created such anguish and uncertainty; feelings only altered when the roar of an airplane engine conspired a life-changing serendipity for a young boy in the 1930s. In that young boy's mind was fuelled the desire to be free of unrelenting brutish abuse. Flying was a dream to be fulfilled.

As an independent-minded young man he sat in a shot down Junkers in Glasgow. This was the start of his actual flying career. Skilled in aircraft repair and maintenance, he struggled to get out of a reserved occupation. The vast Empire Air Training Scheme and counterpart Joint Air Training Plan provided further skill. Little is comprehended in the UK of the vast Empire Air

Training Scheme or the British and Commonwealth Air Training Plan or Arnold and Towers schemes in the United States, let alone the Joint Air Training Plan in South Africa. Yet without this massive endeavour and series of triumphs of practicality over hard won politics, the Second World War and Britain's role within it would have been sunk. He would become not just any old pilot, but an RAF pilot.

The delight and beauty of flying culminated in poetic coincidence and long term irritation. Magee would be credited, but still he got his 'Wings' and flying dreams had come true. Not bad for the young lad without a college education is the proud boast that he had a Harvard education.

He experienced living in London, Europe and South Africa, and various less romantic destinations, courtesy of His Majesty's Government. There were clean sheets and cocoa too. He was there at the start of commercial aviation as we know it today and a participant in the very cradle of the Cold War with a role in the Berlin Airlift. From the Atlantic Hotel in Hamburg he would see the aftermath of Operation Gomorrah and the emergence of modern Europe.

As he lay before me with life passing and a setting sun, the hero quivered, wheezed and fought, but would not tell his story again. My father's life, its triumphs and failings, are now celebrated. Much of life at the time responded to change and opportunity. Far from the Angus field where he first saw his dream of flying, his life was moulded by circumstances far beyond his control, He should feel no shame. The man is to be celebrated.

Did I realise a different man? Emphatically, no. Youth was older then, and life was tougher. He was the same man, it just so happens that he had led a most remarkable life and I now knew more about it. He felt his life did not matter. I am sorry, but it did and I feel I have now had the most wonderful conversations with my father.

In his heart he was always a flyer and had a sustained love affair with flight. His experiences and memories were ever more distant, but in the joy of solo flight he knew he had realised his ambition. In a life that began with RAF expansion and ended with final payments for his war, he was happiest flying:

> *"Out of life's failures and disappointments I was lucky enough to snatch the fulfilment of my dreams. It's gone now; slipped into the book of memories like a recorded event in a file, but it was real, it was wonderful."*

Photographs &
Bibliography Index

Photographs

Figures I, 3, 4 and 5: Private Collection.

Figures 2, 7 and 8: reproduced by kind permission of British Airways/ BA Archive. See www.bamuseum.com

Figure 6: reproduced by kind permission of the Burnelli Aircraft Corporation. See www.burnelli.com

Bibliography

Anon. *A Short History of the Royal Air Force - Air Publication 125*, Air Council, September, 1929

Armitage, Michael *The Royal Air Force – an Illustrated History*, BCA, 1993

Becker, Capt. Dave *Yellow Wings – The Story of the Joint Air Training Scheme in World War 2* SAAF Museum, 1989

Bramson, Alan and Birch, Neville *The Tiger Moth Story*, Airlife Publishing, 1970

Bowyer, Chaz *Royal Air Force Handbook*, Ian Allan Limited, 1984

Critchley, A.C. *Critch – The Memoirs of Brigadier-General A.C. Critchley*, Hutchinson, 1961

Dunmore, Spencer *Wings for Victory – The Remarkable Story of the British Commonwealth Air Training Plan in Canada*, McClelland and Stewart Inc, 1994

Ford, Donald *The Carnoustie Story*, 2006

Golley, John *Aircrew Unlimited – The Commonwealth Air Training Plan During World War 2*, Patrick Stephens Limited, 1993

Halford-MacLeod, Guy *Britain's Airlines Volume One: 1946-1951*, Tempus, 2006

Hancock, W.K. & Gowing, M.M. *British War Economy* HMSO, 1949

Haslam, E.B. *The History of Royal Air Force Cranwell*, HMSO, 1982

Joubert, Sir Philip *The Third Service – The Story Behind The Royal Air Force*
Thames and Hudson, 1955

Lo Boa, Phil *An Illustrated History of British European Airways*, Browcom, 1989

Lowe, Keith *Inferno – The Devastation of Hamburg 1943*, Viking, 2007

May, Garry *The Challenge of BEA – The Story of a Great Airline's First 25 Years*,
Wolfe Publishing, 1971

Mackenzie King, W.L. *Canada and The Fight for Freedom*, MacMillan, 1944

MacMillan, Capt. Norman, The *Royal Air Force in the World War Vol 1 1919-
1940* George Harrap & Co, 1942

Ministry of Defence, *A Brief History of the Royal Air Force*, HMSO, 1994

Ministry of Information (Introduction by Overy, Richard) *What Britain
Has Done 1939-1945*, Atlantic Books, 2007

Monk, F.V. & Winter, H.T., *The Royal Air Force*, Blackie and Son
Limited, 1939

Partridge, Eric *A Dictionary of RAF Slang* Michael Joseph, First Edition, 1945

Phipp, Mike *The Brabazon Committee and British Airliners, 1945-1960*
Tempus, 2007

Richards, Denis *The Fight at Odds The Royal Air Force Volume 1* HMSO, 1974

Sargent, Eric *The Royal Air Force 2nd Edition* Sampson Low, Marston &
Co, 1941

Sims, Charles, *The Royal Air Force – The First Fifty Years*, Adam & Charles
Black, London, 1968

Smith, Graham, *Essex and Its Race for The Skies*, Countryside Books, 2007

Smith, Peter C, *T-6 A Pictorial Record of The Harvard, Texan and Wirraway*,
Airlife Publishing, 1995

Smuts, J.C., *Jan Christian Smuts* , Cassel & Co, 1952

Stewart, Major Oliver, *The Royal Air Force in Pictures*, Second Edition,
Country Life, 1941

Stewart, Major Oliver, *The Royal Air Force in Pictures*, Third Edition,
Country Life, 1942

Stewart, Andrew "The 1939 British and Canadian 'Empire Air Training Scheme' negotiations" in The Round Table, Volume 93, Number 377, pp739-754, Routledge, October 2004

Thetford, Owen *Aircraft of the Royal Air Force since 1918*, Putnam and Company, 1957 (revised 1976)

Woodley, Charles *History of British European Airways 1946-1974*, Pen and Sword Books, 2006

If I have left anyone off the list, this is accidental
and not intentional!

Dedication

It has taken some time to bring this book together and I have enjoyed every moment of it. Realising a life was what I set out to do and I hope I have achieved this. Fundamentally, the book is for my father and a wider family I may one day meet.

To the many people whom I spoke to, corresponded with, some of whom clarified and offered information – thank you. To John and Frankie, huge thanks for making it real.

For her love, patience and understanding in wondering what on earth I was doing and why I was pre-occupied in a black and white or sepia world, I must thank my wife, Kaeren.